THE
POET'S
MARKETPLACE

THE

definitive

sourcebook

on where to get

your poems

published

Joseph J. Kelly

THE POET'S MARKETPLACE

RUNNING PRESS
Book Publishers
Philadelphia ♦ Pennsylvania

9 8 7 6 5 4 3 2 1
The digit on the right indicates the number of this printing.

Library of Congress Cataloging in Publishing Data:
Main entry under title:
The Poet's marketplace.
1. Poetry—Marketing.   2. Publishers and publishing—
United States—Directories.   3. American periodicals—
Directories.   I. Kelly, Joseph J.
PN1059.M3P6 1984   070.5′.025′73   84–2053

ISBN: 0–89471–257–8 (paperback)
ISBN: 0–89471–264–0 (lib. bdg.)

Cover design by Toby Schmidt.
Typography: Goudy Oldstyle by rci, Philadelphia, Pennsylvania.
Printed by Port City Press.

This book can be ordered by mail from the publisher.
Please include 95¢ for postage. **But try your bookstore first.**

Running Press
Book Publishers
125 South 22nd Street
Philadelphia, Pennsylvania 19103

CONTENTS

INTRODUCTION
WHAT IS THE MARKET FOR POETRY?

From one point of view, the phrase "poet's marketplace" is an oxymoron like "darkness visible," "pleasurable pain," or "military intelligence." It is *utopia*—the good place that is no place.

In a country where there are relatively few readers of serious books, and still fewer readers of literature, fewest of all are the readers of poetry. Publishers simply cannot afford to publish many poetry manuscripts, print many copies, or pay very much. The general public, by and large, isn't interested.

Poets whose books are published receive few or no reviews, get minimal publicity, if any, and thus gain almost as little recognition as money. Grants and awards don't amount to much.

Given this harsh reality, one might think that poets would despair and give up writing. Perhaps they would if they expected something else. But, as in so many other areas, poets are realists in that they know what their rewards will *not* be. Poetry may be their life and their vocation; but they know that it can't be their livelihood. From poetry alone they can usually expect only the wages of a dabbling freelancer: annual earnings in one to three figures.

There are exceptions, of course; and in their wake there are many whose noble infirmity keeps them flooding the publishing world with their work. Literary fame is a fairly common yearning—and not at all a contemptible one.

Yet, in reality, poets are more apt to expect too little than too much. Because they work without financial motive, on material that demands the utmost personal involvement and concentration, they necessarily pay little attention to the interests of readers. To write with their minds on the popular reader rather than the subject would be to dilute their poetry into rhetoric. Even more than other writers, poets see their task as writing a very personal truth, and do not hope for a very wide readership.

And because the creative act of poetry is so personal, many poets also consider efforts to sell their work (even in the limited market) as hucksterism of the worst sort—a search for a marketplace for one's soul. They prefer to mail their poems out wherever they choose, half-hoping that their worth will be recognized, but not really expecting that they will connect with a proper editor.

In their attitude toward marketing, in fact, many poets sell themselves short and restrict the poetry market even further—and unnecessarily so. Poets must certainly uphold the distinction between poetry and rhetoric—even more so today, when "causes" proliferate. But they must recognize that all work sent out to be published has *some* prospective readership; and they should seek that readership in the same ways other writers do. This doesn't mean selling out and writing to order: it simply means knowing where readers receptive to your work are likely to be located and directing your poems their way. It only makes sense to submit work to publishers that are the most likely to publish it, and not to waste time and postage on extreme long-shots.

Also, poetry marketing means taking advantage of the many opportunities that still exist for poets, even within the limited field. Contests, requests for poetry on a theme or in a specified form, special issues of periodicals—these are not necessarily lures to seduce the muse: they can be invitations to expand your craft and add important credits to your résumé. If Ben Jonson could make poetry out of the Jacobean court, and Andrew Marvell out of Cromwell's campaign in Ireland, today's poets should be able to make poetry out of requests for specific themes or subject matter—especially when their inspiration has flagged on their own projects. Often enough, you may already have some work that fits the requirements, or which can be fitted with a little revision. As in the case of strict metrical forms, publishers' requirements sometimes inspire new material or suggest new ways to handle existing poems. Knowing that poetry can be generated from just about anything, and that beginning a poem often is a way of finding one, you can also benefit from exploring this part of the marketplace.

Although harsh, then, the marketplace can be a poet's friend—not a rich friend, but a benefactor nonetheless. Although small, the marketplace is large enough for any poet to feel at home in, without feeling complacent.

THE SCOPE OF THIS BOOK

This book's basic purpose is to help serious poets find the right outlets for their work and gain appropriate rewards for it. It is not a guide for hacks and dilettantes. *The Poet's Marketplace* encourages poets to seize the real opportunities open to them, serving as an essential handbook to the "business" end of a poet's creative life—the one volume for you to consult before sending out your work. It's a place where you can go window-shopping to see which "window" will best display your poems.

Following this introductory chapter are guidelines on how to use the directory effectively (Chapter 1) and on submitting a manuscript and keeping market information current (Chapters 2 & 3). Next come the directory listings of magazine publishers (Chapter 4), chapbook publishers (Chapter 5), book publishers (Chapter 6), alternative markets (Chapter 7), contests and awards (Chapter 8), grants (Chapter 9), and writers' associations (Chapter 10). Following these directory entries is a list of additional markets to query. The indexes, designed to help you find just what you want, provide geographical and subject indexes by directory category—and a list of periodical markets that pay.

SOURCES

In providing market information, *The Poet's Marketplace* takes its place beside a number of valuable directories, each of them useful to poets in its own way. The following books are available to writers at a reasonable cost:

The CCLM Literary Magazine Directory 1983. Coordinating Council of Literary Magazines, 2 Park Avenue, New York, NY 10016 ($5.00). This is a list of 340 literary magazines, arranged alphabetically and indexed by state. The 2-column page format makes the book easy to skim for poetry markets, and the directory entries are especially valuable for descriptions of the magazines in their editors' own words.

The International Directory of Little Magazines and Small Presses. Len Fulton and Ellen Ferber, eds. 19th edition. Paradise, CA: Dustbooks, 1983 (Box 100, Paradise, CA 95967, $17.95). The fullest listing of little magazines, with detailed entries, the *ID* offers access to poetry markets through its 8-page index to about 600 poetry publications.

1984 Writer's Market. Bernadine Clark, ed. Cincinnati: Writer's Digest Books, 1983 ($18.95). A standard reference book for writers, *WM* lists 132 poetry magazines and 78 literary and "little" magazines, with good detail on the kind of poetry wanted and editorial needs in other genres.

Poetry Marketing. Lincoln Young. Kingsport, TN: Five Arts Press, 1982 ($5.00). A 40-page pamphlet that lists 125 paying markets, many of them specialty magazines outside the usual channels for poetry submissions. Also offers advice on marketing and submitting poetry manuscripts.

Others may be consulted at a library:

Directory of Publishing Opportunities in Journals and Periodicals. 5th edition. Chicago: Marquis Academic Media, 1981. A listing of 136 poetry and fiction markets in North America and Britain, this directory is especially valuable for its information on editorial needs and advice on manuscript submissions.

Literary Market Place 1984. New York: R. R. Bowker, 1983. *LMP* lists about 70 book publishers of poetry, and contains lists of literary awards, prize contests, and fellowships and grants.

Magazine Industry Market Place 1982. New York: R. R. Bowker, 1981. A "Literature and Poetry" index on page 330 leads to entries on about 130 well-known magazines publishing poetry and/or literary criticism.

THE
POET'S
MARKETPLACE

1 | HOW TO USE THIS BOOK EFFECTIVELY

TAKING MARKETING SERIOUSLY

With the financial rewards of poetry so small, and recognition so hard to come by, it's essential that you not waste your time, effort, and money on futile submissions. Writers who send work out blindly to every magazine or publisher, or who mail occasional submissions to publications with whom they aren't familiar, are only subsidizing the Post Office and the stationery manufacturers. Besides, sending poems to editors who aren't likely to be interested needlessly undermines your confidence in your own work.

If, instead, you know where your work stands a chance of being accepted, and restrict your submissions only to those places, you not only increase the possibility of publication, but save time for more writing and more profitable submissions. With such restricted submissions also comes an increase in personal rejection letters. That too is a benefit, for it assures you that you are actually being read and allows you to build self-confidence.

For reading the entries in Chapters 4 through 8, then, it's best to take the descriptions literally. Assume that the editors *do* know what they want! Some poets, after flipping through a magazine, become convinced that the editors will prefer their work to the "garbage" that they're presently publishing. Although it is true that editors want to upgrade the quality of their poems, poets forget that editors try to publish the sort of material they like. And in such cases, it is impossible to convert them. The best way to know a publication's individual tastes is to carefully read its directory description and study a sample issue or two. As one editor has told me: "Nothing beats the *involvement* of reading. It seems to me that it's necessary for writers to be familiar with the magazines that publish them: that is, that people should —ideally—send their work to magazines that they, themselves, *care* about and wish to be a part of."

Restricting your submissions will by no means limit your market. With enormous diversity the rule in modern poetry, periodical and book publishers will continue to publish all kinds and styles of poetry. All restricting your submissions will do is increase your chances for success.

You can also help ease the burden of editors. One, who speaks for many, has written, "No matter how accurately I describe the kind of poetry we will accept, we will continue to get thousands of unacceptable ditties. It is the nature of the beast." Prove him wrong!

2 | HOW TO SUBMIT A POETRY MANUSCRIPT

You should always check to see if the publication you have in mind has special requirements, as listed in this book and in other directories. In the absence of guidelines for submitting manuscripts, you can also determine a periodical's wants by querying the editor with a self-addressed, stamped envelope (SASE). Poets reckless enough to send blind submissions can at least request that writers' guidelines be sent if (or rather, *when*) the manuscript is returned.

FORMAT

If there are no special requirements for format, then adhere to the following rules for submitting poetry manuscripts. It's always safe to presume that editors are not shallow people and, according to Oscar Wilde, "It is only the shallow people who do not judge by appearances."

What Kind of Page?

1. Use non-Corrasable 8½" by 11" paper. Use photocopies only if the publication accepts them—and then only when they're the best copies you can get.
2. Type your name and address in the upper left-hand corner.
3. Type the number of lines of poetry in the upper right-hand corner.

4. Center the poem's title about 8 to 10 lines down from the top of the page.
5. Double-space the lines of the poem.
6. A few lines below the end of the poem, type your name once again.
7. Type no more than one poem on a page.
8. If your poem continues for more than one page, type the poem's title and page number at the top right-hand corner of each page after the first—directly across from your name and address.
9. Use a paper clip to bind your pages, or else leave them unfastened. Do not staple them.

Pointers for Cover Letters

Cover letters are generally optional. Many publications do not require cover letters, and some actually oppose them because they may interfere with the judgment of the quality of the work submitted. A one-page letter/résumé, though, that can be skimmed or put aside quickly, should do you no harm, and may do you some good.

However:

1. Keep it short—one page at the most!
2. Restrict it to a list of your publications and awards, as if it were a résumé or bibliography—which it is.
3. Do *not* make it a defense of, or apology for, your work.

SASE

On all correspondence with publishers, always, *always* enclose a self-addressed, stamped envelope. The absence of a SASE induces poetry manuscripts to be filed in the trash immediately. Be sure that the SASE is large enough to hold all the poems you submit without refolding them, and bears sufficient postage: namely, the same amount of postage you put on the outside mailing envelope. Have the Post Office weigh your envelope *before* you seal it. (In submissions to Canadian journals, include an International Reply Coupon, available from the Post Office.) The envelope should be a standard white office envelope, about $4\frac{1}{8}$" by $9\frac{1}{2}$" or 5" by 10".

Copyright Notice

There is no need to put the © copyright symbol on your

manuscripts. In most cases, the publisher obtains the copyright, pays for first publication rights only, and then allows all other rights to revert to the author on request. Publishers who want the transfer of exclusive rights must gain the poet's signature on a written contract.

For information on current copyright law, which guarantees protection during your lifetime plus 50 years, whether or not you publish, write for the free copyright information kit from the Copyright Office, Library of Congress, Washington, DC 20559, or call (202) 287-8700.

RECORD-KEEPING

For every poetry submission or query, you need to keep an accurate record that measures the degree of your success, gauged by your own standards. A journal and two index-card files—one for poems, and one for publishers—provide a basic system.

Journal entries should be arranged chronologically by date of submission, with a listing under each date of the poems submitted and the publications submitted to. With a journal record, you can follow up submissions with queries when the decision date is well past and, most importantly, divide the number of submissions by the number of acceptances to calculate the year's success rate. You can also calculate the cost in postage and stationery for tax purposes.

On the "poem"cards, each headed with the title of the poem, enter the date of submission and the publisher sent to, and then later the date of the response and the verdict. On the "publisher" cards, headed with the publisher's name, you can record the date the poem was submitted and the title, and later the date of the response and the verdict. In this way, you can chart both the success of each poem and the responsiveness of individual publishers.

Also essential to record-keeping is maintaining files of acceptance letters and "friendly rejections." In both cases, the files remind you where to submit again, and—for a beginning writer—provide support in times of countless form rejections. Also, some poets may want to rank the journals and book publishers in their personal directory of markets by the kind of rejection they received. Give an A for personal rejections, B for form letters, and C for no responses.

3 | KEEPING MARKET INFORMATION CURRENT

THE USE OF AVAILABLE JOURNALS

Given the ephemeral nature of little magazines and poetry markets in general, to say nothing of the continuing changes in editorship, addresses, and deadlines, it's absolutely necessary to update the listings given in books such as this and the *International Directory*. Fortunately, a number of magazines keep the writer apprised of the latest market news. One of the best is *Coda: Poets and Writers Newsletter*, edited by Darlyn Brewer (201 West 54th Street, New York, NY 10019). Its five yearly issues (available for a $10 subscription) list awards, grants, and publishing opportunities, and contain valuable articles on the writing trade. Comparable is *Small Press Review*, edited by Len Fulton and Ellen Ferber (Box 100, Paradise, CA 95969). *SPR*, available monthly for a yearly subscription of $14, supplements the *International Directory*.

Yet another valuable source is the annual list of over 100 poetry markets in the March issue of *The Writer*, a monthly that sells for $15 a year (8 Arlington Street, Boston, MA 02116). Also containing market information, Judson Jerome's monthly column in *Writer's Digest* gives poets excellent general advice, full of wit and judgment. (Subscription address: 205 West Center Street, Marion, OH 43305. Price: $18.)

Additional sources for poetry markets include:

AWP Newsletter, Kate McCune, Editor; Old Dominion University, Norfolk, VA 23508. (Subscription rate $7; sample copy $1.)

Bloomsbury Review, Tom Auer, Editor; Box 8928, Denver, CO 80201. (Subscription rate $6; sample copy $2.)

Cross-Canada Writers Quarterly, Ted Plantos, Editor; Box 277, Station F, Toronto, Ontario, M4Y 2L7 Canada. (Subscription rate $10 Canada; $11 U.S. and foreign; sample copy $2.95.)

Golden Eagle, Moreag E. Wood, Editor; 2 Marina Point, Danbury, CT 06810. (Sample copy $1.50.)

League Boots, Bayside Publishing, Box 1949, Everett, WA 98206. (Subscription rate $12; sample copy $1.)

Library Journal, "Magazines" section, R. R. Bowker & Co., Inc., 205 East 42nd Street, New York, NY 10017. (Subscription rate $55; sample copy $3.50.)

Literary Magazine Review, G. W. Clift, Editor; English Department, Kansas State University, Manhattan, KS 66506. (Subscription rate $10; sample copy $3.)

Literary Markets, Bill Marles, Editor; 4340 Coldfall Road, Richmond, British Columbia, V7C 1P8, Canada. (Subscription rate $9; sample copy $1.)

New Pages: News and Reviews of the Progressive Booktrade, Casey Hill and Grant Burns, Editors; 4426 South Belsay Road, Grand Blanc, MI 48439. (Subscription rate $15; sample copy $1.)

Small Press, John F. Baker, Editor; R. R. Bowker, 205 East 42nd Street, New York, NY 10017. (Subscription rate $18; sample copy $3.50.)

Small Press News, Diane Kruchkow, Editor; Weeks Mills, New Sharon, ME 04955. (Subscription rate $10; sample copy $1.25.)

Stony Hills, Diane Kruchkow, Editor; Weeks Mills, New Sharon, ME 04955. (Subscription rate $4; sample copy $1 plus 50¢ postage.)

Writer's Newsletter, Mike Wilkerson and Thomas Hastings, Editors; 316 North Jordan, Bloomington, IN 47405. (Subscription rate $4; sample copy $1.)

UPDATING YOUR PERSONAL DIRECTORY
Some poets may update their personal directory simply by

annotating their copy of *The Poet's Marketplace* or the *International Directory*. Others change the entries in a notebook directory of markets or a card file. In any case, don't forget to mark along with the change the source from whom you got it and the date. This will prevent those confusing occasions when you are not sure whom to contact or what editorial policies are still in effect.

4 | THE MAGAZINE MARKET

Relatively few poets manage to get a book into print, and so for most people, poetry publication means periodical publication—usually in little magazines. The *International Directory* lists some 600 poetry magazines, ranging from those that photocopy 100 copies of any one issue and pay nothing, up to those whose pages are professionally typeset, with circulations in the thousands, and who pay a rate of $50 a poem or more. With the addition of a few large publications like *The Atlantic Monthly*, *The Nation*, and *The New Republic*, little magazines comprise the center of the poet's marketplace.

One obvious but painful fact is that poets themselves need to support this market for it to survive. Ironically, in a time when few people read poetry, relatively few poets read it either! Yet poetry magazines must rely on their subscriptions in order to keep publishing. While a poet's small book budget must necessarily go toward collections of established writers, some portion of it must go toward supporting those journals where you yourself want to be printed. Of course you need to buy samples as part of your marketing effort, but you also need to buy subscriptions to show your confidence in contemporary poetry as a vital concern—not a luxury or frivolity. Also, as one editor puts it, it is simply "not *honorable* for would-be contributors to send submission after submission to a magazine they wish to appear in, without subscribing. Especially nowadays, when magazines need and deserve the loyalty of readers who admire them, in a time of budgetary difficulties."

Another striking thing about the magazines listed below is their extreme specialization. In one way, this is deplorable, because many publications tend to substitute for sheer quality in poetry various forms of "right thinking"—feminist, fascist, Marxist, whatever. Yet this same specialization allows you, the poet, to market your work better, if only by exclusion. Also, it helps you determine more easily, by your own analysis, what is bogus and what is real.

Typically, a young poet will begin by submitting his work to nearby college publications (many of which accept poems by outsiders) and then go on to the little magazines, looking at first for good circulation figures and later the cash reward. By and large, you'll have your best luck with magazines in your own geographical region—provided that your work is right for them to begin with. You can assume that, in close decisions on a manuscript, there will be a bias in favor of a writer from the magazine's local area. (For useful background on the little magazine market, consult Elliott Anderson and Mary Kinzie, *The Little Magazine in America: A Modern Documentary History.* Yonkers: Pushcart Press, 1976.)

A basic rule is that the more poetry a magazine publishes, the better your chances of getting published. It is easier to get poems accepted by an all-poetry magazine than by an omnibus literary journal that prints only three or four poems per issue.

The selected list of magazines that follows, drawn from sources cited in the Introduction and Chapter Three, includes *only* those magazines presently accepting unsolicited manuscripts. With a few exceptions, chosen for their quality or reputation, all have a circulation of 500 or more. Where a phone number is not given, the periodical in question prefers that all correspondence be in writing.

Adrift, 239 East 5th Street #4D, New York, NY 10003. Founded 1982. Circulation: 1,500. Quality poetry of Irish, Irish-American, and general interest. Poets recently published: James Liddy, Leland Bardwell, Tom McKeown, Eamonn Wall. Besides poetry, publishes fiction, prose, and autobiography. Size: 32 pages in an 8½" by 11" format. Subscription rate: $7 for 2 issues; sample copy $3.50.
☐Received 1,000 poetry mss. in 1982; accepted 25. Pay varies, depending on

funding, from $10 to $200. Copyright reverts to author. Contact: Thomas Mc Gonigle, Editor. Send 3 to 4 poems. Simultaneous and photocopied submissions acceptable. Decision in 1 to 3 weeks.

The Agni Review, Box 229, Cambridge, MA 02238. (617) 491–1079. Founded 1972. Circulation: 1,200. High-quality poetry, long and short, in formal or free verse. Poets recently published: Derek Walcott, Jorie Graham, Michael Benedikt, William Harmon. Besides poetry, publishes fiction and interviews. Size: 136 pages in a 5½″ by 8½″ format. Subscription rate: $8 for 2 issues; sample copy $3.95.
□Received 3,500 poetry mss. in 1982; accepted 100. Pays 3 free copies. Copyright reverts to author. Contact: Sharon Dunn, Editor. Send 3 to 5 poems. Simultaneous and photocopied submissions acceptable. Decision in 5 weeks.

America, 106 West 56th Street, New York, NY 10019. (212) 581–4640. Founded 1909. Circulation: 35,000. Poetry in contemporary idiom, built around a single image, that seizes the reader's attention from the first line and holds it throughout. Mostly poetry of a spiritual nature and religious poetry without clichés. No experimental forms. Poets recently published: James Hearst, Babette Deutsch, Norma Farber, Robert Siegel. Besides poetry, publishes articles and opinion pieces on world affairs and religious concerns, literary articles, book and film reviews, and a religious page. Size: 22 pages in an 8¼″ by 10½″ format. Subscription rate: $21 for weekly issues (biweekly in July and August); sample copy 75¢.
□Received between 500 and 1,000 poetry mss. in 1982; accepted 30. Pays $1.40 per line and 2 copies. Copyright reverts to author. Contact: John Moffitt, Poetry Editor. Send 2 to 3 poems, each 10 to 30 lines long. No simultaneous submissions. Photocopies acceptable. Decision in 2 weeks.

The American Poetry Review, 1616 Walnut Street, Room 405, Philadelphia, PA 19103. (215) 732–6770. Founded 1972. Circulation: 23,000. Open to all kinds of poetry. Poets recently published: Seamus Heaney, John Ashbery, Sandra McPherson, Paul Goodman. Besides poetry, publishes essays, translations, reviews, and fiction. Size: 48 pages in a 10″ by 14″ format. Subscription rate: $8.50 for 6 issues; sample copy free.
□Received 5,000 poetry mss. in 1982; accepted 250. Pays $1 per line on publication and 2 or more free copies. Copyright reverts to author. Prizes of $1,000, $500, and $250 for the best poetry to appear in the magazine each year. Contact: The Editors. Send up to 10 poems. No simultaneous submissions; photocopies acceptable. Decision in 8 weeks.

The American Scholar, 1811 Q Street N.W., Washington, DC 20009. (202) 265–3808. Founded 1932. Circulation: 30,000. Quality poetry. Poets recently published: Eric Tretheway, Robert Pack, Alan Shapiro, Gregory Djanikan. Besides poetry, publishes articles and book reviews. Size: 144

pages in a 6½" by 10" format. Subscription rate: $12 for 4 issues; single copy, $4.

□Received 7,000 poetry mss. in 1982; accepted 23. Pays $50 per poem and 3 free copies. Copyright reverts to author. The Mary Elinore Smith Poetry Prize is announced each spring. The winning poet is published in the spring issue. Contact: Lisa McAuliffe, Poetry Editor. Send 3 poems, each no longer than 34 lines. Simultaneous and photocopied submissions acceptable. Decision in 2 to 4 weeks.

Antaeus, 18 West 30th Street, New York, NY 10001. (212) 685–8240. Founded 1970. Circulation: 5,000. Poetry of all kinds. Poets recently published: Robert Hass, Robert Pinsky, Carolyn Kizer. Besides poetry, publishes fiction and documents. Size: 175 pages in a 6½" by 9" format. Subscription rate: $16 for 4 issues; sample copy $5.

□Received 1,500 poetry mss. in 1982; accepted 15. Pays $5 per printed page and 2 free copies on publication. Copyright reverts to author. Contact: Daniel Halpern, Editor; Megan Ratner, Associate Editor. Send 5 to 8 poems. No simultaneous submissions; no submissions in the summer months (June through October). Photocopies acceptable. Decision in 6 to 8 weeks.

The Antigonish Review, Box 135, St. Francis Xavier University, Antigonish, Nova Scotia, B2G 1CO Canada. (902) 867–2157. Founded 1970. Circulation: 1,000. Poetry of all kinds, except political and erotic. Poets recently published: John Wain, Omar Pound, Irving Layton, Peter Sanger. Besides poetry, publishes fiction, light critical articles, and book reviews. Size: 130 pages in a 6" by 9" format. Subscription rate: $8 for 4 issues; sample copy $2.

□Received 650 poetry mss. in 1982; accepted 90. Pays 2 free copies. Copyright reverts to author. Contact: George Sanderson, Editor. Send 6 poems, each no longer than 50 lines. No simultaneous submissions; photocopies acceptable. Decision in 8 weeks.

Antioch Review, Box 148, Yellow Springs, OH 45387. (513) 767–7386. Founded 1941. Circulation: 4,000. High-quality poetry; no light or inspirational verse. Poets recently published: Charles Wright, Larry Levis, Karen Fish, Sharon Olds. Besides poetry, publishes fiction and essays. Size: 128 pages in a 6" by 9" format. Subscription rate: $15 for 4 issues (individuals), $20 (libraries and institutions). Sample copy: $3 for back issue, $4.50 for current issue.

□Received 3,000 to 4,000 poetry mss. in 1982; accepted 40. Pays $10 a page and 2 free copies on publication. Buys reprint rights. Contact: David St. John, Poetry Editor. Send 1 to 6 poems. No simultaneous submissions; no submissions in the summer. Photocopies acceptable. Decision in 6 weeks.

Apalachee Quarterly, Box 20106, Tallahassee, FL 32316. Founded 1972. Circulation: 400. High-quality poetry that uses language in inventive, subtle ways. No pornography, racism, or sexism. Poets recently published: Peter Meinke, G. S. Sharat Chandra, David Kirby. Also publishes fiction. Size: 50 to 75 pages in a 6¼" by 9¼" format. Subscription rate: $8 for 4 issues; sample copy $2.

☐Received 1,200 poetry mss. in 1982; accepted 9. Pays 2 free copies; pays cash if funding is available. Copyright reverts to author. Occasional prizes for best poems in specified theme issues. Uses an independent judge for the contest. Contact: The Editors. Send 3 to 5 poems, preferably short, each no longer than 2 pages. Simultaneous and photocopied submissions acceptable. Decision in 4 to 6 weeks. May be slow to respond during the summer.

The Archer, Box 41, Camas Valley, OR 97416. (503) 445-2327. Founded 1951. Circulation: 500. All types of poetry, but no extreme avant-garde or surrealistic work, or poems with obscene language. No poems on suicide or homosexuality. Poets recently published: Frederic Raborn, B. Z. Niditch, Josepha Emms. Besides poetry, publishes very short prose and (rarely) fiction. Size: 32 pages in a 5½" by 8½" format. Subscription rate: $4 for 4 issues; sample copy $1. (Rates may change in 1984.)

☐Received 6,000 poetry mss. in 1982; accepted 300. Pays 1 free copy. Copyright reverts to author. Poetry contests on specified themes award about $30 in cash and free subscriptions or books. One contest planned on comets in advance of return of Halley's Comet. Write for details. Contact: Wilfred Brown, Editor. Send no more than 4 poems, each under 30 lines. Simultaneous and photocopied submissions acceptable. Decision in 1 or 2 weeks. May be slow to respond during the summer.

Arizona Quarterly, Main Library B-541, University of Arizona, Tucson, AZ 85721. (602) 621-6396. Founded 1945. Circulation not available; state supported. Poetry that has something to say and says it well. Poets recently published: Howard G. Hansen, F. C. Rosenberger, Bernard Rogers, A. P. Phillips. Besides poetry, publishes stories, articles, and book reviews. Size: 96 pages in a 6" by 9" format. Subscription rate: $5 for 4 issues; sample copy $1.50.

☐Received 1,500 poetry mss. in 1982; accepted 15. Pays 10 free copies. Copyright reverts to author. Annual award for the best poem published in that year. Contact: A. F. Gegenheimer, Editor. Send 1 to 5 poems, each no more than 30 lines. No previously published or simultaneous submissions. Photocopies acceptable. Decision in 3 weeks. Slow to respond during the summer.

The Atlantic Monthly, 8 Arlington Street, Boston, MA 02116. (617) 536-9500. Founded 1857. Circulation: 440,000. Poetry of all kinds for the general reader. Poets recently published: Stanley Kunitz, William Matthews, May Swenson, Tess Gallagher. Besides poetry, publishes articles on politics, literature, science, and art. Size: 100 to 128 pages in an 8" by 11" format. Subscription rate: $18 for 12 issues; sample copy $2.

□Received 70,000 poetry mss. in 1982; accepted 50. Pays cash and 2 free copies on acceptance. Copyright reverts to author. Contact: Peter Davison, Poetry Editor. Send 5 or 6 previously unpublished poems. No simultaneous submissions; photocopies acceptable. Decision in 3 weeks.

The Bellingham Review, 412 North State, Bellingham, WA 98225. (206) 734–9781. Founded 1977. Circulation: 700. Poetry of all kinds. Poets recently published: Laurel Speer, Mark McCloskey, Peter Nicoletta, Christina V. Pacosz. Besides poetry, publishes fiction, drama, reviews, drawings, and photography. Size: 52 pages in a 5½″ by 8½″ format. Subscription rate: $4 for 2 issues; sample copy $2.
□Received "countless" poetry mss. in 1982; accepted 80. Pays one free copy and a free subscription. Copyright reverts to author. Contact: Knute Skinner and Stanley J. Hodson, Poetry Editors. Send 1 to 10 poems, each no more than 4 pages. Manuscripts not read from June 1 to September 15. Simultaneous and photocopied submissions acceptable. Decision in 8 weeks.
□Signpost Press Poetry Chapbook Competition pays $50 and 50 free copies of the book. Sample publication: Jim Daniels, *On the Line.* Send a 20-page ms. and a $4 reading fee between September 1 and December 31. The winner will be announced in March. Write for full details.

Beloit Poetry Journal, Box 154, RFD 2, Ellsworth, ME 04605. (207) 667–5598. Founded 1950. Circulation: 1,100. The best new poetry of any form, content, or school. Criteria are excellence, imagination, and power. Poets recently published: James Bertolino, Stephen T. Butterfield, Lola Haskins. Also publishes reviews by the editors. Size: 40 pages in a 5½″ by 8¼″ format. Subscription rate: $6 for 4 issues; sample copy $1.
□Received 4,000 poetry mss. in 1982; accepted 66. Pays 3 free copies. Copyright reverts to author. Contact: David M. and Marion K. Stocking, Editors. Send 3 to 6 poems. No simultaneous submissions; photocopies acceptable. Decision in 12 weeks.
□Beloit Poetry Journal Chapbooks complement the unsolicited submissions. Pays in free copies. Sample publication: Richard Pao-Llosa, Ed. and Trans., *New Latin American Poems.*

Bitterroot, Box 51, Blythebourne Station, Brooklyn, NY 11219. Founded 1962. Circulation: 1,000. Original poetry, fantastic, close to the earth, or cabalistic. Interested in young, unpublished poets, including those in prison. Poets recently published: Harry Smith, Gayle Elen Harvey, John Tagliabue, Arthur Dobrin. Also publishes translations. Size: 72 pages in a 5½″ by 8½″ format. Subscription rate: $7 for 3 issues; sample copy $2.75.
□Received "thousands" of poetry mss. in 1982; accepted about 250. Pays 1 free copy; will pay cash if a pending grant comes through. Copyright reverts to author. William Kushner and Heershe David Badannek poetry contests offer prizes ranging from $25 to $100. Write for guidelines. Contact: Menke Katz, Editor. Send 3 or 4 poems, each no longer than 50 lines. No simultaneous or photocopied submissions. Decision in 6 weeks.

The Black Warrior Review, Box 2936, University, AL 35486. (205) 348-5065. Founded 1974. Circulation: 1,000 to 1,500. Quality poetry with an original voice. Poets recently published: James Tate, Dave Smith, Michael Pettit, Mary Ruefle. Besides poetry, publishes fiction, essays, and reviews. Size: 128 pages in a 9" by 6" format. Subscription rate: $5.50 for 2 issues; sample copy $3.
☐Received 1,500 to 2,000 poetry mss. in 1982; accepted 45. Pays 2 free copies. Copyright reverts to author. Contact: John C. Morrison, Poetry Editor. Send any number of poems. Simultaneous and photocopied submissions acceptable. Decision in 3 to 8 weeks.
☐Black Warrior Chapbook Series pays 2 free copies. Sample publication: Mary Ruefle, *8 Poems.* Decision in 3 to 8 weeks.

Black Willow, 401 Independence Drive, "Sunrise," Harleysville, PA 19438. (215) 362-5546. Founded 1982. Circulation: 300. Poetry in the vein of Richard Hugo, Robert Lowell, Anne Sexton, William Stafford, and Robert Frost. Poets recently published: R. T. Smith, Fred Chappell, Roy Scheele. Publishes poetry only. Size: 52 pages in a 5½" by 8½" format. Subscription rate: $7 for 2 issues; sample copy $3.
☐Received 1,300 poetry mss. in 1982; accepted 147. Pays 2 free copies. Copyright reverts to author. Contact: Harold Fleming, Editor; Eileen Davenport, Associate Editor. Send at least 4 poems. Simultaneous and photocopied submissions acceptable. Decision in 6 weeks.
☐Black Willow Chapbook Series pays 10% royalties and offers a 25% discount on author's purchases. Open to contemporary and traditional poetry. Sample publication: Mark De Foe, *Bringing Home Breakfast.* Send a ms. of 20 pages, including front matter. Decision in 10 to 12 weeks.

The Bloomsbury Review, Box 8928, Denver, CO 80201. (303) 455-0593. Founded 1980. Circulation: 8,000. Contemporary, non-rhyming poetry in open forms. Poets recently published: William Pitt Root, Duane Niatum, Robert Burlingame, Del Marie Rogers. Besides poetry, publishes features, book reviews, and interviews. Size: 32 pages in a 10" by 13" format. Subscription rate: $12 for 12 issues; sample copy $2.
☐Received 1,000 poetry mss. in 1982; accepted 50. Pays $5 to $15 per poem and 10 free copies. Copyright reverts to author. Contact: Ray Gonzalez, Poetry Editor. Send 5 to 8 poems, each no longer than 65 lines. No previously published work or simultaneous submissions. Photocopies acceptable. Decision in 6 weeks.

Blue Unicorn, 22 Avon Road, Kensington, CA 94707. (415) 526-8439. Founded 1977. Circulation: 500. Poetry that shows originality in imagery, thought, and music. Memorable and communicative poetry in both traditional and free verse. Poets recently published: Charles Edward Eaton, Josephine Miles, Peter Wild, Norma Farber. Publishes poetry only. Size: 48 to 50 pages in a 5½" by 8½" format. Subscription rate: $9 for 3 issues; sample copy $3.

☐Received 20,000 poetry mss. in 1982; accepted about 200. Pays 1 free copy. Copyright reverts to author. Annual Blue Unicorn contests award cash prizes of $100, $75, and $50, and 6 honorable mentions. Write for rules and deadlines. Contact: The Editors. Send 3 to 5 poems, each no more than 1 page long. No simultaneous submissions; clear photocopies acceptable. Decision in 2 to 3 months.

Boston Review, 991 Massachusetts Avenue, Cambridge, MA 02138. (617) 492–5478. Founded 1975. Circulation: 10,000. Quality poetry. Poets recently published: Mekeel McBride, James Merrill, Jay Parini. Besides poetry, publishes fiction, feature articles, and book reviews. Size: 36 pages in a tabloid format. Subscription rate: $9 for 6 issues; sample copy $2.50.
☐Received 500 poetry mss. in 1982; accepted 10. Pays $25 per poem and 2 free copies. Copyright reverts to author. Contact: Poetry Editor. Send no more than 5 poems, each under 50 lines long. No simultaneous or photocopied submissions. Decision in 6 weeks.

boundary 2, State University of New York at Binghamton, Binghamton, NY 13901. (607) 798–2743. Founded 1972. Circulation: 1,000 to 1,500. Postmodern and experimental poetry. Poets recently published: Jerome Rothenberg, Robert Creeley, David Ignatow, Diane Wakoski. Besides poetry, publishes fiction, criticism, and articles on theory. Size: 300 pages in a 9″ by 5¾″ format. Subscription rate: $15; sample copy $5.
☐Received 450 poetry mss. in 1982; accepted 20. Pays 15 free copies. Copyright reverts to author. Contact: William Spanos, Editor. Send 2 to 4 poems. No simultaneous submissions. Photocopies acceptable. Decision in 6 to 16 weeks.

California Quarterly, Department of English, University of California, Davis, CA 95616. (916) 752–2272. Founded 1971. Circulation: 700. Serious contemporary poetry. Poets recently published: Lyn Lifshin, Joyce Carol Oates, Sandra Gilbert, Anne Perlman. Besides poetry, publishes interviews, fiction, and graphics. Size: 80 pages in an 8½″ by 5½″ format. Subscription rate: $7 for 4 issues; sample copy $2.
☐Received 3,000 poetry mss. in 1982; accepted 75. Pays $3 per poem and 2 copies. Copyright reverts to author. Contact: Poetry Editor. Send 3 to 5 poems. No simultaneous submissions. Photocopies acceptable. Decision in 4 weeks. Manuscripts not read between July 1 and October1.
☐Occasional contests include the Hart Crane Memorial Poetry Contest. Write with SASE for details.

Calliope, Creative Writing Program, Roger Williams College, Bristol, RI 02809. (401) 255–2185. Founded 1977. Circulation: 300. Poetry of various styles, with a preference for concrete images over abstract messages. Poets recently published: Lucien Stryk, George E. Murphy, Pamela Harrison. Besides poetry, publishes fiction, interviews, occasional reviews of other little magazines. Size: 40 pages in a 5½" by 8½" format. Subscription rate: $1.50 for 2 issues; sample copy $1.

☐Received 2,000 poetry mss. in 1982; accepted 40 to 50. Pays 2 free copies and a year's subscription. Copyright reverts to author. Contact: Martha Christina, Editor. Send no more than 5 poems. No simultaneous submissions. Photocopies acceptable. Manuscripts not read from May through August. Decision in 3 weeks.

Calyx: *A Journal of Art and Literature by Women*, Box B, Corvallis, OR 97339. (503) 753-9384. Founded 1976. Circulation: Over 2,000. Well-written poetry. Poets recently published: Jana Harris, Colleen McElroy, Lyn Lifshin, Eleanor Wilner. Besides poetry, publishes fiction, reviews, and art. Size: 80 to 100 pages in a 7" by 8" format. Subscription rate: $10 for 3 issues; sample copy $4 plus 75¢ postage.

☐Received 1,000 to 2,000 poetry mss. in 1982; accepted 45. Pays 1 free copy for each poem published. Copyright reverts to author. Contact: Poetry Editor. Send no more than 6 poems. No simultaneous submissions; photocopies acceptable. Decision in 6 months.

The Cape Rock, Southeast Missouri State University, Cape Girardeau, MO 63701. (314) 651-2158. Founded 1964. Circulation: 200 to 250. Quality poetry in all forms; nothing didactic, sentimental, or cute. Poets recently published: Martin Robbins, Laurie Taylor, Laurel Speer, Louis Mc Kee. Also publishes photography. Size: 56 pages in a 6" by 9" format. Subscription rate: $3 for 2 issues; sample copy $2.

☐Received 2,000 poetry mss. in 1982; accepted 90. Pays 2 free copies. Copyright reverts to author. Contact: Harvey Hecht, Editor. Send any number of poems, each under 70 lines. Prefers no simultaneous submissions. Photocopies acceptable. Decision in 4 to 12 weeks. Slow to respond from June through August.

Carolina Quarterly, Greenlaw Hall 066-A, University of North Carolina, Chapel Hill, NC 27514. (919) 962-0244. Founded 1948. Circulation: 800 to 1,000. Quality poetry of all kinds. Poets recently published: Albert Goldbarth, Richard Kenney, William Stafford, John Hollander. Besides poetry, publishes short fiction, reviews, graphic art, and photography. Size: 100 pages in a 6" by 9" format. Subscription rate: $9 for 3 issues; sample copy $4.

☐Received 2,000 poetry mss. in 1982; accepted 40. Pays $5 per poem and 2 free copies. Copyright reverts to author. Contact: Ellen Caldwell, Poetry Editor. Send 3 to 5 poems, each no longer than 100 lines. No simultaneous submissions. Prefers no photocopies. Decision in 12 to 15 weeks.

Cedar Rock, 1121 Madeline, New Braunfels, TX 78130. (512) 625-6002. Founded 1976. Circulation: 2,000. Serious, readable, and dramatic poetry, in free or conventional forms. No light or religious verse. Poets recently pub-

lished: Marge Piercy, Judson Jerome, Charles Bukowski, Archibald MacLeish. Besides poetry, publishes fiction, essays, and reviews. Size: 28 pages in an 11½" by 14½" tabloid format. Subscription rate: $6 for 4 issues; sample copy $2.50.
☐Received 700 poetry mss. in 1982; accepted 75. Pays $10 to $200 a poem on acceptance, and 1 free copy. Copyright reverts to author. Contact: David C. Yates, Poetry Editor. Send 4 to 6 poems under 25 lines. No simultaneous submissions; photocopies acceptable. Decision in 4 weeks.
☐Cedar Rock Press Chapbook Series publishes poets whose work has appeared in the magazine. Pays royalties. Sample publication: Judson Jerome, *Thirty Years of Poetry, 1949–1979.*

The Centennial Review, 110 Morrill Hall, Michigan State University, East Lansing, MI 48824. (517) 355–1905. Founded 1960. Circulation: 1,200. Poetry of all kinds, with a preference for good free verse and organic form poems. Especially interested in women poets. No long poems or sequences. Poets recently published: Joyce Carol Oates, Susan Fromberg Schaeffer, David Ignatow, David Citino. Besides poetry, publishes essays on interdisciplinary topics and literature, including contemporary work. Size: 85 to 100 pages in a 6" by 9" format. Subscription rate: $5 for 4 issues; sample copy $1.50.
☐Received 3,000 poetry mss. in 1982; accepted 25. Pays one year's free subscription and 2 free copies. Copyright reverts to author. Contact: Linda W. Wagner, Poetry Editor. Send 3 to 5 poems, each under a page in length. No simultaneous or photocopied submissions. Decision in 2 weeks.

The Chariton Review, Northeast Missouri State University, Kirksville, MO 63501. (816) 785–4499. Founded 1975. Circulation: 600. Quality contemporary poetry in traditional and open forms. Poets recently published: Lucien Stryk, Al Goldbarth, David Ray, Ron Wallace. Besides poetry, publishes fiction and translations of fiction and poetry. Size: 100 pages in a 6" by 9" format. Subscription rate: $4 for 2 issues; sample copy $2.
☐Received 2,000 poetry mss. in 1982; accepted 40 to 50. Pays $5 per published page and 1 free copy. Buys first North American serial rights. Contact: Jim Barnes, Editor. Send 4 to 7 poems. No simultaneous or photocopied submissions. Decision in 2 weeks.

Chelsea, Box 5880, Grand Central Station, New York, NY 10163. Founded 1958. Circulation: 1,100 to 1,500. Sophisticated avant-garde or traditional poetry; superior translations. Poets recently published: Amy Clampitt, Philip Dacey, Jane Flanders, José Emilio Pachéco. Besides poetry, publishes short stories, short plays, essays, art, and photography. Size: 182 pages in a 6" by 9" format. Subscription rate: $9 for 2 issues or 1 double issue; sample copy $4.50.
☐Received 700 poetry mss. in 1982; accepted 25. Pays 2 free copies. Copyright reverts to author. Contact: Sonia Raiziss, Editor; Alfredo de

Palchi, Brian Swann, Richard Foerster, Associate Editors. Send 5 to 8 poems. No simultaneous submissions; photocopies acceptable. Decision in 6 to 8 weeks, except when preparing special issues.

Chicago Review, Faculty Exchange, Box C, University of Chicago, Chicago, IL 60637. (312) 753-3571. Founded 1946. Circulation: 3,000. Quality poetry. Poets recently published: Turner Cassity, Alan Shapiro, Pattiann Rogers, W. S. Di Piero. Besides poetry, publishes fiction, essays, criticism, and interviews. Also sponsors a speaker series that includes poetry readings. Size: 150 pages in a 6″ by 9″ format. Subscription rate: $12 for 4 issues; sample copy $3.50.
☐Received 1,500 poetry mss. in 1982; accepted 75. Pays 2 free copies and a year's free subscription. Copyright reverts to author. Contact: Michael Donaghy and Michael Alper, Poetry Editors. Send any number of poems. No simultaneous submissions; photocopies acceptable. Decision in 4 to 6 weeks.

The Chowder Review, 648 Canton Avenue, Milton, MA 02186. Founded 1973. Circulation: 800 to 1,000. A variety of types of poetry. Poets recently published: William Dickey, Robert Pack, Laura Jensen, Pattiann Rogers. Besides poetry, publishes articles, reviews, and interviews. Size: 110 pages in an 8½″ by 5½″ format. Subscription rate: $9 for 3 issues; sample copy $3.50.
☐Received 7,500 poetry mss. in 1982; accepted 120. Pays $10 to $50 when funds are available plus 2 free copies. Copyright reverts to author. Contact: Ron Slate, Editor. Send 5 poems. No simultaneous submissions; photocopies acceptable. Decision in 3 weeks.
☐Chowder Chapbooks competition results in publication and payment of a flat fee and copies. Sample publication: Paul Zimmer, *Earthbound Zimmer.* Send for guidelines with SASE. Appropriate mss. of 32–40 pages will be read.

Cimarron Review, 208 Life Sciences East, Oklahoma State University, Stillwater, OK 74078. (405) 624-6573. Founded 1967. Circulation 500. Quality poetry dealing with contemporary issues or offering insights into the past. Subject matters less than vision and technique. Poets recently published: Bruce Weigl, Thomas Reiter, W. C. Bowie, H. A. Maxson. Besides poetry, publishes fiction, essays, and photography. Size: 64 pages in a 6″ by 9″ format. Subscription rate: $10 for 4 issues; sample copy free.
☐Received around 1,000 poetry mss. in 1982; accepted about 30. Pays $12.50 per poem when CCLM grant is available; otherwise pays 6 free copies. Copyright reverts to author. Contact: Terry Hummer, Poetry Editor. Send 2 to 5 poems, each no more than 2 pages long. Simultaneous and photocopied submissions acceptable. Decision in 3 weeks.

College English, Department of English, Indiana University, Bloomington, IN 47405. (312) 335-8183. Founded 1965. Circulation: 10,000. Poems of all kinds, especially those of fewer than 50 to 60 lines. Poets recently published: Rennie McQuilin, Ralph Burns, Brian O'Neill, Charles Guilford. Besides poetry, publishes essays on the teaching of literature and creative writing; occasional interviews with poets. Size: 112 pages in an 8½" by 9½" format. Subscription rate: $30 for 8 issues, with membership in the National Council of Teachers of English. Sample copy: $2.50.

☐Received 1,000 poetry mss. in 1982; accepted 25. Pays 6 free copies. Copyright reverts to author. Contact: Brian O'Neill, Poetry Consultant. Send 3 to 4 poems. Simultaneous and photocopied submissions acceptable. Decision in 12 weeks.

Colorado State Review, English Department, 322 Eddy, Colorado State University, Fort Collins, CO 80523. (303) 491–6428. Founded 1977. Circulation: 500. Poetry with magical realism; translations. Poets recently published: Floyce Alexander, Patricia Goedicke, Vern Rutsala, Lyn Lifshin. Besides poetry, publishes interviews, reviews, and essays on contemporary poetry. Size: 80 pages in an 8½" by 5½" format. Subscription rate: $5 for 2 issues; sample copy $2.

☐Received 500 poetry mss. in 1982; accepted 60. Pays 2 free copies, and a year's free subscription. Copyright reverts to author. Contact: Bill Tremblay, Poetry Editor; Mary Crow, Translations Editor. Send 1 to 5 poems. No simultaneous submissions; no submissions between January 1 and April 30. Photocopies acceptable. Decision in 12 weeks.

Commonweal, 232 Madison Avenue, New York, NY 10016. (212) 683–2042. Founded 1924. Circulation: 18,000. Quality poetry. Poets recently published: Josephine Jacobsen, Hillel Schwartz, Anne Porter, Jane Flanders. Besides poetry, publishes editorials, articles on public affairs, and reviews of the arts. Size: 32 pages in an 8¼" by 11" format. Subscription rate: $24 for biweekly issues; sample copy $1.25.

☐Received 400 poetry mss. in 1982; accepted 25. Pays 40¢ a line and 2 free copies. Copyright reverts to author. Contact: Rosemary Deen, Poetry Editor. Send 3 to 4 poems, each no longer than 40 lines. Manuscripts not read during July and August. Simultaneous and photocopied submissions acceptable. Decision in 4 weeks.

Confrontation, English Department, Long Island University, Brooklyn, NY 11201. (212) 403–1050. Founded 1968. Circulation: 2,000. Literate, crafted poetry with intensity of feeling. Poets recently published: Philip Appleman, Susan Fromberg Schaeffer, Jane Mayhall, Jane Flanders, Harvey Shapiro. Besides poetry, publishes occasional interviews, and essays on poetry. Size: 160 to 190 pages in a 5" by 7" format. Subscription rate: $5 for 2 issues; sample copy: back issue $1.50, current issue $3.

☐Received 2,000 poetry mss. in 1982; accepted 200. Pays $5 to $40 per poem and 1 free copy. Buys rights for future anthologies. Contact: Poetry Editors. Send 4 to 5 poems. Simultaneous submissions acceptable if editors are notified. Photocopies acceptable. Manuscripts not read during July and August. Decision in 4 to 6 weeks.

Connecticut River Review, 184 Centerbrook Road, Hamden, CT 06518. (203) 281–0235. Founded 1974. Circulation: 500. Well-crafted and deeply felt poetry of all kinds. No surrealism. Poets recently published: Geraldine C. Little, Ruth Lisa Schechter, Mark Johnston. Publishes poetry only. Size: 36 pages in a 5½" by 8½" format. Subscription rate (including membership in the Connecticut Poetry Society): $15; sample copy $3.75.
☐Received 1,000 poetry mss. in 1982; accepted 58. Pays 2 free copies. Copyright reverts to author. The annual Brodine Award gives 3 prizes of $100, $50, and $25, and several honorable mentions. Contact: Virginia Brady Young, Executive Editor; May Harding and Peter Ulisse, Assistant Editors. Send 4 to 5 poems, each no more than 35 lines long, prior to the September 15 and March 15 deadlines. Do not include a letter or a lengthy biography. No simultaneous submissions; photocopies acceptable. Decision in 12 weeks.

Corona, Department of History and Philosophy, Montana State University, Bozeman, MT 59715. (406) 994–4395. Founded 1980. Circulation: 2,000. Quality poetry of all kinds. Poets recently published: Richard Hugo, Donald Hall, X. J. Kennedy, Ken McCullough. Besides poetry, publishes fiction, articles, satire, plays, cartoons, art, photography, and music. Size: 125 to 140 pages in a 7" by 10" format. Subscription rate: $7 for 1 issue; sample copy $7.
☐Received "too many" mss. in 1982; accepted 10 poetry mss. Pays $10 per poem and 2 free copies. Copyright reverts to author. Contact: Lynda or Michael Sexson, Editors. Send any number of poems. Simultaneous and photocopied submissions acceptable. Decision in 1 to 12 weeks.

Cosmopolitan, 224 West 57th Street, New York, NY 10019. Founded 1885. Circulation: 2,983,978. Poetry on male-female relationships, from a woman's point of view. Poets recently published: Erica Jong, Merrit Malloy, Alan Dugan. Besides poetry, publishes articles, fiction, and fillers. Size: 300 to 325 pages in an 8" by 10⅞" format. Subscription rate: $24 for 12 issues. No samples; $2.25 is the newsstand price.
☐Received about 10,000 poetry mss. in 1982; accepted about 15 to 20. Pays $25 and up for poems. Buys all rights. Contact: Roni Benson, Poetry Editor. Send a few poems. Simultaneous and photocopied submissions acceptable. Decision in 2 weeks.

Cottonwood Magazine, Box J, Student Union, Kansas University, Lawrence, KS 66045. Founded 1965. Circulation: 800. "Solidly built," non-academic poetry. Poets recently published: Victor Contoski, Harley Elliott, Patricia Traxler. Besides poetry, publishes fiction, reviews, interviews, and photographs. Size: 120 pages in a 9" by 6" format. Subscription rate: $9 for 3 issues; sample copy $2.
☐Received 600 poetry mss. in 1982; number of acceptances not available. Pays 2 free copies. Copyright reverts to author. Contact: Erleen Christensen, Poetry Editor. Send 5 poems. No simultaneous submissions. Photocopies acceptable. Decision in 9 weeks.

The Country Poet, RD #3, Dodgeville, WI 53533. Founded 1951. Discontinued 1955; revived 1983. Circulation: under 1,000. Good seasonal poetry and current poetry of any type with depth but not obfuscation. No Jack Frosts, red-bellied robins, or gypsy autumns. Poets recently published: Marcia Lee Masters, May Sarton, William Stafford, Hans Juergensen. Publishes poetry only. Size: 36 to 48 pages in a 5½" by 8½" format. Subscription rate: $3.50 for 4 issues; sample copy $1.
☐Received 117 poetry mss. from August 1 to September 1, 1983; accepted 40. Pays one penny for each subscriber on the roll at the time the issue is mailed. Copyright reverts to author. Contact: Edna Meudt, Editor. Send 3 to 5 poems. No simultaneous submissions; photocopies acceptable. Decision in 6 weeks.

Crab Creek Review, 30 F Street N. E., Ephrata, WA 98823. (206) 634-3199. Founded 1983. Circulation: 500. Formal or free verse, with clear and precise imagery and voice, and wit in the use of sound and language. Poets recently published: Mark Halperin, Joan Kaplinski, Sheila Nickerson, Tony Moffeit. Besides poetry, publishes fiction and essays under 3,500 words. Size: 32 pages in a 7½" by 11" format. Subscription rate: $8 for 3 issues; sample copy $3.
☐Received 150 to 200 poetry mss. in 1982; accepted 45. Pays 2 free copies. Copyright reverts to author. Contact: Linda Clifton, Co-Editor. Send 1 to 4 poems, each under 40 lines, beginning in March 1984. No simultaneous submissions; photocopies acceptable. Decision in 8 weeks.

Croton Review, Box 277, Croton-on-Hudson, NY 10520. Founded 1978. Circulation: 2,000. Quality poetry that shows craft, imagination, substance, and originality. No racist or pornographic material. Poets recently published: Lyn Lifshin, Marge Piercy, James Miller, Joan Colby. Besides poetry, publishes short fiction, essays, and translations. Size: 32 pages in a tabloid format. Subscription rate: $7 for 1 issue; sample copy $7.
☐Received "thousands" of poetry mss. in 1982; accepted 25. Pays a cash amount dependent on a grant, plus 1 free copy. Copyright reverts to author. Poetry Contest for 1984 awarded prizes of $50, $75, and $100. Query about future contests. Contact: The Editors. Send 3 to 5 poems, each under 75 lines. Manuscripts read only from September to February. Simultaneous submissions acceptable if editors are notified. Photocopies acceptable. Decision in 12 weeks.

Cumberland Poetry Review, Box 120128, Acklen Station, Nashville, TN 37212. (615) 373-8948. Founded 1981. Circulation: 500. Poetry of all kinds. Poets recently published: Seamus Heaney, Elder Olson, Richard Eberhart, C. H. Sisson. Besides poetry, publishes poetry criticism and articles on contemporary poetry. Size: 100 pages in a 6" by 9" format. Subscription rate: $9 for 2 issues; sample copy $6.
☐Received 300 poetry mss. in 1982; accepted 50. Pays 2 free copies.

Copyright reverts to author. Contact: The Editors. Send 3 to 6 poems, each no more than 2 pages long. Simultaneous and photocopied submissions acceptable. Decision in 12 weeks.

CutBank, English Department, University of Montana, Missoula, MT 59812. Founded 1972. Circulation: 600. Quality poetry. Poets recently published: Richard Hugo, Dick Allen, Madeline De Frees, Harry Humes. Besides poetry, publishes short stories, reviews, articles, interviews, art, and photography. Size: 112 pages in a 5½" by 8½" format. Subscription rate: $7.50 for 2 issues; sample copy $2.50.
☐Received 1,000 poetry mss. in 1982; accepted 60. Pays 2 free copies. Copyright reverts to author. Contact: Suzanne Hackett and Jon Davis, Co-Editors. Send 5 to 6 poems. No simultaneous submissions; photocopies acceptable. Decision in 6 to 8 weeks. Slow to respond during the summer.

Dark Horse, Box 9, Somerville, MA 02143. Founded 1974. Circulation: 700. Honest, well-crafted, emotionally intense poetry. Poets recently published: Nancy Cherry, Alice Fulton, Ernest Kroll, Carolyn White. Besides poetry, publishes short fiction, reviews, contest notices and manuscript-wanted notices. Size: 24 pages in an 11" by 17" format. Subscription rate: $6 for 4 issues, $10 for 8 issues (individual); $10 for 4 issues (institutional); sample copy $2.
☐Received 900 poetry mss. in 1982; accepted 70. Purchases non-exclusive anthology rights. Pays 2 free copies. Contact: John Elder and Seth Steinzor, Poetry Editors. Send 6 to 10 poems of any length. Simultaneous and photocopied submissions acceptable. Decision in 16 weeks.

Descant, Box 314, Station P, Toronto, Ontario, M5S 2S8 Canada. Founded 1970. Circulation: 800. Poetry in a variety of styles. Poets recently published: John Hollander, Peter Redgrove, Ralph Gustaphson, Dennis Lee. Besides poetry, publishes plays, short stories, articles, essays, graphics, and photography. Size: 150 pages in a 5¾" by 8½" format. Subscription rate: $18 for 4 issues (in Canada); sample copy $6.50 (in Canada).
☐Received 300 to 350 poetry mss. in 1982; accepted 50. Pays 1 free copy and offers a 40% discount on additional copies. Copyright reverts to author. Contact: Editors of *Descant*. Send at least 3 poems. No simultaneous submissions or previously published work. Photocopies acceptable. Decision in 16 weeks.

Descant, Department of English, Texas Christian University, Fort Worth, TX 76129. (817) 921-7240. Founded 1956. Circulation: 450. Poetry of all kinds. Rarely uses poetry longer than 40 lines or posing unusual requirements with typography. Poets recently published: Walter McDonald, Kate Jennings, Ramona Weeks, Peter Wild. Also interested in interviews, but has not published any. Size: 90 pages in a 6" by 9" format. Subscription rate: $6.50 for 2 issues; sample copy $2.50.

☐Received 6,000 poetry mss. in 1982; accepted 50 to 60. Pays in free copies. Copyright reverts to author. Contact: Betsy Colquitt, Editor. Send 4 to 5 poems. Manuscripts not read during the summer. Simultaneous and photocopied submissions acceptable. Decision in 6 weeks.

The Devil's Millhopper, Route 3, Box 29, Elgin, SC 29045. (803) 438-2764. Founded 1975. Circulation: 300 to 400. Poetry of all kinds, from traditional to experimental, with a special interest in narrative. Poets recently published: Sydney Lea, Jared Carter, Robert Dana, William Stafford. Usually publishes poetry only, with occasional other material solicited from writers. Size: 20 to 60 pages in a 5½" by 8½" format. Subscription rate: $5 for 2 issues; sample copy $2.50.
☐Received 4,000 poetry mss. in 1982; accepted 60. Pays 2 free copies. Buys rights to republish. Contact: Jim Peterson, Poetry Editor. Send 1 to 7 poems. No simultaneous submissions; photocopies acceptable. Decision in 4 weeks.
☐Devil's Millhopper Chapbook Series, founded 1983, pays $50 flat fee and 50 free copies to the winner of a competition. Considers mss. of 30 pages (including front matter) submitted before February 1. Decision in 8 weeks.

Earthwise Publications (Earthwise Poetry Journal, Earthwise Newsletter, Tempest: Avant-Garde Poetry), Box 680-536, Miami, FL 33168. (305) 688-8558. Founded 1978. Circulation: 300 (*Earthwise Poetry Journal*). Free verse, especially avant-garde and experimental. No pornography. Poets recently published: Karla Hammond, Albert Huffstickler, Ricardo Pau-Llosa, David Yates. Besides poetry, publishes interviews, essays, articles, and short fiction under 1,200 words. Size: 60 pages in a 5½" by 8½" format. Subscription rate: $16 for 4 issues; sample copy $3.63.
☐Received 1,500 poetry mss. in 1982; accepted 100 to 150. Pays $2 to $5 per poem. Copyright reverts to author. Contact: Sally Newhouse, Poetry Editor. Send 3 to 5 poems, each no longer than one page unless it's a narrative. Include a brief biography and a list of publications and contests won. Manuscripts not read from June 15 to September 15. Prefers no simultaneous submissions. Clear photocopies acceptable. Decision in 6 to 8 weeks.
☐The Earthwise Annual Summer Competition offers prizes ranging from $15 to $100 for poems on a specified theme. Send up to 5 poems, with an entry fee of $2.50 for the first poem and $1.25 for each additional one. The 1983 deadline was September 30.
☐The annual T. S. Eliot Chapbook Competition awards a cash prize of $200, publication, and 100 free copies of the book. Send a manuscript of 15 to 25 poems with a reading fee of $10. The 1983 deadline was November 1, with the decision due in January 1984. Write for current information.
☐Earth Series Chapbooks offers a subsidization plan and pays royalties when all copies are sold. Sample publication: Margaret Key Biggs, *Sister to the Sun*. Send one page of your manuscript on a theme announced in *Earthwise Newsletter*. Decision in 6 to 8 weeks.

Epoch, 251 Goldwin Smith, Cornell University, Ithaca, NY 14853. (607)

256–3385. Founded 1947. Circulation: 900 to 1,000. Quality poetry. Poets recently published: Robert Kelly, Josephine Miles, Michael Ondaatje, Fred Chappell. Besides poetry, publishes personal essays, fiction, reviews, drama, and symposia (occasionally on poetry). Size: 80 pages in a 6″ by 9″ format. Subscription rate: $8 for 3 issues; sample copy $3.

☐Received 2,000 poetry mss. in 1982; accepted 27. Pays in free copies; cash payment if state or federal grants are available. Copyright reverts to author. Contact: Poetry Editor. Send any number of poems. No simultaneous submissions; photocopies acceptable. Decision in 8 weeks. Slow to respond during the summer.

Family Circle, 488 Madison Avenue, New York, NY 10022. (212) 593–7930. Circulation: 8 million. Poetry of interest to women and the family. Humorous verse only if it is very good. Poets recently published: Barbara Crooker, Dorothy Raemsch, Jean Boyce. Besides poetry, publishes a variety of articles and features of interest to women. Size: 200 pages in an 8″ by 10½″ format. Subscription rate: $12.75 for 17 issues; single issue 75¢.

☐Received 2,000 to 3,000 poetry mss. in 1982; accepted 7 or 8. Pays $50 per poem and 1 free copy. Copyright reverts to author. Contact: Eleanore Lewis, Poetry Editor. Send no more than 10 poems, each no more than 25 lines long. No simultaneous submissions. Photocopies acceptable. Decision in 3 weeks.

Feminist Studies, Women's Studies Program, University of Maryland, College Park, MD 20742. (301) 454–2363. Founded 1972. Circulation: 5,000. Poetry that focuses on women's experiences or is imbued with feminist consciousness. Poets recently published: Honor Moore, Marilyn Hacker, Frances Jaffer, June Jordan. Besides poetry, publishes essays and criticism. Size: 218 pages in a 6″ by 9″ format. Subscription rate: $18 for 3 issues; sample copy $8.

☐No figures given for mss. received and accepted in 1982. Pays 1 free copy. May purchase additional rights if author agrees. Contact: Claire G. Moses or Rachel DuPlessis, Poetry Editors. Send any number of poems. Simultaneous and photocopied submissions acceptable. Decision in 6 weeks.

The Fiddlehead, The Observatory, University of New Brunswick, Fredericton, New Brunswick E3B 5A3, Canada. (506) 454–3591. Founded 1945. Circulation: 1,100. Quality poetry. Poets recently published: Dermot McCarthy, Derek Wynand, Joseph Sherman, Eric Cashen. Also publishes short fiction. Size: 110 to 120 pages in a 6″ by 9″ format. Subscription rate: $13 for 4 issues; sample copy $4.25.

☐Received 1,200 poetry mss. in 1982; accepted 60 to 120. Pays $10 per printed page and 1 free copy. Copyright reverts to author. Contact: Robert Gibbs and Robert Hawkes, Poetry Editors. Send 6 to 10 poems. No simultaneous submissions. Clear photocopies acceptable. Decision in 8 weeks.

Field, Rice Hall, Oberlin College, Oberlin, OH 44074. (216) 775–8408. Founded 1969. Circulation: 2,000. The best poetry, in translation too. Poets recently published: Jean Valentine, Sandra McPherson, Miroslav Holub, Charles Wright. Also publishes essays on poetics by working poets. Size: 100 pages in a 5½″ by 8½″ format. Subscription rate: $7 for 2 issues; $14 for 4 issues; sample copy $3.50 postpaid.
□Received 15,000 poetry mss. in 1982; accepted 150. Pays $20 to $30 per page and 2 free copies on publication. Copyright reverts to author. Contact: Stuart Friebert and David Young, Editors. Send 5 to 8 poems. No simultaneous submissions; photocopies acceptable. Decision in 3 weeks.
□Field Translation Series, founded in 1978, publishes translations of the best world poetry. Sample publication: Eugenio Montale, *The Storm and Other Poems,* trans. Charles Wright. Pays royalties and free copies. Send a ms. of 100 to 200 pages. Decision in 10 weeks.

Footwork, Passaic County College, College Boulevard, Paterson, NJ 07509. (201) 279–5000. Founded 1979. Circulation: 1,000. High-quality poetry. Poets recently published: Joseph Bruchac, Lyn Lifshin, Ruth Lisa Schechter, James McCartin. Besides poetry, publishes short stories and artwork. Size: 72 pages in an 8½″ by 11″ format. Subscription rate: $3 for 1 annual issue; sample copy $1.50.
□Received 2,000 poetry mss. in 1982; accepted 70. Pays 1 free copy. Copyright reverts to author. Contact: Maria Gillan, Poetry Editor. Send 3 poems. Simultaneous and photocopied submissions acceptable. Manuscripts not read from May through September. Decision in 12 weeks.
□Yearly poetry contest offers cash prizes for first, second, and third places, and about 20 honorable mentions. Winning poems are published in an anthology. Write for guidelines.

Gargoyle, Box 3567, Washington, DC 20007. (202) 333–1544. Founded 1976. Circulation: 1,100. Poetry that makes an adventurous and/or imaginative use of language; that effects an intelligent and imaginative marriage of style and subject. Poets recently published: Amy Gerstler, Rodger Kamenetz, David McAleavey, Robert Peters. Besides poetry, publishes fiction, graphics, interviews, and reviews. Size: 120 pages in an 8½″ by 11″ format; as many as 460 pages in a 6″ by 9″ format. Subscription rate: $7 for 2 issues; $8 for institutions. Sample copy $4.
□Received about 3,500 poetry mss. in 1982; accepted about 7. Pays 1 free copy and allows 50% off on additional copies. Copyright reverts to author. Contact: Gretchen Johnsen. Send 5 poems of about 5 to 25 lines. No simultaneous submissions; photocopies acceptable. Decision in 4 weeks.

The Georgia Review, University of Georgia, Athens, GA 30602. (404) 542-3481. Founded 1947. Circulation: 4,400. Quality poetry. Poets recently published: Robert Penn Warren, Mary Oliver, Gerald Stern, Rita Dove.

Besides poetry, publishes fiction, essays, and book reviews. Size: 240 pages in a 6¾" by 10" format. Subscription rate: $9 for 4 issues; sample copy $3.
☐Received 6,250 poetry mss. in 1982; accepted 78. Pays a minimum of $1 per line and 2 free copies. Copyright reverts to author. Contact: Stanley W. Lindberg, Editor; Stephen Corey, Assistant Editor. Send 3 to 5 poems. No simultaneous submissions; photocopies acceptable. Manuscripts not read during June, July, and August. Decision in 6 to 8 weeks.

Good Housekeeping, 959 Eighth Avenue, New York, NY 10019. (212) 262-5700. Founded before 1900. Circulation: 20 million. Poetry about the home and family, preferably short, simple, and rhymed. Poets recently published: Lois Duncan, Alma Denny, Michael Drury. Besides poetry, publishes short stories, novel condensations, articles, and recipes. Size: 300 pages in a glossy magazine format. Subscription rate: $12 for 12 issues. No samples.
☐Received 6,000 poetry mss. in 1982; accepted 10. Pays $5 per line and one free copy. Copyright reverts to author. Contact: Arleen Quarfoot, Poetry Editor. Send any number of poems, each no longer than 20 lines. Simultaneous and photocopied submissions acceptable. Decision in 4 to 6 weeks.

Great River Review, 211 West 7th, Winona, MN 55987. (507) 454-6564. Founded 1977. Circulation: 1,000. High-quality poetry that uses the image as the basis of expression. Poets recently published: Thomas McGrath, Frannie Lindsey, Alvin Greenberg, Marisha Chamberlain. Besides poetry, publishes fiction and book reviews. Size: 160 pages in an 8" by 6" format. Subscription rate: $7 for 2 issues; sample copy $3.50.
☐Received 800 poetry mss. in 1982; accepted 20. Pays 2 free copies. Copyright reverts to author. Contact: Paul Wadden, Poetry Editor. Send 4 to 6 poems. No simultaneous submissions; photocopies acceptable. Decision in 7 weeks.

The Greenfield Review, RD 1, Box 80, Greenfield Center, NY 12833. (518) 584-1728. Founded 1969. Circulation: 1,200. Contemporary poetry, translations from little-translated languages, multi-cultural work. Poets recently published: John Logan, N. Scott Momaday, Jayne Cortez, Martha McFerren. Besides poetry, publishes short stories, reviews, and interviews. Size: 220 pages in a 5½" by 8½" format. Subscription rate: $8 for 2 issues; sample copy $3.
☐Received 2,500 poetry mss. in 1982; accepted 200. Usually pays in free copies. Copyright reverts to author. Contact: Joseph Bruchac, Editor. Send 3 to 6 poems. Manuscripts not read from June through August. No simultaneous or photocopied submissions. Decision in 2 weeks.
☐Greenfield Review Press Chapbook Series pays in royalties and free copies. Sample publication: Kwesi Brew, *African Panorama*. Reports on manuscripts with a multi-cultural focus in 2 weeks. Not accepting manuscripts until 1985.

The Greensboro Review, Department of English, University of North Carolina–Greensboro, Greensboro, NC 27412. (919) 379–5384. Founded 1966. Circulation: 500. Quality poetry. Poets recently published: J. B. Goodenough, Ernest Kroll, Sister Bernetta Quinn, Turner Cassity. Also publishes fiction. Size: 104 pages in a 6″ by 9″ format. Subscription rate: $5 for 2 issues; sample copy $2.50.
□Received 200 poetry mss. in 1982; accepted 20. Pays 3 free copies. Copyright reverts to author. Contact: Sarah Lindsay, Poetry Editor, or Lee Zacharias, Editor. Send 1 to 6 poems during the months of January, February, September, and October only. No simultaneous submissions. Prefers no photocopies. Decision in 6 weeks.

Gryphon, Department of Humanities, LET 370, University of South Florida, Tampa, FL 33620. (813) 974–2260. Founded 1974. Circulation: 300 to 400. Eclectic poetry of high quality; good humorous poetry. No work in the manner of Charles Bukowski. Poets recently published: Will Inman, Edna Meudt, Lyn Lifshin. Besides poetry, publishes fiction and one-act plays. Size: 50 to 60 pages in an 8″ by 11″ format. Subscription rate: $6 for 3 issues; sample copy $2.
□Received 600 poetry mss. in 1982; accepted 150. Pays 1 free copy. Copyright reverts to author. Contact: Dr. Hans Juergensen, Poetry Editor. Send no more than 4 poems. No simultaneous submissions; photocopies acceptable. Decision in 6 to 9 weeks.

G. W. Review, Box 20, Marvin Center, George Washington University, Washington, DC 20052. Founded 1980. Circulation: 1,000. Quality poetry, especially narrative poetry. Poets recently published: Lucille Clifton, Gary Fincke, David McAleavey, Sister Mary Lucina. Also publishes fiction. Size: 24 pages in a 6″ by 9″ format. Subscription rate: $5 for 5 issues; sample copy free with a 6″ by 9″ envelope and 63¢ postage.
□Received 1,000 poetry mss. in 1982; accepted about 100. Pays 3 free copies. Copyright reverts to author. Contact: C. J. Hall, Editor-in-Chief. Send no more than 7 poems. Manuscripts not read from April through August. No simultaneous submissions; photocopies acceptable. Decision in 4 weeks.

Hanging Loose, 231 Wyckoff Street, Brooklyn, NY 11217. Founded 1966. Circulation: 1,200. High-quality poetry. Poets recently published: Jack Anderson, Donna Brook, Carol Cox, Paul Violi. Also publishes fiction. Size: 72 to 80 pages in an 8½″ by 7″ format. Subscription rate: $5.50 for 3 issues; sample copy $3.
□No figures given for mss. received and accepted in 1982. Pays variable amount per poem on acceptance and 3 free copies. Buys additional rights. Contact: R. Hershon, D. Lourie, M. Pawlak, or R. Schreiber, Poetry Editors. Send 4 to 6 poems. No simultaneous submissions; photocopies acceptable. No decision time given.

The Harbor Review, English Department, University of Massachusetts/Boston, Boston, MA 02125. Founded 1982. Circulation: 500. Poetry about people and places; poetry that says complex things simply. Poets recently published: Jared Carter, Ron Schreiber, Helena Minton, Judith Steinbergh. Besides poetry, publishes fiction, interviews, and one-page book reviews. Size: 40 pages in a 5½" by 8" format. Subscription rate: $7 for 3 issues; sample copy $2.50.
☐Received 1,000 to 1,500 poetry mss. in 1982; accepted 15. Pays 2 free copies. Copyright reverts to author. Contact: Stephen Strempek, Poetry Editor. Send 3 to 5 poems. No simultaneous submissions; photocopies acceptable. Decision in 4 weeks.

Helicon Nine: The Journal of Women's Arts & Letters, Box 22412, Kansas City, MO 64113. (913) 381–6383. Founded 1979. Circulation: 2,000. Quality poetry. Poets recently published: Joyce Carol Oates, Roberta Gould, Virginia Scott Miner. Besides poetry, publishes fiction, articles, and art. Size: 96 pages in a 7" by 10" format. Subscription rate: $15 for 3 issues; sample copy $7.50.
☐Received 400 to 500 poetry mss. in 1982; accepted 16. Pays 1 free copy. Copyright reverts to author. Contact: Pat Breed, Poetry Editor. Send any number of poems, each no more than 2 pages long. Simultaneous and photocopied submissions acceptable. Decision in 6 weeks.

The Hollins Critic, Box 9538, Hollins College, VA 24020. (703) 362–6316. Founded 1964. Circulation: 550. Short poems interesting from a technical point of view or for originality of content (or both). Poets recently published: David Citino, Joan Colby, Stephen Ajay, Lyn Coffin. Besides poetry, publishes essays and book reviews. Size: 20 pages in an 8" by 11" format. Subscription rate: $5 for 5 issues; $6.50 foreign. Sample copy: $1.50; $2 foreign.
☐Received 95 poetry mss. in 1982; accepted 24. Pays $25 per poem and 5 free copies. Copyright reverts to author. Awards a prize for the best poem published in that year, with funds available from a grant. Contact: John Rees Moore, Editor. Send 1 to 5 poems, each no longer than 35 lines. No simultaneous or photocopied submissions. Decision in 6 weeks. Slow to respond during the summer.

Hollow Spring Review of Poetry, Hollow Spring Press, RD 1, Chester, MA 01011. Founded 1975. Circulation: 1,200. Poetry in all forms by serious writers. Poets recently published: Leo Connellan, Donald Junkins, Elaine Ferranna. Besides poetry, publishes articles, interviews, satire, criticism, reviews, art, and news items. Size: 64 pages in a 5½" by 8½" format. Subscription rate: $6 for 2 issues; sample copy $1.50.
☐Received 500 poetry mss. in 1982; accepted 170. Pays 2 free copies. Copyright reverts to author. Contact: Alex Harvey, Editor. Send 4 to 6

poems with a reading fee of $1. No simultaneous or photocopied submissions. Decision in 3 weeks.

☐Hollow Spring Poetry Series involves a negotiated contract with authors for a chapbook publication. Sample publication: Louis Phillips, *Bulkington*. Send a query letter; if approved, a ms. of 48 to 64 pages will be read. Decision in 5 to 7 weeks.

Home Planet News, Box 415 Stuyvesant Station, New York, NY 10009. (212) 769-2854. Founded 1979. Circulation: 1,000 to 2,000. Strong, energetic poetry of all kinds. Will not publish anything racist, anti-Semitic, or sexist. Poets recently published: Daniel Berrigan, Charles Bukowski, Jan Clausen, Julian Beck, Judith Malina. Besides poetry, publishes fiction, articles, reviews, interviews, and cartoons. Size: 24 pages in an 8" by 12" format. Subscription rate: $6 for 4 issues; sample copy $1.25.

☐Received 500 poetry mss. in 1982; accepted 100. Pays 4 free copies and a gift subscription. Copyright reverts to author. Contact: Enid Dame or Donald Lev, Poetry Editors. Send 3 to 5 poems, each under 32 lines. No simultaneous submissions; photocopies acceptable. Decision in 2 to 3 months.

Hot Water Review, Box 8396, Philadelphia, PA 19101. Founded 1976. Circulation: 500 to 1,000. Speculative and imagist poetry, offshoots of the New York School. Very little "traditional" poetry. Poets recently published: Andrei Codrescu, Ron Padgett, Diane Devennie, Richard Kostelanetz. Besides poetry, publishes art, photography, occasional short fiction, essays. Size: 80 pages in an 8" by 8" format. Subscription rate: $5 for 1 issue; sample copy $5.

☐Received 100 unsolicited poetry mss. in 1982; accepted 3. Pays 1 free copy. Copyright reverts to author. Contact: Peter Bushyeager, Editor. Send no more than 8 poems, each no longer than 6 pages. Simultaneous and photocopied submissions acceptable. Decision in 8 weeks. After the first rejection, one must subscribe to be read.

Images, English Department, Wright State University, Dayton, OH 45435, (513) 873-2443. Founded 1974. Circulation: 1,000. High-quality poetry. Poets recently published: Joan Colby, Will Inman, Jared Carter, Christopher Bursk. Publishes poetry only. Size: 12 pages in an 11½" by 16" format. Subscription rate: $3 for 3 issues; sample copy $1.

☐Received 1,000 poetry mss. in 1982; accepted 70. Pays 3 free copies. Copyright reverts to author. Contact: Gary and Dorothea Pacernick, Editors. Send any number of poems, each no more than 150 lines. No simultaneous submissions; photocopies acceptable. Decision in 4 weeks.

Indiana Review, 316 North Jordan Avenue, Bloomington, IN 47405. (317) 335-3439. Founded 1981. Circulation: 350. Poetry with both breadth and depth, strong stylistically and large in scope. Poets recently published: David Wagoner, Lisel Mueller, Linda Pastan, William Stafford. Besides poetry, publishes fiction, and essays on contemporary fiction and poetry. Size: 100 pages in a 9″ by 6″ format. Subscription rate: $8 for 3 issues; sample copy $4. □Received 600 poetry mss. in 1982; accepted 70. Pays $5 a page and 2 free copies. Copyright reverts to author. Contact: Jane Hilberry, Poetry Editor. Send about 3 poems. Simultaneous and photocopied submissions acceptable. Decision in 6 weeks.

Inlet, Department of English, Virginia Wesleyan College, Norfolk, VA 23502. (804) 461–3232. Founded 1971. Circulation: 1,000. Poetry of any type, under 40 lines. No explicit sexual or scatological language. Poets recently published: Janet Lembke, Maurice Ferguson, Bob Libertelli, Brenda Nasio. Also publishes short fiction. Size: 30 pages in a 7″ by 8″ format. Subscription rate: voluntary contribution; sample copy free.
□Received 350 poetry mss. in 1982; accepted 30. Pays 4 free copies; more on request. Copyright reverts to author. Contact: Rick Hite, Poetry Editor. Send 1 to 5 poems, between September 1 and March 1 only. No simultaneous or previously published submissions. Clear photocopies acceptable. Decision in 4 weeks.

International Poetry Review, Box 2047, Greensboro, NC 27402. (919) 273–1711. Founded 1975. Circulation: 400 to 500. Previously unpublished translations of contemporary poets; original poetry in English. Poets recently published: William Stafford, William Barnstone, Charles Edward Eaton. Publishes poetry only. Size: 128 pages in a 6″ by 9″ format. Subscription rate: $6 for 2 issues; sample copy $3.
□Received 1,500 poetry mss. in 1982; accepted 63. Pays 1 or 2 free copies. Copyright reverts to author. Occasional contests, though none projected as of September 1983. Past ones judged by William Meredith (1980) and Gregory Rabassa and Fred Chappell (1982). Contact: Evalyn P. Gill, Editor. Send 5 poems or at least 100 lines, with a biography for contributors' notes. No simultaneous submissions; photocopies acceptable. No decision time given.

Jewish Currents, 22 East 17th Street, Suite 601, New York, NY 10003. (212) 924–5740. Founded 1946. Circulation: 4,000. Poetry on Jewish themes, Jewish content, or with a Jewish frame of reference, suitable for a secular (rather than religious) Jewish publication. Poets recently published: Regina Krummel, B. Z. Nidich, Aaron Kramer, I. E. Ronch. Besides poetry, publishes stories and articles. Size: 48 pages in a 5½″ by 8½″ format. Subscription rate: $12 for 11 issues; sample copy free with 50¢ postage.
□Received 100 poetry mss. in 1982; accepted 15. Pays 6 free copies and a year's gift subscription. Copyright reverts to author. Joseph Shachow Award ($200) for longtime service to the magazine; Avrom Jenofsky Award ($100) for services to Yiddish in translation. Contact: Morris V. Schappes, Editor; Lawrence Bush, Assistant Editor. Send 3 to 4 poems. No simultaneous submissions; photocopies acceptable. Decision in 8 weeks.

Kalliope: A Journal of Women's Art, 3939 Roosevelt Boulevard, Jacksonville, FL 32205. (904) 387–8211. Founded 1979. Circulation: 1,000. Poetry by women. Nothing sexist, racist, or homophobic. Poets recently published: Denise Levertov, Marge Piercy, Kathleen Spivack, Gail White. Besides poetry, publishes fiction, black-and-white photography and art, essays, interviews, and reviews. Size: 72 to 80 pages in a 9″ by 6″ format. Subscription rate: $9 for 3 issues in U. S. and Canada, £6 in U. K., $13 elsewhere. Sample copy $3.50.
□Received 4,000 poetry mss. in 1982; accepted 60. Pays 3 free copies or a year's free subscription. Copyright reverts to author. Contact: Sharon Wilson, Poetry Editor. Send 3 to 7 poems with a biographical note. No simultaneous submissions; photocopies acceptable. Decision in 8 to 12 weeks except for summer submissions, which will not be reported on until fall.

Kansas Quarterly, Denison Hall, Kansas State University, Manhattan, KS 66506. (913) 532–6716. Founded 1968. Circulation: 1,100 to 1,350. Poetry of various kinds, but no humorous verse, doggerel, or limericks. Poets recently published: Shannon Keith Kelley, Tom Liske, Roy Scheele, R. T. Smith. Besides poetry, publishes short fiction and critical and historical articles in special numbers. Size: 176 pages in a 6″ by 9″ format. Subscription rate: $12 for 4 issues; sample copy $4.
□Received several thousand poetry mss. in 1982; accepted 300 to 350. Pays 2 free copies. Copyright reverts to author. The Kansas Arts Commission Awards give 7 or 8 prizes ranging from $25 to $200 for the best poems published, selected by a distinguished writer/judge. The Seaton Awards recognize poetry by Kansas residents or natives. Write for details. Contact: The Editors. Send 1 to 10 poems, nothing very long (e.g., 400 lines). Prefers no simultaneous submissions; photocopies acceptable. Decision in 12 weeks. May be slow to respond during the summer.

Kavitha, 4408 Wickford Road, Baltimore, MD 21210. (301) 467–4316. Founded 1982. Circulation: 500. Quality poetry, both traditional and free verse. Poets recently published: Gary Fincke, Sandra Kohler, Jean Hollander, Joan Colby. Publishes poetry only. Size: no set number of pages, in a 6″ by 9″ format. Subscription rate: $3.50 for one issue, $6 for two; sample copy $3.50.
□Received 4,000 poetry mss. in 1982; accepted 40. Pays 1 free copy. Copyright reverts to author. Contact: Thomas Dorsett, Poetry Editor. Send 4 to 5 poems, ideally in the 20- to 40-line range. Prefers no simultaneous submissions. Photocopies acceptable. Decision in 6 weeks.

kayak, 325 Ocean View Avenue, Santa Cruz, CA 95062. Founded 1964. Circulation: 1,100. High-quality modernist, imagist, or surrealist poetry. Poets recently published: Hayden Carruth, James Tate, Charles Simic, W. S. Merwin. Besides poetry, publishes criticism and artwork. Size: 72 pages in a 5½″ by 8½″ format. Subscription rate: $5 for 3 issues; sample copy $2.

☐Received 3,000 poetry mss. in 1982; accepted 150. Pays in free copies. Copyright reverts to author. Contact: The Editors. Send 4 to 5 poems. Sometimes accepts simultaneous submissions. Photocopies acceptable. Decision in 3 weeks.

Lake Street Review, Box 7188, Powderhorn Station, Minneapolis, MN 55407. Founded 1976. Circulation: 600. Poetry of all kinds. Poets recently published: Roy C. McBride, Jonathan Sisson, Patricia Monaghan. Besides poetry, publishes fiction, drawings, and songs. Size: 40 pages in a 7" by 8½" format. Subscription rate: $6 for 4 issues; sample copy $1.50.
☐Received "many" poetry mss. in 1982; accepted 50. Pays 2 free copies. Copyright reverts to author. Contact: Kevin Fitzpatrick, Editor. Send 3 to 5 poems. No simultaneous submissions; photocopies acceptable. Decision in 8 weeks.

Laurel Review, Department of English, West Virginia Wesleyan College, Buckhannon, WV 26201. (304) 473–8006. Founded 1960. Circulation: 500. Poetry that is intelligent, lucid, well-crafted, and evocative, especially by Appalachian writers. Poets recently published: Judy Moffett, Carol Frost, Charles Edward Eaton, David Hopes. Besides poetry, publishes fiction, plays, reviews, and interviews. Size: 60 pages in a 6" by 9" format. Subscription rate: $6 for 2 issues; sample copy $2.50.
☐Received 300 poetry mss. in 1982; accepted about 100. Pays 2 free copies and $5 per poem if grant money is available. Copyright reverts to author. Contact: Mark De Foe, Poetry Editor. Send 4 or 5 poems. Simultaneous and photocopied submissions acceptable. Decision in 12 weeks. Slow to respond during the summer.

Lettres From Limerick, 1212 Ellsworth Street, Philadelphia, PA 19147. (215) 271–1403. Founded 1982. Circulation: 1,000. Limericks only. Poets recently published: Norman Cousins, Clifton Fadiman, John Ciardi, Isaac Asimov. Besides limericks, publishes news and articles about them. Size: 16 pages in an 8½" by 11" format. Subscription rate: $20 for 4 issues; sample copy $5.50.
☐Received "scores" of limericks in 1982; accepted "most" of them. No cash payment, and usually no payment in copies. Copyright reverts to author. Contact: J. Beauregard Pepys, Editor. Send any number of limericks. Simultaneous and photocopied submissions acceptable. Decision in 4 weeks. Readers must subscribe to be published.

Light Year, Bits Press, Department of English, Case Western Reserve University, Cleveland, OH 44106. (216) 795–2810. Founded 1974. Circulation: 2,500. Light verse and funny poems. Poets recently published: John Updike, X. J. Kennedy, Donald Hall, Marge Piercy. Publishes poetry only, in an annual publication marketed as a book. Size: 150 pages in a 6¼" by 4¼" hardcover format. Subscription/List Price: $12.95; sample copy for poets: $9.

☐Received 3,000 poetry mss. in 1982; accepted 134. Pays 1 free hardcover copy for the first poem and $7.50 for more than one poem or a long poem. Copyright reverts to author. Contact: Robert Wallace, Editor. Send 4 to 6 poems, each under 30 lines, before March 1. No simultaneous submissions, but previously published work is acceptable if no permission fee is required. Photocopies acceptable. Decision in 4 weeks.

☐Light Year Chapbook Series pays free copies. Normally by invitation only, it seeks excellent poetry of all kinds. Sample publication: Gerald Costanzo, *Wage the Improbable Happiness*. Send query letter; if approved, a ms. of 20 pages or less will be read. Decision in 6 weeks.

The Limberlost Review, Box 771, Hailey, ID 83333. Founded 1976. Circulation: 500. Publishes poetry in all styles and forms. Poets recently published: Charles Bukowski, Lawrence Ferlinghetti, John Clellon Holmes, Ed Dorn. Also publishes interviews. Size: 50 to 60 pages in a 5½" by 8½" format. Subscription rate: $4 each for 2 issues, sold individually. Sample copy $4.

☐Received several hundred poetry mss. in 1982; acceptance rate varies, since some issues are devoted to work of one poet. Pays 1 or 2 free copies. Copyright reverts to author. Contact: Richard Ardinger, Editor. Send 4 poems. No simultaneous or photocopied submissions. Decision in 8 to 10 weeks.

☐Limberlost Press Chapbooks pays in free copies. Sample publication: William Studebaker, *Trailing the Rain*. Reads mss. of 24 to 40 pages. Decision in 6 to 8 weeks.

The Literary Review, Fairleigh Dickinson University, 285 Madison Avenue, Madison, NJ 07940. (201) 377-4050. Founded 1957. Circulation: 1,000. Quality poetry in various forms; no abstract, intellectualized, or sentimental work. Poets recently published: Richard Eberhart, David Citino, Greg Kuzma, Duane Locke. Besides poetry, publishes occasional interviews, reviews, and fiction. Size: 120 pages in a 6" by 9" format. Subscription rate: $12 for 4 issues; $15 foreign. Sample copy $4.50; $5.50 foreign.

☐Received 1,600 poetry mss. in 1982; accepted 100. Pays 2 free copies. Copyright reverts to author. Annual Charles Angoff Award for the 3 to 5 best pieces published in a volume. Contact: Walter Cummins, Martin Green, and Harry Keyishian, Editors. Send 3 to 5 poems. Simultaneous and photocopied submissions acceptable. Decision in 8 to 10 weeks.

Little Balkans Review, 601 Grandview Heights Terrace, Pittsburg, KS 66762. (316) 231-7000, Ext. 431; evenings (316) 231-1589. Founded 1980. Circulation: 1,200. Quality poetry of all kinds. Poets recently published: Charles Simic, James Tate, William Stafford, Elizabeth Layton. Besides poetry, publishes fiction, articles, interviews, photography, and artwork. Size: 96 pages in a 5½" by 8½" format. Subscription rate: $10 for 4 issues; sample copy $2.

☐Received 10,000 poetry mss. in 1982; accepted 80. Pays 3 free copies. Copyright reverts to author. Contact: Gene De Gruson, Poetry Editor. Send no more than 5 poems. Manuscripts not read during August and September. No simultaneous or photocopied submissions. Decision in 6 weeks.
☐Kansas Poetry Contest winners are published each spring. For guidelines write to Ossie E. Tranbarger, 619 West Main, Independence, KS 67301.

The Lyric, 307 Dunton Drive, S. W., Blacksburg, VA 24060. Founded 1921. Circulation: 1,000. Traditional poetry, preferably rhymed. Poets recently published: John Robert Quinn, Jess Perlman, Sara Henderson Hay. Publishes poetry only. Size: 22 pages in a $5\frac{3}{16}$" by $7\frac{3}{4}$" format. Subscription rate: $6 for 4 issues; sample copy $2.
☐Received 4,000 poetry mss. in 1982; accepted 170. Pays 1 free copy. Copyright reverts to author. Quarterly and annual prizes include the College Contest, which pays between $25 and $200 in prizes to poets still in undergraduate school. Contact: Leslie Mellichamp, Editor. Send a maximum of 5 poems, each under 35 lines. Simultaneous and photocopied submissions acceptable. Decision in 3 to 4 weeks.

Madison Review, Helen C. White Hall, University of Wisconsin–Madison, Madison, WI 53706. (608) 263-3705. Founded 1979. Circulation: 400. Poetry of all kinds. Poets recently published: Philip Dacey, Sarah Brown Weitzman, Naomi Shahib Nye. Also publishes short fiction. Size: 120 pages in an $8\frac{1}{2}$" by $5\frac{1}{2}$" format. Subscription rate: $10 for 4 issues; sample copy $2.
☐Received 500 poetry mss. in 1982; accepted 28. Pays 2 free copies. Copyright reverts to author. Contact: Poetry Editor. Send no more than 4 poems, each no more than 2 pages long. Manuscripts not read from May 15 to September 1. No simultaneous submissions. Prefers nonphotocopied submissions. Decision in 10 weeks.

Magical Blend, Box 11303, San Francisco, CA 94101. (415) 282-9338. Founded 1979. Circulation: 10,000. Metaphysical poetry or poetry that expresses insight into the struggle of and harmony of the spirits. No overtly sexual work; nothing either airy-fairy or morbidly dark. Poets recently published: Dave Rudhyar, Michael Moorcock, Justin Green. Besides poetry, publishes fiction, articles, comics, interviews, four-color photography, and black-and-white art. Size: 72 pages in an $8\frac{1}{2}$" by 11" format. Subscription rate: $12 for 4 issues; sample copy $3.50.
☐Received "tons" of poetry mss. in 1982; accepted 80. Pays 3 free copies. Copyright reverts to author. Contact: Mary R. Webster, Poetry Editor. Send 2 poems only, each no more than 1 page. Simultaneous and photocopied submissions acceptable. Decision in 8 weeks.

Magic Changes, 553 West Oakdale #317, Chicago, IL 60618. (312) 327-5606. Founded 1979. Circulation: 500. Poetry on the themes of space, music, cities, and wilderness. Poets recently published: A. D. Winans, Margaret Kaminsky, Sri Chinmoy. Besides poetry, publishes short fiction, reviews, interviews, and drawings. Size: 100 pages in an 8½″ by 11″ format. Subscription rate: $10 for 2 issues; sample copy $5 payable to John Sennett. ☐Received 2,000 to 3,000 poetry mss. in 1982; accepted 100. Pays 1 or 2 free copies. Copyright reverts to author. Contact: John Sennett, Editor. Send 4 poems. No simultaneous submissions; photocopies acceptable. Decision in 2 weeks.

Maize: Notebooks of Xicano Art and Literature, The Colorado College, Box 10, Colorado Springs, CO 80903. (303) 636–3249. Founded 1977. Circulation: 3,000. Contemporary Third World poetry, with social awareness. Poets recently published: Joseph Tyler, Ernesto Cardenal, Roque Dalton. Besides poetry, publishes fiction, drama, and literary criticism. Size: 112 pages in a 5½″ by 8½″ format. Subscription rate: $8 for 2 issues; sample copy $5. ☐Received 75 poetry mss. in 1982; accepted 20. Pays 3 free copies. Copyright reverts to author. Contact: Xelina R. Urista, Poetry Editor. Send 5 to 10 poems, each no longer than 80 lines (40 lines maximum preferred). Simultaneous and photocopied submissions acceptable. Decision in 8 to 12 weeks. ☐Maize Chapbook Series, beginning in fall 1982, will pay in free copies. Will read socially conscious poetry mss. of 50 poems. Decision in 12 weeks.

Malahat Review, Box 1700, University of Victoria, Victoria, British Columbia, V8W 2Y2 Canada. (604) 721–8524. Founded 1967. Circulation: 800 to 900. Quality poetry of all kinds. Poets recently published: Phyllis Webb, Mark De Foe, David Helwig. Besides poetry, publishes fiction and translations. Size: 150 pages in a 6″ by 9″ format. Subscription rate: $15 for 3 issues; sample copy $5 plus $1 mailing charge. ☐Received 400 poetry mss. in 1982; accepted 20. Pays $12.50 per poem or page, plus 2 free copies. Copyright reverts to author. Contact: Stephen Scobie, Poetry Editor. Send any number of poems. Simultaneous and photocopied submissions acceptable. Decision in 4 weeks.

Manhattan Poetry Review, 36 Sutton Place South, 11 D, New York, NY 10022. (212) 355–6634. Founded 1982. Circulation: 1,000. High-quality poetry of all kinds. Nothing handwritten, ungrammatical, or obscene. Poets recently published: Theodore Weiss, Marge Piercy, Frederick Morgan, David Ignatow. Publishes poetry only. Size: 80 pages in a 5½″ by 8″ format. Subscription rate: $10 for 2 issues; sample copy $5 plus 88¢ postage. ☐Received more than 1,000 poetry mss. in 1982; accepted 120. Pays 1 free copy; in the future, funds may become available for cash payment. Copyright reverts to author. Contact: Elaine Reiman–Fenton, Editor. Send 3 to 5 poems, each no more than one page long, and a brief publications biography. Manuscripts not read during the summer. No simultaneous submissions; photocopies acceptable. Decision in 12 to 15 weeks. ☐A contest will be held in 1984–85 for new poets without a book-length publication. Will accept 1 poem less than 30 lines long per entrant. Send SASE for rules and deadlines.

The Manhattan Review, 304 Third Avenue, 4A, New York, NY 10010. Founded 1980. Circulation: 500. High-quality poetry of all kinds. Poets recently published: Peter Redgrove, Christopher Bursk, A. R. Ammons, Anselm Parlatore. Also publishes interviews conducted by the editor. Size: 64 pages in a 5½" by 8½" format. Subscription rate: $4 individual, $6 institution, for 1 or 2 issues. Sample copy $4 or $6.
☐Received 100 unsolicited poetry mss. in 1982; accepted none. Pays 2 free copies. Copyright reverts to author. Contact: Philip Fried, Editor. Send 3 to 5 poems with a note on previous publications. Absolutely no simultaneous submissions. Photocopies discouraged. Decision in 8 weeks, except in the summer, when fewer manuscripts are read.

Many Smokes Earth Awareness Magazine, Box 9167, Spokane, WA 99209. (509) 258-7755. Founded 1965. Circulation: 5,000. Short poetry on earth awareness, Native Americans, or female energy. No hip or gutter language or negativity. Poets recently published: P. J. Brown, Evelyn Eaton, Cloud Anderson, Marcia Starck. Besides poetry, publishes articles and book reviews on the history and spirituality of Native Americans. Size: 40 pages in an 8½" by 11" format. Subscription rate: $4 per year; sample copy $1.
☐Received 75 poetry mss. in 1982; accepted 20. Pays 3 free copies or more as requested. Not copyrighted. Contact: Matthew Ryan, Poetry Editor. Send 1 to 6 poems, each no longer than 1 page. Simultaneous and photocopied submissions acceptable. Decision time variable.

Me Magazine, Box 1132, Peter Stuyvesant Station, New York, NY 10009. (212) 673-2705. Founded 1980. Circulation: Over 1,000. Intermedia poetry and visual poetry. Poets recently published: Roland Legiardi Laura, Mark Melnicove, Bern Porter, Margaret Dunbar. Besides poetry, publishes art, collages, criticism, and reviews. Size: 8 to 12 pages in an 8½" by 11" format. Subscription rate: $20 for 4 issues; sample copy $5.
☐Received 1,000 poetry mss. in 1982; accepted 30. Pays 1 to 5 free copies. Copyright reverts to author. Contact: Poetry Editor. Send 3 poems. Manuscripts not read during the summer. Simultaneous and photocopied submissions acceptable. Decision in 3 weeks.
☐Post Me poetry stamp series pays free copies. Sample publication: Carlo Pittore, *Bean Porter Commemorative Stamp Series*. Accepts visual poetry or boldly represented, concise poems. Decision in 3 weeks.

Memphis State Review, Department of English, Memphis State University, Memphis, TN 38152. (901) 454-2668. Founded 1980. Circulation: 2,000. High-quality poetry with a sense of style, energetic imagery, and emotional honesty. Poets recently published: W. D. Snodgrass, John Allman, Edward Hirsch, Roberta Spear. Besides poetry, publishes fiction, assigned

reviews and interviews, and translations. Size: 60 pages in a 7½" by 10" format. Subscription rate: $3 for 2 issues; sample copy $2.
☐Received 1,300 poetry mss. in 1982; accepted 43. Pays 2 free copies. Copyright reverts to author. Annual Hohenberg Award gives $100 for the best poem published in that year. Contact: William Page, Editor. Send 3 to 5 poems. Manuscripts not read during July and August. No simultaneous submissions; photocopies acceptable. Decision in 8 weeks.

Mendocino Review, Box 888, Mendocino, CA 95460. (707) 964–3831. Founded 1972. Circulation: 5,000. Poetry of all kinds. Nothing political or religious. Poets recently published: Paul McHugh, Don Shanley, Luke Breit, Eric Claessens. Besides poetry, publishes fiction, articles, art, and photography. Size: 200 pages in a 7¼" by 10½" format. Subscription rate: $5.95 for 1 issue; sample copy free with submission of poetry.
☐Received 100 poetry mss. in 1982; accepted 50. Pays in free copies. Copyright reverts to author. Contact: Camille Ranker and Amanda Avery, Poetry Editors. Send 3 to 6 poems. Simultaneous and photocopied submissions acceptable. Decision in 6 to 8 weeks. Slow to respond from September to mid-November.

Michigan Quarterly Review, 3032 Rackham Building, Ann Arbor, MI 48109. (313) 764–9265. Founded 1962. Circulation: 2,000. Poetry of all kinds, with the taste and skill appropriate to a university-based journal. Poets recently published: James Merrill, Diane Ackerman, Phyllis Janowitz, Stephen Sandy. Besides poetry, publishes essays on literature, and interviews with authors. Query first on both. Size: 160 pages in a 6" by 9" format. Subscription rate: $13 for 4 issues; sample copy $2.
☐Received 300 to 400 poetry mss. in 1982; accepted 20 to 30. Pays $10 per printed page and 2 free copies. Copyright reverts to author. Contact: Laurence Goldstein, Editor. Send 3 to 5 poems, each no more than 3 pages. No simultaneous submissions; photocopies acceptable. Decision in 3 to 5 weeks. Slow to respond during July and August.

Mid-American Review, 106 Hanna Hall, Department of English, Bowling Green State University, Bowling Green, OH 43403. (419) 372–2725. Founded 1980. Circulation: 500. Poetry that emanates from strong, evocative imagery, that uses language as an integral part of the work, and that has a strong, consistent voice. No adolescent romantic verse, sentimentality, or philosophic treatises in verse. Poets recently published: David Citino, David Baker, Jeff Gundy, Dave Kelly. Besides poetry, publishes fiction, critical essays on contemporary writing, and book reviews. Size: 200 pages in a 5½" by 8½" format. Subscription rate: $6 for 2 issues; sample copy $2.
☐Received 400 poetry mss. in 1982; accepted 65. Pays $5 per page and 2 free copies. Copyright reverts to author. James Wright Award of $200 for the best poem published in that year. Contact: George Looney or Robert Early, Editors. Send 3 to 5 poems. No simultaneous submissions; photocopies acceptable. Decision in 2 to 4 weeks.

Midway Review, 2358 West 63rd Street, Chicago, IL 60636. (312) 238-8254. Founded 1979. Circulation: 1,000 to 2,000. Quality contemporary and avant-garde poetry. Poets recently published: Tymoteusz Karpowicz, Phyllis Janik, Paul Hoover, John Dickson. Besides poetry, publishes fiction, comment, reviews, photography, and illustrations. Size: 48 to 60 pages in an 8½″ by 11″ format. Subscription rate: $7 for 2 issues; sample copy $3.50. □Received 500 poetry mss. in 1982; accepted 60. Pays up to $25 and 1 free copy. Copyright reverts to author. Contact: Peter S. Cooper and Grace Kuikman, Editors. Send 3 to 5 poems, each no longer than 60 lines. Will respond to each submission personally, with no form letters. No simultaneous submissions; photocopies acceptable. Decision in 6 weeks.
□Little Sister Awards pay cash prizes ranging from $50 to $500 and publication in the magazine. Send no more than 3 poems, each under 32 lines, with a $5 entry fee and SASE. Deadline for 1984: March 1.
□Midway Review Chapbook Series in preparation. Query for details.

Midwest Arts & Literature, Box 1623, Jefferson City, MO 65102. (314) 893-5834. Founded 1978. Circulation: 500. Poetry of all kinds except pornography. Poets recently published: Howard Nemerov, Mona Van Duyn, Ann Marx, Judith Saul Stix. Besides poetry, publishes fiction, essays, black-and-white photo essays, articles on the arts, and cartoons and jokes with an arts focus. Size: 12 pages in an 11¼″ by 17¼″ tabloid format. Subscription rate: $15 for 2 issues; sample copy $2.50.
□Received 75 to 100 poetry mss. in 1982; accepted 25 to 35. Pays 1 free copy and offers additional copies at $1 each. Copyright reverts to author. Contact: Sharon D. Hanson, Managing Editor. Send 3 poems, each no more than 35 lines. Simultaneous submissions acceptable; photocopies acceptable if clean and clear. Decision in 2 to 4 months.
□Chapbook division and writing contest under consideration for 1985. Query then.

Midwest Poetry Review, Box 776, Rock Island, IL 61201. Founded 1980. Circulation: 10,000. Poetry of all kinds, modern and traditional. Poets recently published: Lolette Barlow, Barbara Rebbeck, Patricia Hladik, William Dougherty. Besides poetry, publishes poetry commentary and letters. Size: 48 pages in a 5¼″ by 8½″ format. Subscription rate: $15 for 4 issues; sample copy $2.
□Received 10,000 poetry mss. in 1982; accepted 250. Pays $5 to $25 per poem on acceptance. Copyright reverts to author. Grand Contest in March offers $1350 in prizes in 25 awards, the top prize being $500. Each issue awards $200 in prizes. Contact: Tom Tilford and Grace Keller, Editors. Must be a subscriber to be read. Send 5 poems. Simultaneous and photocopied submissions acceptable. Decision in 2 weeks.

Minetta Review, 21 Washington Place, Box 65, New York, NY 10003. (212) 598-2141. Founded 1980. Circulation: 3,000. Quality poetry of all kinds on contempory themes. Poets recently published: Galway Kinnell and Philip Schultz. Besides poetry, publishes fiction, drama, criticism, and interviews. Size: 60 pages in a variable format. Subscription rate: none; sample copy free.

☐Received 50 poetry mss. in 1982; accepted 13. Does not pay. Copyright reverts to author. Contact: Laurel Saville or Leslie Abbattiello. Send no more than 7 poems, each no longer than 3 pages. Manuscripts not read during the summer. Simultaneous and photocopied submissions acceptable. Decision in 8 weeks.

the minnesota review, Department of English, Oregon State University, Corvallis, OR 97331. (503) 754-3244. Founded 1960. Circulation: 1,200. Poetry that is politically engaged, from a (broadly speaking) leftist and/or feminist perspective. No restrictions on form. Poets recently published: Jonathan Holden, Roque Dalton, Zoe Anglesey, Joan Joffe Hall. Besides poetry, publishes fiction, essays, interviews, and reviews. Size: 160 pages in a 5½" by 8½" format. Subscription rate: $7 for 2 issues; sample copy $3.

☐Received 800 poetry mss. in 1982; accepted 31. Pays 3 free copies. Copyright reverts to author. Contact: Richard Daniels and Anne Krosby, Editors. Send 3 to 5 poems, each no longer than 100 lines. No simultaneous submissions; photocopies acceptable. Decision in 14 weeks.

Modern Haiku, Box 1752, Madison, WI 53701. (608) 255-2660. Founded 1969. Circulation: 510. Well-crafted haiku. Poets recently published: Raymond Roseliep, Virginia Brady Young, Ann Atwood, Gunther Klinge. Besides haiku, publishes articles on haiku and reviews of haiku books. Size: 60 to 64 pages in a 5⁷⁄₁₆" by 8⁷⁄₁₆" format. Subscription rate: $8.75 for 3 issues; sample copy $2.75.

☐Received 8,000 haiku in 1982; accepted 440. No payment, but prizes of $120 in cash and other awards given for meritorious work in each issue. Cash awards will increase in the future. Copyright reverts to author. Contact: Robert Spiess, Editor. Send at least 3 poems. No simultaneous submissions or previously published work. Photocopies acceptable. Decision in 6 weeks.

Modern Maturity, 215 Long Beach Boulevard, Long Beach, CA 90801. Founded in the 1950s. Circulation: 8 million. A variety of types of poetry. Poets recently published: Maria Gleason, Elva Mc Allister, Sheryl Nelms, Winston Smith. Besides poetry, publishes articles and tips. Size: 120 pages in an 8½" by 11" format. Subscription rate: $5 for 6 issues; sample copy free.

☐Received 2,000 poetry mss. in 1982; accepted 50. Pays $35 and up per poem. Prefers to buy first rights. Contact: Annette Winter, Poetry Editor. Send no more than 10 poems, each under 40 lines. Four month deadline for seasonal material. Prefers no simultaneous submissions. Photocopies acceptable. Decision in 4 weeks.

Modern Poetry in Translation—See Chapter 6.

The Montana Review, Box 2248, Missoula, MT 59806. (406) 243–6736. Founded 1979. Circulation: 500. Quality poetry. Poets recently published: David Wagoner, James Wright, Mekeel McBride, Laura Jensen. Besides poetry, publishes fiction, articles, interviews, and book reviews. Size: 100 to 125 pages in a 5½" by 8½" format. Subscription rate: $7 for 2 issues; sample copy $4 current, $3 back issue.

☐Received 1,000 poetry mss. in 1982; accepted 20. Pays a free subscription, including 3 free copies of the issue the work appears in. Buys additional rights if the poems are included in a book or chapbook accepted by Owl Creek Press. Contact: Rich Ives. Send 3 to 4 poems. Simultaneous and photocopied submissions acceptable. Decision in 2 weeks.

☐Owl Creek Press Chapbook Series pays 10% of press run in free copies. Sample publication: Richard Wrigley, *The Glow.* Reads mss. of any length over 20 pages. Decision in 4 weeks.

MSS Magazine, State University of New York–Binghamton, Binghamton, NY 13901. Founded 1961. Circulation: 750 to 1,000. High-quality poetry—well-crafted, heartfelt, original, beautiful. Nothing commercial, shoddy, or greeting card. Committed to new and unestablished writers. Poets recently published: James Dickey, Linda Pastan, William Stafford, Andrew Hudgins. Besides poetry, publishes fiction, essays, illustrations. Size: 250 pages in a 6" by 9" format. Subscription rate: $10 for 3 issues; sample copy $4.

☐Received 2,000 poetry mss. in 1982; accepted 60. Pays $25 per poem and 2 free copies. Copyright reverts to author. Contact: L. M. Rosenberg, Poetry Editor. Send 3 to 7 poems. Manuscripts not read from June 1 to September 1. No simultaneous submissions; photocopies acceptable. Decision in 2 to 6 weeks.

Negative Capability, 6116 Timberly Road North, Mobile, AL 36609. (205) 661–9114. Founded 1981. Circulation: 1,000. Open to all kinds of poetry: traditional, free verse, prose poems, eye poems. Nothing tasteless or obscene. Poets recently published: John Updike, X. J. Kennedy, Marge Piercy, William Stafford. Besides poetry, publishes black-and-white artwork, interviews, music, essays, critical articles, and fiction. Size: 140 pages in a 5½" by 8½" format. Subscription rate: $12 for 4 issues; sample copy $3.50.

☐Received 6,000 poetry mss. in 1982; accepted 240. Pays 1 free copy. Copyright reverts to author. Contact: Sue Walker, Editor. Send 3 to 5 poems. No simultaneous submissions; photocopies acceptable. Decision in 4 weeks.

☐Annual Eve of St. Agnes Contest each January. Write for guidelines. Also publishes books of poetry. Sample publication: Maurice Gandy, *An Uncharted Inch.* Send ms. of 50 to 70 pages. Decision in 2 weeks. Pays royalties.

New CollAge Magazine, 5700 North Tamiani Trail, Sarasota, FL 33580. (813) 355–7671, Ext. 203. Founded 1970. Circulation: 1,000. Serious poetry of strong imagery and sustained tone, which avoids the tick-tock effusions of everyday sentiment. Biased toward closed form, but finds little of it worth printing; also likes new slants on traditional prosodies. Poets recently published: Ruth Daigon, Stephen Corey, Sue Walker, H. R. Coursen. Besides poetry, publishes occasional reviews and interviews. Size: 32 pages in a 5½" by 8½" format. Subscription rate: $6 for 3 issues; sample copy $2.

□No figures given for mss. received and accepted in 1982. Pays 3 free copies. Copyright reverts to author. Contact: A. McA. Miller, General Editor; Carol Mahler, Co-Editor. Send 3 poems. Manuscripts not read from June through August. No simultaneous submissions; photocopies acceptable. Decision in 2 to 4 weeks.

New England Sampler, RFD 1, Box M 119, Brooks, ME 04921. (207) 525-3575. Founded 1980. Circulation: 2,000. Wholesome, short, lyrical poems on nature, people, or New England. Poets recently published: William Dougherty, Nellie Hill, Gladys Verville Deane. Besides poetry, publishes fiction, articles, and interviews. Size: 52 pages in a 5½" by 8½" format. Subscription rate: $7.50 for 8 issues; sample copy $1.

□Received 500 poetry mss. in 1982; accepted 50. Pays 2 free copies. Copyright reverts to author. Contact: Arnold Perrin, Poetry Editor. Send 3 to 5 poems. No simultaneous submissions; photocopies acceptable. Decision in 3 weeks.

□Annual poetry contest awards prizes of $10 to $50. Write for guidelines. Submit work by May 15 with a $2 entry fee.

New Letters, 5346 Charlotte, University of Missouri–Kansas City, Kansas City, MO 64110. (816) 276-1168. Founded 1971. Circulation: 2,000 to 2,500. Quality poetry. Poets recently published: William Stafford, Patricia Goedicke, Mbembe, Ronald Perry. Besides poetry, publishes fiction, essays, reviews, and artwork. Size: 128 pages in a 6" by 9" format. Subscription rate: $15 for 4 issues; sample copy $2.50.

□Received "thousands" of poetry mss. in 1982; number accepted not given. Pays $5 to $10 per poem and 2 free copies. Copyright reverts to author. Contact: Poetry Editors. Send about 4 poems. Manuscripts not read from May 15 to September 15. Prefers submissions by subscribers. No simultaneous or photocopied submissions. Decision in 4 weeks.

New Mexico Humanities Review, Box A, New Mexico Tech, Socorro, NM 87801. (505) 835-5200. Founded 1978. Circulation: 650. All kinds of poetry. Poets recently published: Peter Wild, Peter Klappert, Fred Chappell. Besides poetry, publishes fiction, essays, book reviews, artwork, photography, and interviews. Size: 100 pages in a 6" by 9" format. Subscription rate: $8 for 3 issues; sample copy $3.

□Received 600 poetry mss. in 1982; accepted 50. Buys reprint rights. Pays $10 a poem and 2 free copies. Contact: Jerry Bradley, Poetry Editor. Send no more than 5 poems. No simultaneous submissions; photocopies acceptable. No decision time given.

the new renaissance, 9 Heath Road, Arlington, MA 02174. Founded 1968. Circulation: over 1,300. Poetry of most kinds, including traditional and free verse, blank and rhymed verse. No haiku. Poets recently published: David Hopes, Joan Colby, Ruth Feldman, William Dubie. Besides poetry, publishes articles, fiction, essays, interviews, reviews, and artwork. Size: 104 to 120 pages in a 6" by 9" format. Subscription rate: $9.50 for 3 issues; sample copy $2.10 back issue; $4.25 current.
☐Received 375 to 430 mss. in 1982; accepted 50 to 55. Buys all rights. Pays $13 and up per poem and 1 free copy. Contact: Stanwood Bolton, Poetry Editor, or Margot Lockwood, Guest Poetry Editor for issue #20. Send 3 to 6 poems, no longer than 2 typed pages each, with a check for $2.10 or $2.90 for a past issue. Prefers poems typed double-spaced. Simultaneous submissions acceptable if editor is notified. Photocopies acceptable. No readings from July 1 to September 10 or from December 10 to January 14. Decision in 3 to 5 months; sometimes within 2 months.

The New Republic, 1220 19th Street N. W., Washington, DC 20036. (202) 331–7494. Founded 1914. Circulation: 100,000. Good poetry. Poets recently published: Frank Bidart, Robert Hass, Irving Feldman, Daniel Halpern. Besides poetry, publishes articles, essays, and reviews. Size: 40 pages in an 8¼" by 11" format. Subscription rate: $45 for 52 weekly issues; sample copy $1.50.
☐Received 5,000 to 7,000 poetry mss. in 1982; accepted 50. Pays $20 per poem and 3 free copies. Copyright reverts to author. Contact: Robert Pinsky, Poetry Editor. Send 5 poems, each no longer than one page of the magazine. Simultaneous and photocopied submissions acceptable. Decision in 5 weeks. May be slow to respond during the summer.

The New Yorker, 25 West 43rd Street, New York, NY 10036. Founded 1925. Circulation: 500,000. High-quality poetry. Poets recently published: Louise Gluck, Robert Penn Warren, W. S. Merwin, Roger Shattuck. Besides poetry, publishes fiction, articles, and reviews. Size: 130 to 190 pages in an 8¼" by 11" format. Subscription rate: $32 a year; newsstand price $1.50.
☐No figures given for mss. received and accepted in 1982. Pays variable rate on acceptance. Contact: The Editors. No simultaneous submissions; no submissions in the summer, unless the poem is timely. Photocopies acceptable. Decision in 8 to 10 weeks.

Nightsun, Department of Philosophy, Frostburg State College, Frostburg, MD 21532. (301) 689–4249. Founded 1981. Circulation: 500 to 1,000. Quality poetry on announced topics for each issue. Poets recently published: Peter Wild, Brian Swann, Duane Locke, William Stafford. Besides poetry, publishes reviews, essays, and interviews. Size: 110 pages in a 5½" by 8½" format. Subscription rate: $6 plus 85¢ postage for 1 issue; sample copy $3.
☐Received 300 to 400 poetry mss. in 1982; accepted 30. Pays 1 free copy. Copyright reverts to author. From August to December, reads only poems

by subscribers. Contact: Jorn K. Bramann. Send about 5 poems. Simultaneous and photocopied submissions acceptable. Tries to respond in 4 weeks, but decision sometimes takes a long time.

□Nightsun Books negotiates contracts with authors of chapbooks. Sample publication: Frank Graziano, *Ubermenschen*. Write for details.

Nimrod, Arts & Humanities Council of Tulsa, 2210 South Main, Tulsa, OK 74114. (918) 584–3333, Ext. 19. Founded 1956. Circulation: 1,000 to 2,000. Quality poetry. Poets recently published: Rita Dove, Peter Wild, Stephen Dunning. Publishes poetry and short fiction. Size: 110 pages in a 6" by 9" format. Subscription rate: $10 for 2 issues; sample copy $5.

□Received 3,000 poetry mss. in 1982; accepted 65. Pays in free copies. Copyright reverts to author. Contact: Markham Johnson, Poetry Editor. Send between 2 and 8 poems. No simultaneous submissions. Photocopies acceptable. Decision in 1 to 10 weeks.

□Pablo Neruda Prize for Poetry awards prizes of $500 and $250 for a substantial effort in a single poem or a sequence of related poems. Send SASE for detailed instructions. The 1984 deadline is April 1; there is an entry fee of $5.

Nit & Wit, Chicago's Arts Magazine, Box 14685, Chicago, IL 60614. (312) 248–1183. Founded 1977. Circulation: 25,000. Serious poetry of high quality. Poets recently published: Matthew Graham, Richard Behm, Neurine Wiggin, Leslie Adrienne Miller. Besides poetry, publishes features, interviews, reviews, fiction, photography, and artwork. Size: 68 to 76 pages in an 8½" by 11" format. Subscription rate: $9 for 6 issues; sample copy $2.

□Received 2,000 poetry mss. in 1982; accepted 60. Pays 1 free copy with discount on additional copies. Copyright reverts to author. Annual Poetry Contest offers awards up to $250. Write for guidelines. Contact: Robin Hemley, Poetry Editor. Send 3 to 5 poems with a cover letter and your name in the upper right-hand corner of each page. No simultaneous or photocopied submissions. Decision in 6 weeks.

North Country Anvil, Box 37, Millville, MN 55957. (507) 798–2366. Founded 1972. Circulation: 1,500. Poetry with a strong understanding of form, love of language, and a commitment to artistic values. No overtly political poetry, but work that adds an emotional and human dimension to a political magazine with a decentralist point of view. Poets recently published: Rodney Nelson, John Solensten, Meridel LeSueur, Barton Sutter. Besides poetry, publishes articles, criticism, reviews, interviews, letters, and fiction. Size: 48 pages in an 8½" by 11" format. Subscription rate: $8.50 for 5 issues; sample copy $2.

□Received "several hundred" poetry mss. in 1982; accepted 6. Pays 3 free copies, or more as requested. Copyright reverts to author. Contact: Steven and Barbara Whipple. Send a representative group of poems. No simultaneous submissions; photocopies acceptable. Decision in 8 weeks. Slow to respond during the harvest season.

Northwest Review, 369 PLC, University of Oregon, Eugene, OR 97403. (503) 686-3957. Founded 1957. Circulation: 1,200. Poetry that meets the one criterion of excellence. Poets recently published: Alan Dugan, Olga Broumas, Willis Barnstone, Hans Magnus Enzenberger. Besides poetry, publishes fiction, essays, book and film reviews, and artwork. Size: 180 pages in a 6″ by 9″ format. Subscription rate: $8 for 3 issues; sample copy $2.50. ☐Received 1,000 poetry mss. in 1982; accepted 30. Pays 3 free copies. Copyright reverts to author. Occasional poetry contests when support for them can be generated. Contact: Maxine Scates, Poetry Editor. Send 5 to 8 poems of any length. Crisp, clean copies are appreciated. No simultaneous submissions; photocopies acceptable. Decision in 8 weeks.

Not Man Apart, 1045 Sansome Street, San Francisco, CA 94111. (415) 433-7373. Founded 1970. Circulation: 35,000. Nature poetry and political poetry. Poets recently published: Susan Ventors, Dave Whitman, Sylvia Williams. Besides poetry, publishes environmental news, features, and reviews. Size: 24 pages in a 10″ by 13″ tabloid format. Subscription rate: $15 for 12 issues; sample copy free.
☐Received 40 poetry mss. in 1982; accepted 12. Pays up to 5 free copies. Copyright reverts to author. Contact: G. Smith, Poetry Editor. Send 1 to 3 poems. Simultaneous and photocopied submissions acceptable. No decision time given.

The Ohio Journal, English Department, Ohio State University, 164 West 17th Avenue, Columbus, OH 43210. (614) 389-2361. Founded 1972. Circulation: 1,000. High-quality poetry. Poets recently published: David Wagoner, Howard Nemerov, David Young, Albert Goldbarth. Besides poetry, publishes fiction, reviews, essays, photography, and art. Size: 56 pages in an 8½″ by 11″ format. Subscription rate: $4 for 2 issues; sample copy $3. ☐Received 2,000 poetry mss. in 1982; accepted 60. Pays 2 free copies. Copyright reverts to author. Annual President's Award of $100 for poetry. Contact: David Citino, OSU at Marion, 1465 Mount Vernon Avenue, Marion, OH. Send 3 to 10 poems. No simultaneous or photocopied submissions. Decision in 4 weeks.

The Old Red Kimono, Box 1864, Rome, GA 30163. (404) 295-6312. Founded 1975. Circulation: 500. Poetry of all kinds. Poets recently published: Ken Anderson, Carol Hyatt, Lyn Lifshin. Also publishes short fiction. Size: 50 pages in a variable format. Subscription rate: free; sample copy free. ☐Received about 500 poetry mss. in 1982; accepted 70. Pays 1 free copy. Copyright reverts to author. Contact: Jo Anne Starnes. Send 3 to 5 poems, each no longer than 30 lines. No simultaneous submissions. Photocopies acceptable. Decision in 4 weeks.

Open Places, Box 2085, Stephens College, Columbia, MO 65201. (314) 442-2211. Founded 1966. Circulation: 1,500. High-quality poetry. No sexism. Poets recently published: Sharon Olds, Marge Piercy, Marilyn Hacker, Tom Disch. Also publishes reviews. Size: 76 pages in an 8½" by 5½" format. Subscription rate: $8 for 2 issues; sample copy $4.

☐Received 2,500 poetry mss. in 1982; accepted 20. Pays $10 to $25 per page, depending on funding, and 6 free copies. Copyright reverts to author. Contact: Eleanor M. Bender, Poetry Editor. Send 4 to 6 poems. Manuscripts not read during December and January, and from May through September. No simultaneous submissions; photocopies acceptable. Decision in 4 weeks.

Orpheus, 8812 Pico Boulevard, Suite 203, Los Angeles, CA 90035. (213) 271–1460. Founded 1978. Circulation: 1,000. Original poetry in English only. No political poems. Poets recently published: Greg Kuzma, William Pillin, Wanda Coleman. Publishes poetry only. Size: 50 pages in a 7¼" by 11½" format. Subscription rate: $12.50 for 3 issues; sample copy $4.50.

☐Received 1,200 poetry mss. in 1982; accepted 50. Pays $5 to $40 per poem and 1 or 2 free copies. Sometimes buys additional publication rights. Contact: P. Schneidre, Poetry Editor. Send 3 to 6 poems of any length. No simultaneous submissions; no poor photocopies. Decision in 2 weeks.

☐Chapbook series, *tadbooks* (sample publication: Herbert Morris, *Afghanistan*), pays an advance representing 12.5% of the retail price of one-third of the edition. Considers mss. of 5 to 20 pages. Decision in 4 weeks.

Outerbridge, English A323, The College of Staten Island, 715 Ocean Terrace, Staten Island, NY 10301. (212) 390–7654. Founded 1975. Circulation: 500. Well-crafted, professional poems. No "found" poems or experimental verse. Poets recently published: Naomi Rachel, Marilyn Throne, Barry Spacks, Hillel Schwartz. Besides poetry, publishes short stories and occasional excerpts from novels. Size: 120 pages in an 8" by 5" format. Subscription rate: $4 for 1 issue; sample copy $2.

☐Received 300 to 400 poetry mss. in 1982; accepted 40 to 45. Pays 2 free copies. Copyright reverts to author. Contact: Charlotte Alexander, Editor. Send 3 to 5 poems, each no longer than about 3 pages. Prefers no simultaneous submissions. Photocopies acceptable. Manuscripts not read during July and August, and responses slow in late spring. Otherwise, decision in 8 weeks.

Overtone Series, 4421 Chestnut Street #3, Philadelphia, PA 19104. (215) 386–4279. Founded 1973. Circulation: 2,500. Experimental, Black, and concrete poetry. Poets recently published: Etheridge Knight, Thomas Lux, Marilyn Waniek. Besides poetry, publishes fiction, interviews, criticism, artwork, and graphics. Size: 60 pages in a 5½" by 8½" format. Subscription rate: $8 for 4 issues; sample copy $2.

☐Received 200 poetry mss. in 1982; accepted 1 chapbook and 10 poems. Pays 5 free copies. Copyright reverts to author. Contact: Otis and Beth Brown, Poetry Editors. Send 5 poems. Simultaneous and photocopied submissions acceptable. Decision in 6 weeks.

☐Overtone Series Chapbooks publishes mss. of 20 to 25 pages with a $5 reading fee. Sample publication: E. Ethelbert Miller, *Poems for the Holy in Paradise*. Pays in free copies.

Owlflight, c/o Unique Graphics, 1025 55th Street, Oakland, CA 94608. (415) 655–3024. Founded 1981. Circulation: 1,000 to 1,500. Poetry in any form or style that is oriented toward science fiction and fantasy. Poets recently published: Bruce Boston, Robert Frazier, Janet Fox, Christine Zawadiwsky. Besides poetry, publishes fiction, articles, and reviews. Size: 64 pages in an 8½" by 11" format. Subscription rate: $10 for 3 issues; sample copy $4.
☐Received 500 poetry mss. in 1982; accepted 25. Pays $1 minimum per poem and 1 to 3 free copies. Copyright reverts to author. Contact: Millea Kenin, Editor. Send up to 10 poems, each no longer than 100 lines. Simultaneous submissions acceptable if acknowledged as such in a cover letter. Photocopies acceptable. Decision in 4 weeks.
☐Occasional theme anthologies are published under the Unique Graphics label. Occasional contests are announced to subscribers via news releases. Send SASE for details and deadlines.

The Pale Fire Review, 162 Academy Avenue, Providence, RI 02908. Founded 1980. Circulation: 500. Poetry in all forms on any subject matter except erotica. Poets recently published: Sue Standing, Fanny Howe, Nancy Condee, Michael Shorb. Besides poetry, publishes fiction, short plays, essays, and line drawings. Size: 64 to 80 pages in an 8½" by 5¼" format. Subscription rate: $10 for 3 issues; sample copy $4.
☐Received 2,500 poetry mss. in 1982; accepted 50. Pays 1 free copy. Copyright reverts to author. Contact: Catherine Reed or Steven Strang, Editors. Send 8 poems of any length. Simultaneous and photocopied submissions acceptable. Decision in 3 weeks.

Panjandrum Poetry Journal, 11321 Iowa Avenue, Suite 1, Los Angeles, CA 90025. (213) 477–8771. Founded 1971. Circulation: 1,000 to 1,500. Surrealist and experimental poetry. Poets recently published: Jerome Rothenberg, Michael McClure, John Logan. Besides poetry, publishes short fiction and prose poems. Size: 84 to 145 pages in a variable format. Subscription rate: $14 for 3 issues; sample copy $4.95 plus $1 for shipping.
☐Received 1,000 poetry mss. in 1982; accepted "very few." Pays 2 free copies. Copyright reverts to author. Contact: Dennis Koran, Editor. Send 5 to 7 poems. No simultaneous submissions. Photocopies acceptable. Decision in 6 weeks. Not reading until November 1984.
☐Panjandrum Books Chapbooks Series pays in royalties for surrealist and experimental mss. under 60 pages in length. Sample publication: Clayton Eshleman, *Visions of the Fathers of Lascaux*. Decision in 6 weeks.

Paris Review, 541 East 72nd Street, New York, NY 10021. (212) 861–0016. Founded 1953. Circulation: 7,000. Quality poetry of all kinds. Poets recently published: Frank Bidart, May Sarton, Alfred Corn. Besides poetry, publishes fiction, features, and interviews. Size: 250 pages in an 8½" by 5¼" format. Subscription rate: $16 for 4 issues; sample copy $5.75.

☐Received 5,000 poetry mss. in 1982; accepted 30 to 40. Pays $15 to $100 per poem and 2 free copies. Copyright reverts to author. Contact: Jonathan Galassi, Poetry Editor. Send any number of poems. Simultaneous and photocopied submissions acceptable. Decision in 16 weeks.

☐The Bernard F. Conners Prize for Poetry awards $1,000 and publication for the best previously unpublished poem over 300 lines submitted. Translations (with accompanying original text) are also eligible. Send the ms. between April 1 and May 1. The winner will be announced in the fall issue.

Partisan Review, 121 Bay Street Road, Boston, MA 02215. (617) 353-2460. Founded 1938. Circulation 8,500. Lyrical and experimental poetry. Poets recently published: Rachel Hadas, Kathleen Spivack, Aaron Bulman, Philip Appleman. Besides poetry, publishes fiction, interviews, book reviews, and articles on culture, the arts, and politics. Size: 160 pages in a 6" by 9" format. Subscription rate: $14 for 4 issues; sample copy $4.

☐Received 500 poetry mss. in 1982; accepted 30. Pays a minimum of $25 per poem and 1 free copy. Copyright reverts to author. Contact: William Phillips, Editor. Send any number of poems. Simultaneous and photocopied submissions acceptable. Decision in 16 weeks; slow to respond during the summer. Wait 6 months before inquiring about mss.

Passages North, William Bonifas Fine Arts Center, Escanaba, MI 49829. Founded 1979. Circulation: 1,200. High-quality contemporary poetry. Poets recently published: Jack Driscoll, Joan Colby, Jim Daniels, Eve Shelnutt. Besides poetry, publishes short fiction, interviews, and graphics. Size: 24 pages in an 11" by 14" format. Subscription rate: $2 for 2 issues; sample copy $1.50 including postage.

☐Received 1,200 poetry mss. in 1982; accepted 80. Pays 3 free copies; honoraria when grant money available. Copyright reverts to author. Contact: Editors. Send 4 to 6 poems, each no longer than 40 lines. Simultaneous submissions acceptable if editor is notified. Photocopies acceptable. Decision in 6 weeks. January and August are good months; slow to respond in November and December and from May through July.

☐Prizes for the best poem or poems in an issue are offered when grant money is available and are announced beforehand in poetry news sources.

Passaic Review, Forstmann Library, 195 Gregory Avenue, Passaic, NJ 07055. (201) 471-8077. Founded 1979. Circulation: 1,000. Poetry with a natural voice and energy. Aims at a mix of established and new poets. Poets recently published: Allen Ginsberg, David Ignatow, Barbara Holland, Lyn Lifshin. Besides poetry, publishes fiction, art, interviews, and reviews. Size: 50 pages in a 5½" by 8½" format. Subscription rate: $6 for 2 issues; sample copy $3 and 75¢ postage.

☐Received 400 poetry mss. in 1982; accepted 50. No payment. Copyright reverts to author. Contact: Richard and Lorraine Quatrone, Editors. Send any number of poems, of any length. Simultaneous and photocopied submissions acceptable. Decision in 16 weeks.

Pembroke Magazine, Box 60—Pembroke State University, Pembroke, NC 28372. (919) 521–4214, Ext. 433. Founded 1969. Circulation: 500. Poetry of all kinds. Poets recently published: Felix Pollak, Fred Chappell, A. R. Ammons, Ron Schreiber. Besides poetry, publishes short stories, essays, interviews, and reviews. Size: 200 pages in a 6″ by 9″ format. Subscription rate: $3 for 1 issue; sample copy $3.
☐Received 3,650 poetry mss. in 1982; few accepted due to lack of space. Pays 1 free copy. Copyright reverts to author. Contact: Shelby Stephenson, Editor. Send 3 to 5 poems. No simultaneous submissions; clear photocopies acceptable. Decision in 4 weeks.

Phantasm, Box 3606, Chico, CA 95927. (916) 342–6582. Founded 1976. Circulation: 1,000. Poetry of all kinds. Poets recently published: Elizabeth Revere, Hillel Schwartz, Mary Norbert Korte, John Beecher. Besides poetry, publishes feature articles, interviews, literary news, book reviews, columns, editorials, and announcements. Size: 72 pages in an 8½″ by 11″ format. Subscription rate: $8 for 4 issues; sample copy $3.
☐Accepted about 1% of the poetry mss. received in 1982. Pays $2 for each issue in which poetry appears, plus 1 free copy. Copyright reverts to author. Contact: Phillip Hemenway, Poetry Editor. Send 2 to 4 poems, each no longer than 1 page. No simultaneous submissions; photocopies acceptable. Decision in 20 weeks.
☐Phantasm Supplements Chapbook Series (sample publication: Joanna Thompson, *Into Dark*) pays a small cash fee. Send query letter. Decision in 24 weeks.

Pig Iron, Box 237, Youngstown, OH 44501. (216) 744–2258. Founded 1975. Circulation: 1,000. In 1984 desires poetry with psychological insight, and humorous poetry. Poets recently published: James C. Kilgore, Terry Wright, Grace Butcher. Besides poetry, publishes fiction, nonfiction, and art. Size: 96 pages in an 8½″ by 11″ format. Subscription rate: $7 for 2 issues; sample copy $2.50.
☐Received 1,000 poetry mss. in 1982; accepted 100. Pays $2 per poem and 2 free copies. Copyright reverts to author. Contact: Terry Murcko, Poetry Editor. Send up to 10 poems, each no longer than 100 lines. No simultaneous submissions; photocopies acceptable. Decision in 12 weeks.

The Pikestaff Forum, Box 127, Normal, IL 61761. (309) 452–4831. Founded 1977. Circulation: 1,000. Both traditional and experimental poetry, grounded in lived experience and reflective of the human condition with clear, precise images and concrete detail. No inspirational uplift, vague abstraction, prose tricked out in short lines, workshop pieces, or private confessions. Poets recently published: Jared Carter, Joan Colby, Guy R. Beining, Raymond Roseliep. Besides poetry, publishes short stories, novel excerpts, drama, work by young writers (7 to 17), interviews, book reviews of small press publications, and opinion on literature and the small-press scene. Size: 32 to 40 pages in a tabloid newsprint format. Subscription rate: $10 for 6 issues; sample copy $2.

☐Received 1,800 poetry mss. in 1982; accepted 54. Pays 3 free copies and a 50% discount on additional ones. Copyright reverts to author. Contact: Robert D. Sutherland, Editor. Send no more than 6 poems. Prefers no simultaneous submissions; expects to be told if they are. Photocopies acceptable. Decision in 12 weeks.

☐Pikestaff Poetry Chapbook Series (sample publication: Frannie Lindsay, *The Horse We Lie Down In*) pays a portion of the press run in free copies. Reads mss. of 8 to 10 poems that make up a thematically organized whole, with a discernible focus or identity. Decision in 12 weeks.

Plainsong, Box U245, Western Kentucky University, Bowling Green, KY 42101. (502) 781-3468 or (502) 745-3046. Founded 1979. Circulation: 400. Poems about places, short poems that move swiftly, poems with form that is alive but invisible, poems that imply more than they say, humorous poems, poems in which there are real human voices. Poets recently published: William Stafford, Robert Bly, Ted Kooser, Marvin Bell. Besides poetry, publishes reviews, interviews, and articles, by invitation only. Size: 48 to 56 pages in a 6″ by 9″ format. Subscription rate: $7 for 2 issues; sample copy $3.50.

☐Received about 1,000 poetry mss. in 1982; accepted about 100. Pays $8 per page and 3 free copies in 1983-84. Copyright reverts to author. Contact: Frank Steele, Peggy Steele, or Elizabeth Oakes, Editors. Send 1 to 10 poems. No simultaneous submissions; photocopies acceptable. Decision in 3 to 4 weeks.

Plains Poetry Journal, Box 2337, Bismarck, ND 58202. (701) 222-0728. Founded 1981. Circulation: Over 200. Finely crafted poetry, skillful in its use of language. No conversational, broken-prose free verse, or "Hallmark" verse. Poets recently published: Rodney Nelson, Edward Watkins, Jane Greer, Robert N. Feinstein, William F. Dougherty. Also publishes essays on poetry—no reviews. Size: 40 pages in a 5½″ by 8½″ format. Subscription rate: $10 for 4 issues; sample copy $2.50.

☐Received 2,500 poetry mss. in 1982; accepted 160. Pays 2 free copies. Copyright reverts to author. Contact: Jane Greer, Editor. Send 5 to 8 poems. Simultaneous and photocopied submissions acceptable. Decision in 1 week.

☐Stronghold Press Chapbook Series (sample publication: William Burns, *Under Pressure*) pays a negotiable percentage after costs are met. Send query letter; if approved, mss. of 40 to 60 pages are read. Decision in 1 week.

Poem, Department of English, University of Alabama at Huntsville, Huntsville, AL 35899. Founded 1967. Circulation: 500 to 600. Poetry in traditional

and nontraditional forms, on all themes. No translations or previously published work. Poets recently published: Charles Edward Eaton, Ronald Wallace, Norman Nathan. Publishes poetry only. Size: 70 pages in a 4½" by 7¼" format. Subscription rate: $5.50 for 3 issues; sample copy $2.50.
☐Received 10,000 poetry mss. in 1982; accepted 175. Pays 1 free copy. Copyright reverts to author. Contact: Robert L. Welker, Editor. Send 3 to 5 poems under 40 lines in length. No simultaneous submissions; photocopies acceptable. Decision in 4 weeks.

Poet and Critic, Department of English, Iowa State University, Ames, IA 50011. (515) 294-2180. Founded 1963. Circulation: 600. Poetry of all kinds. Poets recently published: Jordan Smith, Laura Jensen, Jim Heynen, Sandra Gilbert. Besides poetry, publishes essays, some fiction, prose poems, and reviews. Size: 72 pages in a 6" by 9" format. Subscription rate: $9 for 3 issues; sample copy $3.
☐No figures given for mss. received and accepted in 1982. Pays 2 free copies. Copyright reverts to author. Spring issue each year publishes the best poetry by graduate students in writing programs. Contact: Michael Martone, Editor. Send 3 to 4 poems. No simultaneous submissions. Photocopies acceptable. Decision in 4 weeks.

Poet Lore, 4000 Albemarle Street, N.W., Washington, DC 20016. (202) 362-6445. Founded 1889. Circulation: 400. Poetry of all kinds, with a special interest in narrative poetry and translations of contemporary world poets. Poets recently published: Linda Pastan, Susan Astor, Albert Goldbarth, Roger Finch. Also publishes reviews of poetry books. Size: 64 pages in a 6" by 9" format. Subscription rate: $12 for 4 issues; sample copy $2.50.
☐No figures given for mss. received and accepted in 1982. Pays 2 free copies. Copyright reverts to author. Contact: Susan Davis, Managing Editor. Send 3 to 5 poems. No simultaneous submissions; photocopies acceptable. Decision in 12 to 16 weeks.

Poetry, Box 4348, 601 South Morgan Street, Chicago, IL 60680. (312) 966-7803. Founded 1912. Circulation: 7,000. High-quality poetry in all forms, on all subject matter. Poets recently published: David Wagoner, Richard Kenney, Ai, Gary Soto. Besides poetry, publishes reviews of poetry books, news notes, and a list of books received. Size: 64 pages in a 5½" by 9" format. Subscription rate: $20 in the U. S., $24 foreign; sample copy $2.60.
☐Received "60,000" poetry mss. in 1982; accepted 300. Pays $1 per line and 2 free copies. Copyright reverts to author. Contact: Joseph Parisi, Acting Editor. Send about 6 poems. No simultaneous submissions. Photocopies acceptable. Decision in 4 to 6 weeks.
☐Annually awards about 7 prizes in November for the best poems published in the preceding 2 volumes. All poems published in the magazine are automatically considered for the awards. In November 1982, the awards, ranging from $100 to $1,000, included the Oscar Blumenthal Prize ($100), The

Frederick Bock Prize ($300), The English-Speaking Union Prize ($1,000), The Jacob Glatstein Memorial Prize ($100), The Bess Hokin Prize ($200), The Levinson Prize ($750), and The Eunice Tietjens Prize ($200).

Poetry Canada Review, Box 1280, Station A, Toronto, Ontario, M5W 1G7 Canada. (416) 927-8001. Founded 1979. Circulation: 2,000. Short lyrics that meet the criterion of excellence. No spiritualism, beautifulism, or moralism. Poets recently published: Irving Layton, Margaret Atwood, Gwendolyn MacEwen, Michael Ondaatje. Besides poetry, publishes reviews, articles, and lists of markets. Size: 20 pages in an 11¼" by 15" format. Subscription rate: $8 for 4 issues; sample copy $3.50 prepaid.
□Received 1,300 poetry mss. in 1982; accepted 65. Pays $5 per poem and 2 free copies. Copyright reverts to author. Annual Editor's Prizes are selected from the previous 4 issues each fall. Contact: Clifton Whiten (Canadian), Rosalind Eve Conway (International), Poetry Editors. Send 6 to 12 poems. No simultaneous or photocopied submissions. Decision in 1 to 4 weeks.

Poetry Flash, Box 4172, Berkeley, CA 94704. (415) 548-6871. Founded 1972. Circulation: 7,000 to 7,500. Short poems or poems on poetry, poetry readings, and writing. Poets recently published: David Meltzer, Alan Soldofsky, Dick Bakken, Gellu Naum. Besides poetry, publishes poetry news, calendar items, and poetry reviews. Size: 8 to 12 pages in an 11" by 14" format. Subscription rate: $7 for 12 issues; sample copy free.
□Received 25 poetry mss. in 1982; accepted 5. Pays a year's free subscription and free copies as requested. Copyright reverts to author. Contact: Joyce Jenkins, Editor. Send 5 to 10 poems, each no longer than 20 lines. Simultaneous and photocopied submissions acceptable. Decision in 8 weeks.

Poetry Now, 3118 K Street, Eureka, CA 95501. Founded 1973. Circulation: over 2,500. Quality poetry of all kinds—extremely eclectic in taste. Poets recently published: Richard Eberhart, Charles Bukowski, William Stafford, Marge Piercy. Also publishes an essay-interview with a major American poet, written by the editor. Size: 48 pages in an 11" by 14½" tabloid newspaper format. Subscription rate: $7.50 for 4 issues; sample copy $1.50.
□Received 13,000 poetry mss. in 1982; accepted 400. Pays 2 free copies and 3 tear sheets of the page. Copyright reverts to author. Contact: E. V. Griffith, Editor. Send 3 to 5 poems, each no longer than 30 lines. No simultaneous or photocopied submissions. Decision in 1 to 2 weeks.

Poets On:, Box 255, Chaplin, CT 06235. (203) 455-9671. Founded 1977. Circulation: 450. Well-crafted, humanistic poetry on a specified theme. Poets recently published: Marge Piercy, Seamus Heaney, Charles Edward Eaton, Norma Farber. Publishes poetry only. Size: 46 pages in a 6" by 9" format. Subscription rate: $6 for 2 issues; sample copy $3.
□Received 800 to 1,000 poetry mss. in 1982; accepted 80. Pays 2 free copies. Copyright reverts to author. Contact: Ruth Daigon, Editor. Send 5 poems

on the issue's specified theme and a brief biography. Poems should not exceed 40 lines. Manuscripts not read from June to September. No simultaneous submissions; photocopies acceptable. Decision in 10 weeks.

Portland Review, Box 751, Portland, OR 97211. (503) 229–4468. Founded 1956. Circulation: 400 to 500. Poetry of all kinds, traditional and avant-garde. Poets recently published: Erland Anderson, William Stafford, David Weiss. Besides poetry, publishes short prose, interviews, plays, and photography. Size: 100 to 200 pages in a variable format. Subscription rate: $7 for 2 issues; sample copy $2.
□Received an "unknown" number of poetry mss. in 1982; accepted 40. Pays 1 free copy. Copyright reverts to author. Contact: Nancy L. Moeller, Poetry Editor. Send 3 to 5 poems. Simultaneous and photocopied submissions acceptable. Decision in 4 weeks.

Poultry, A Magazine of Voice, Box 727, Truro, MA 02666. Founded 1979. Circulation: 1,000. Parodies of contemporary poems, styles, manners, classics, and literary foibles. No *ad hominem* attacks on writers; only on their styles, fraudulent mannerisms, etc. Poets recently published: John Ciardi, Paul Zimmer, Al G. Vandenberg, Jonathan Holden. Besides poetry, publishes fiction parodies, interviews, and writing program parodies. Size: 8 pages in a tabloid format. Subscription rate: $2 for 2 issues; sample copy $1.
□Received 200 poetry mss. in 1982; accepted 40. Pays 10 free copies. Copyright reverts to author. Contact: Brendan Galvin, Co-Editor. Send as many poems as you like. No simultaneous submissions; photocopies acceptable. Decision in 4 weeks.

Prairie Schooner, 201 Andrews Hall, University of Nebraska, Lincoln, NE 68588. (402) 472–1800. Founded 1927. Circulation: 2,000. No particular kind of poetry sought. Poets recently published: Susan Fromberg Schaeffer, Lyn Coffin, David Wagoner, Brian Swann. Besides poetry, publishes fiction, interviews, articles, essays, and reviews. Size: 100 pages in a 6″ by 9″ format. Subscription rate: $11 for 4 issues; sample copy $1.
□Received "innumerable" poetry mss. in 1982; accepted 40. Pays 2 free copies. Copyright reverts to author. Awards $300 in prizes for the best poetry published in the year. Contact: Hilda Raz, Poetry Editor. Send 3 to 7 poems. No simultaneous submissions; photocopies acceptable. Decision in 8 weeks.

Primavera, 1212 East 59th Street, Chicago, IL 60637. Founded 1974. Circulation: 1,000. Poetry expressing the experiences of women. Poets recently published: Leslie Adrienne Miller, Judith McDaniel, Harriet Susskind. Besides poetry, publishes fiction and graphics. Size: 100 pages in an 8½″ by 11″ format. Subscription rate: $5 for 1 issue; sample copy $4.
□Received 700 poetry mss. in 1982; accepted 25. Pays 2 free copies. Copyright reverts to author. Poetry contests contingent upon grant money. Query for news. Contact: Editorial Board. Send no more than 6 poems. No

simultaneous submissions; photocopies acceptable. Decision in 6 weeks. Slow to respond during the summer.

PRISM international, Department of Creative Writing, The University of British Columbia, Buch. East 462–1866 Main Mall, Vancouver, British Columbia, V6T 1W5 Canada. (604) 228-2514. Founded 1959. Circulation: 1,000. Poetry that uses the subtle rhythms of speech, strong images, fresh metaphors, and intense patterns of verbal music. Original and subtle work that has a central coherent theme or context. No chatty poems, prose cut arbitrarily into "line" lengths, literary puzzles, "street" rants and rambles, psycho-babble, sentimental poetastry, or hysterical, manufactured angst poems. Poets recently published: Raymond Carver, Al Purdy, Erin Mouré. Besides poetry, publishes short stories, plays, translations, and self-contained novel excerpts of up to 5,000 words. Size: 80 pages in a 9″ by 6″ format. Subscription rate: $10 for 4 issues; sample copy $4.
☐Received 1,700 poetry mss. in 1982; accepted 75. Pays $15 (Canadian) per page and a year's free subscription. Copyright reverts to author. Perodic contests for various genres, topics, and groups of writers. Query for current information. Contact: Richard Stevenson, Editor-in-Chief. Send 4 to 8 poems, each no longer than 66 lines. No simultaneous submissions; photocopies acceptable. Decision in 3 to 6 weeks. Slow to respond during the summer.

Pteranodon, Box 229, Bourbonnais, IL 60914. Founded 1979. Circulation: 500. Poetry of all kinds with a fresh image or view. Poets recently published: Richard Eberhart, William Stafford, Richard Shelton, Jared Carter. Besides poetry, publishes fiction, essays, interviews, graphics, and photography. Size: 40 pages in an 8½″ by 11″ format. Subscription rate: $9.50 for 4 issues; sample copy $2.
☐Received 3,200 poetry mss. in 1982; accepted 41. Pays 1 free copy. Copyright reverts to author. Contact: Patricia Lieb or Carol Schott, Poetry Editors. Send only 4 to 6 poems. No simultaneous or photocopied submissions. Decision in 6 weeks.
☐Pteranodon Chapbook Series (sample publication: Hans Juergensen, *Fire-Tested*) pays 25 free copies, review copies, and 33⅓% off on all books purchased. Publishes mss. of 20 poems or less. Decision in 10 weeks.
☐Pteranodon Prize Poems Contest awards publication in a chapbook anthology with the first place winner's photograph on the cover, and cash prizes ranging from $5 to $20. Send poems of under 75 lines with an entry fee of $1 per poem or $5 for six poems. Send SASE for full information and deadlines.

Pudding Magazine, 2384 Hardesty Drive South, Columbus, OH 43204. (614) 279-4188. Founded 1980. Circulation: 2,000. Experimental and avant-garde poetry, with fresh and dynamic language; concise reflections on intense human situations. Poets recently published: Leonard Nathan, John M. Bennett, Eileen Eliot, Harry Chapin. Besides poetry, publishes articles about the use of poetry and creative writing in human service settings, writing exercises,

line drawings, photography, and letters. Size: 80 pages in a 5½" by 8½" format. Subscription rate: $10 for 3 issues; sample copy $3.50 postpaid.
☐Received "73,000" poetry mss. in 1982; accepted 200. Pays 1 free copy for every poem published. Copyright reverts to author. Contact: Jennifer Groce Welch, Poetry Editor. Send 8 to 25 poems. No simultaneous submissions; photocopies acceptable. Decision in 2 weeks.
☐Annual National Looking Glass Poetry Competition awards $500 for best poem. Send poetry between April 1 and November 30 each year, with an entry fee of $1 per poem. Write for guidelines. National Looking Glass Poetry Chapbook Competition awards publication, 25 free copies, and $84 in cash. Send 10 to 35 poems with a $6 entry fee between January 1 and July 30 of each year.
☐Pudding Publications Chapbook Series (sample publication: Al Ferber, *Gus*) pays 25 free copies. Send mss. of 10 to 50 pages with a $5 reading fee. Decision in 2 weeks.

Pulp, 720 Greenwich Street 4H, New York, NY 10014. Founded 1974. Circulation: 2,000. Open to all kinds of poetry; interested in translations from all languages. Poets recently published: Marge Piercy, Donald A. Sears, Donald Lev, Vincent Spina. Besides poetry, publishes fiction, interviews, and scripts. Size: 16 pages per issue; no format given. Subscription rate: $2 for 2 issues; sample copy $1 payable to Howard Sage.
☐Received more than 500 poetry mss. in 1982; accepted 100. Pays 2 free copies. Copyright reverts to author. Contact: Howard Sage, Editor. Send at least 3 poems. No simultaneous submissions; photocopies acceptable. Decision in 4 to 6 weeks.
☐Query about Pulp Chapbook Series. Sample publication: I. E. Steele, *Between Desire and Consumption*. No payment.

Pulpsmith, 5 Beekman Street, New York, NY 10038. Founded 1964. Circulation: 6,000 to 7,000. Poetry with vivid, original imagery; short lyric poems, ballads, sonnets, and story poems. Poets recently published: Erica Jong, Greg Kuzma, Charles Bukowski, Leo Connellan. Besides poetry, publishes fiction, articles, reviews, and serialized novels. Size: 200 pages in a 5" by 7" format. Subscription rate: $7 for 4 issues; sample copy $2.
☐Received 2,500 poetry mss. in 1982; no figure for acceptance given. Pays $20 to $50 per poem and 2 free copies. Copyright reverts to author. There are three $100 awards in every issue: The Edna St. Vincent Millay Award for a sonnet, The Madeline Sadin Award for a poem by a woman, and The Hank Malone Award for a narrative poem in American idiom. Contact: Joseph Lazarus, Poetry Editor. Send 4 to 5 poems. No simultaneous submissions; photocopies acceptable. Decision in 4 to 6 weeks, except during July and August.

Red Cedar Review, Department of English, 325 Morrill Hall, Michigan State University, East Lansing, MI 48825. (517) 355–9656. Founded 1963.

Circulation: 600. Quality poetry of all kinds. Poets recently published: Diane Wakoski, Carolyn Forché, Lyn Lifshin, Lee Upton. Besides poetry, publishes fiction and book reviews. Size: 80 pages in a 5½" by 8½" format. Subscription rate: $4 for 2 issues; sample copy $1.

☐Received 600 poetry mss. in 1982; accepted 60. Pays 2 free copies. Copyright reverts to author. Annual Creative Writing Contest offers cash awards in poetry for Michigan State students only. Contact: Kathleen Crown, Editor. Send no more than 5 poems, each no longer than 4 pages. Manuscripts not read from June through August. Simultaneous submissions acceptable; no photocopies. Decision in 3 weeks.

Ridge Review, Box 90, Mendocino, CA 95460. (707) 937–4275. Founded 1981. Circulation: 3,000. Regional poetry from Northwest California only. Poets recently published: Kate Dougherty, Karin Faulkner, Judith Tannenbaum. Besides poetry, publishes fiction and non-fiction. Size: 48 pages in a 7" by 10" format. Subscription rate: $7 for 4 issues; sample copy $2.

☐Received 100 poetry mss. in 1982; accepted 20. Pays 2 free copies. Copyright reverts to author. Contact: The Editors. Send about 5 poems. Simultaneous and photocopied submissions acceptable. Decision in 2 weeks.

Ripples, 1426 Las Vegas, Ann Arbor, MI 48103. Founded 1973. Circulation: 1,000. Poetry that's "organic," concerned with natural images. Besides poetry, publishes fiction and reviews. Size: 20 pages in an 8" by 14" or 5½" by 11" format. Subscription rate: $3.50 for 4 quarterly issues; sample copy 75¢.

☐Number of poems received and accepted in 1982 not provided. Pays one free copy, upon publication. Copyright reverts to author. Contact: Karen Schaefer, Editor. Send 1 to 10 poems, "as long as it takes to say it," but not extremely long. Simultaneous submissions acceptable, originals preferred over photocopies. Decision in 1 week.

Room of One's Own, Box 46160, Station G, Vancouver, British Columbia, V6R 4G5 Canada. Founded 1975. Circulation: 1,200. Poetry by women, of interest to women. Poets recently published: Erin Mouré, Jan Conn, Marge Piercy. Besides poetry, publishes fiction and criticism of feminist interest. Size: 82 pages in a 5½" by 8½" format. Subscription rate: $11 for 4 issues; sample copy $2.75.

☐Received "hundreds" of poetry mss. in 1982; accepted 20. Pays $10 and up per poem and 2 free copies. Copyright reverts to author. Contact: Poetry Editor. Send no more than 8 poems. No simultaneous submissions; photocopies acceptable. Decision in 6 to 8 weeks.

San Fernando Poetry Journal, 18301 Halsted Street, Northridge, CA 91325. (213) 349–2080. Founded 1978. Circulation: 500 to 700. Poetry of social protest; frontiers-of-consciousness poetry; poetry of the *Zeitgeist*. Poets recently published: Aaron Kramer, Karla Andersdotter, James Magarian, Jess Graf. Publishes poetry only. Size: 100 pages in a 5¼" by 8¼" format.

Subscription rate: $10 for 4 issues; sample copy $2.50.

□Received 2,000 poetry mss. in 1982; accepted 300. Pays 1 free copy. Copyright reverts to author. Contact: Lori C. Smith, Editor. Send 4 poems. Simultaneous and photocopied submissions acceptable. Decision in 1 week. □Cerulean Press Chapbook Series publishes anti-war poetry. Sample publication: Blair H. Allen, *Atlantis Trilogy*. Pays in free copies. Send query letter; if approved, send a ms. of 16 to 30 pages.

Second Coming Press, Box 31249, San Francisco, CA 94131. Founded 1927. Circulation: 1,000 to 1,500. Beat and Post-Beat poetry and prose poems. Poets recently published: James Purdy, Jack Micheline, Darick Meltzer. Besides poetry, publishes fiction, prose, and one-act plays. Size: 116 to 240 pages in a 6″ by 9″ format. Subscription rate: $5 for 1 issue; sample copy $3.

□Received 500 poetry mss. in 1982; accepted 100. Pays 2 free copies. Copyright reverts to author. Contact: A. D. Winans, Editor. Send 1 to 4 poems. Manuscripts not read during June, July, and August. Simultaneous and photocopied submissions acceptable. Decision in 4 weeks. □Second Coming Press Chapbook Series (sample publication: Gene Fowler, *Felon's Journal*) pays 10% of press run in free copies. Query first with samples; if approved, a ms. of 48 to 64 pages will be read. Decision in 8 weeks. Overstocked through 1984.

Seven, 3630 North West 22, Oklahoma City, OK 73107. Founded 1930. Circulation: 1,000. Classic, traditional poetry and good free verse. Poets recently published: Witter Bynner, Alfred Kreymborg, Margaret Widdemer, Robert P. Tristram Coffin. Publishes poetry only. Size: 7 poems in a 5½″ by 8½″ format. Subscription rate: $7.50 for 4 issues; sample copy $2.

□Received "between 40,000 and 50,000" poetry mss. in 1982; accepted "possibly" 14. Pays $5 per poem on acceptance and six free copies. Copyright usually reverts to author on request. Jesse Stuart Contest for best unpublished poems in the Jesse Stuart tradition. Prizes from $5 to $25. Send for guidelines with SASE. Contact: James Neill Northe, Editor and Publisher. Send 3 to 6 poems. Simultaneous and photocopied submissions acceptable. Decision in 1 week.

The Sewanee Review, University of the South, Sewanee, TN 37375. (615) 598–5931, Exts. 245 & 246. Founded 1892. Circulation 3,400. High-quality poetry of many kinds. Poets recently published: Donald Davie, Vern Rutsala, Dave Smith, Lewis Turco. Besides poetry, publishes short stories, essays, and essay-reviews. Size: 192 pages in a 6″ by 9″ format. Subscription rate: $12 for 4 issues; sample copy $4.75.

□Received 4,360 poetry mss. in 1982; accepted 40. Pays about 60¢ per line and 2 free copies. If the writer wishes, handles reprint-permission requests after a signed transfer of this right. Contact: George Core, Editor. Send no more than 4 to 6 poems, each no longer than 40 lines. No simultaneous submissions; photocopies acceptable, but "much prefers" originals. Decision in 1 to 4 weeks.

Sez, A Multi-Racial Journal of Poetry and People's Culture, Box 8803, Minneapolis, MN 55408. (612) 822-3488. Founded 1978. Circulation: 1,200. Poetry oriented toward working-class, ethnic, and social issues. Favors Midwest poets and poets of color; discourages poets east of the Hudson. Poets recently published: Thomas McGrath, Anya Achtenberg, new poets from Nicaragua and El Salvador. Besides poetry, publishes fiction, articles, interviews, oral histories, and letters. Query before sending. Size: 60 pages in an 8½" by 11" format with glossy cover. Subscription rate: $7 for 4 issues; sample copy $3.50.
□Received 100 poetry mss. in 1982; accepted 15. Pays 2 free copies. Copyright reverts to author. Contact: Jim Dochniak, Editor. Send 4 to 7 poems after purchasing a sample. Manuscripts not read from July through September. Simultaneous submissions acceptable if stated in cover letter. Photocopies acceptable. Decision in 10 weeks.
□Shadow Press, U.S.A. Chapbook Series published on a cooperative basis with individual arrangements made with each author. Sample publication: Mary Fell, *The Triangle Fire.* Send query letter; if approved, a ms. of 10 to 60 pages on working-class and Third World issues will be read. Decision in 10 weeks.

Shenandoah, Box 722, Lexington, VA 24450. (703) 463-9111, Ext. 283. Founded 1950. Circulation: 1,000. Quality poetry. Poets recently published: Richard Wilbur, Daniel Hoffman, Joyce Carol Oates, Irving Feldman. Besides poetry, publishes fiction, essays, interviews, and book reviews. Size: 100 pages in a 6" by 9" format. Subscription rate: $8 for 4 issues; sample copy $2.50.
□Received "hundreds" of poetry mss. in 1982; number accepted not given. Cash payment negotiable; pays 2 free copies and a one-year's free subscription. Copyright reverts to author. Contact: Richard Howard, Poetry Editor. No restrictions on the number of poems that can be submitted. No simultaneous submissions; photocopies acceptable. Decision in 4 weeks.

Sibyl-Child, An Arts and Culture Journal, Box 1773, Hyattsville, MD 20788. Founded 1974. Circulation: 500. Imagistic poetry, narratives, and translations. Poets recently published: Lyn Lifshin, David Hall, Ruthellen Quillen. Besides poetry, publishes stories, reviews, interviews, photography, and graphics. Size: 64 pages in a 5½" by 8½" format. Subscription rate: $9 for 3 issues; sample copy $3.
□Received approximately 100 poetry mss. in 1982; number accepted not given. Pays 2 free copies. Copyright reverts to author. Contact: Nancy Prothro, Saundra Maley, Doris Mozer, Editors. Send 3 to 5 poems. Manuscripts not read during the summer. Simultaneous and photocopied submissions acceptable. Decision in 10 weeks.

□Sibyl-Child Chapbook Series (sample publication: Ruthellen Quillen, *Magdalen*) pays 10 free copies and additional copies at cost. Reads lyric poetry mss. of 25 pages. Decision in 10 weeks.

Silverfish Review, Box 3541, Eugene, OR 97403. (503) 687-9625. Founded 1978. Circulation: 500. Quality poetry and translations. Poets recently published: Katharyn Machan Aal, Robert Ward, Ivan Arquelles, John Morgan. Besides poetry, publishes fiction, reviews, criticism, interviews, and translations. Size: 35 to 40 pages in a 5″ by 8″ format. Subscription rate: $6 for 3 issues; sample copy $2.
□Pays 3 free copies. Copyright reverts to author. Contact: Rodger Moody, Editor. Send 3 to 5 poems. No simultaneous or photocopied submissions. Decision in 2 to 4 weeks.
□Silverfish Review Chapbooks competition awards $250 prize to winning manuscript. Sample publication: Frank Rossini, *Sparking the Rain*. Open to mss. of 24 pages, it publishes the winners in every third issue of the magazine. Decision in 4 weeks.

Sing Heavenly Muse!, Women's Poetry and Prose, Box 14059, Minneapolis, MN 55414. (612) 822-8713. Founded 1978. Circulation: 1,500. Poetry of interest to women. Poets recently published: Joseph Bruchac, Jared Carter, Susan Tichy, Patricia Hampl. Besides poetry, publishes fiction and creative essays. Size: 80 pages in a 6″ by 9″ format. Subscription rate: $9 for 2 issues; sample copy $3.
□Received 200 poetry mss. in 1982; accepted about 30. Usually pays $10 per poem and 2 free copies. Copyright reverts to author. Contact: Sue Ann Martinson, Editor. Send 5 to 7 poems. Simultaneous submissions acceptable if editor is notified. Photocopies acceptable. Decision in 1 to 3 months.
□Poetry contest for unpublished writers planned for 1984. Write for guidelines.

The Slackwater Review, Spalding Hall, Lewis–Clark State College, Lewiston, ID 83501. (208) 746-5541. Founded 1976. Circulation: 500. Quality poetry of all kinds. Poets recently published: David Wagoner, Karen Swenson, John Haines, T. R. Hummer. Besides poetry, publishes fiction, drama, essays, reviews, and interviews. Size: 120 pages in a 5½″ by 8½″ format. Subscription rate: $6 for 2 issues; sample copy $2.
□Received 1,000 poetry mss. in 1982; accepted 50. Pays 2 free copies; 50¢ per line when funds are available. Copyright reverts to author. Contact: Robert Wrigley, Editor. Send 4 to 8 poems. Manuscripts not read from mid-May through early September. No simultaneous or photocopied submissions. Decision in 2 weeks.
□Confluence Press Chapbook Series (sample publication: Greg Keeler, *Spring Catch*) pays in free copies: 10% of a 300–copy run and then additional copies at a 50% discount. Contact: M. K. Browning, Editor. Reads mss. of 15 to 30 pages. Decision in 8 weeks.

Smoke Signals, 1516 Beverly Road, Brooklyn, NY 11226. (212) 856–3643. Founded 1980. Circulation: 1,200. Poetry "on the edge," in the vein of Bukowski, Lally, and Jim Harrison, or biting humor similar to that of Ligi, Mikhail Horowitz, and Andrei Codrescu. No academic or traditional work. Poets recently published: d. a. levy, Charles Bukowski, Jim Harrison, Michael Lally. Besides poetry, publishes fiction, articles, interviews, photography, drawings, and cartoons. Size: 100 pages in an 8″ by 11″ format. Subscription rate: $25 for 4 issues; sample copy $7.
☐Received 1,000 poetry mss. in 1982; accepted 28. Pays 1 free copy. Sometimes buys rights for anthology publication. The Sadakichi-Hartmann Prize awards an entire issue devoted to the poet and an undetermined cash offering. To be awarded in 1985, the Prize is for the life most resembling a poem in the pursuit of an honorable death. Contact: Poetry Editor. Send no more than 5 poems, each no longer than 3 double-spaced pages. Manuscripts not read for 3 months following publication of the magazine. Simultaneous and photocopied submissions acceptable. Decision in 12 weeks.
☐Black Market Press Chapbook Series (sample publication: B. Prune, *How to Jesus on $5 a Day*) pays in royalties and 20 free copies. Query about current manuscript requirements and deadlines. Decision in 12 weeks.

South Carolina Review, English Department, Clemson University, Clemson, SC 29631. (803) 656–3229. Founded 1968. Circulation: 600. Poetry of all kinds. Poets recently published: Larry Lieberman, R. T. Smith, William Aarnes. Besides poetry, publishes fiction and essays. Size: 136 pages in a 6″ by 9″ format. Subscription rate: $5 for 2 issues; sample copy free.
☐Received 500 poetry mss. in 1982; accepted 20. Pays 5 free copies. Copyright reverts to author. Contact: Carol Johnston, Managing Editor. Send any number of poems. Manuscripts not read from May through August. Simultaneous submissions acceptable if editor is notified. Photocopies acceptable. Decision in 12 weeks.

Southern Humanities Review, 9088 Haley Center, Auburn University, Auburn, AL 36849. (205) 826–4606. Founded 1967. Circulation: 1,000. High-quality, carefully crafted poetry. No obscenity. Poets recently published: Marge Piercy, William Stafford, James Applewhite. Besides poetry, publishes short stories, essays, book reviews and book review essays, interviews, and translations. Size: 100 pages in a 7″ by 9″ format. Subscription rate: $8 for 4 issues; sample copy $2.50.
☐Received 1,100 poetry mss. in 1982; accepted 22. Pays 2 free copies. Sometimes buys additional rights; usually, copyright reverts to author. Contact: The Editors. Send 3 to 5 short poems. No simultaneous submissions. Prefers no photocopies. Decision in 6 weeks.

The Southern Review, 43 Allen Hall, Louisiana State University, Baton Rouge, LA 70803. (504) 388–5108. Founded 1965. Circulation: 2,900. Quality poetry on various subjects in a variety of forms. Poets recently published:

Robert Penn Warren, Joyce Carol Oates, Miller Williams, Andrew Hudgins. Besides poetry, publishes short stories, critical essays, reviews, and interviews. Size: 240 pages in a 6¾" by 10" format. Subscription rate: $9 for 4 issues; sample copy $2.50.

☐Received several thousand poetry mss. in 1982; accepted about 50. Pays $20 per page on publication and 2 free copies. Copyright reverts to author. Contact: The Southern Review. Send any number of poems, each no more than 4 pages long. Simultaneous and photocopied submissions acceptable. Decision in 8 weeks.

Southwest Review, Southern Methodist University, Dallas, TX 75275. (214) 692-2263. Founded 1915. Circulation: 1,250. High-quality poetry, both traditional and experimental. Not interested in humorous, religious, or sentimental verse, or unnecessary obscurity and private symbolism. Poets recently published: Charles Black, Brian Swann, William Stafford. Besides poetry, publishes fiction, articles, interviews, and (occasionally) plays. Size: 100 pages in a 6" by 9" format. Subscription rate: $8 for 4 issues; sample copy $2.

☐Received 340 poetry mss. in 1982; accepted 7. Pays $5 per poem and 3 free copies. Copyright reverts to author. The Elizabeth Matchett Stover Award gives $100 for the best poem published in the preceding year. Contact: Charlotte T. Whaley, Editor. Send 3 to 10 poems, each no more than 18 lines. No simultaneous submissions; photocopies acceptable. Decision in 3 months. Slow to respond during the summer.

Stone Country, Box 132, Menemsha, MA 02552. (617) 693-5832 or 645-2829. Founded 1974. Circulation: 900. Poetry notable for its honesty and contemporary language, in forms ranging from the traditional to the experimental. Not for beginners. Poets recently published: Linda Pastan, David Hopes, Elizabeth Bartlett, Harry Humes. Besides poetry, publishes poetry reviews and essays on poetry. Size: 88 pages in a 5½" by 8½" format. Subscription rate: $7.50 for 2 issues; sample copy $3.50.

☐Received 5,000 to 6,000 poetry mss. in 1982; accepted 125 to 130. Pays 1 free copy. Copyright reverts to author. The Phillips Award gives a cash prize of $25 for the poem judged best in each issue. Contact: Judith Neeld, Poetry Editor. Send 5 poems, each no longer than 40 lines. No simultaneous submissions; photocopies acceptable. Decision in 8 to 12 weeks.

☐Stone Country Press Chapbook Series publishes poetry on a cooperative basis with the author. Reads mss. of 16 to 100 pages. Query first; as of October 1983, plans for future poetry chapbooks were on hold.

Street Magazine, Box 555, Port Jefferson, NY 11777. Founded 1973. Circulation: 750. Poetry on announced themes. Poets recently published: Anselm Hollo, Ray Freed, Kathryn Nocerino, Roberta Metz. Besides poetry, publishes short stories, essays, and interviews. Size: 100 pages in a 5½" by 8½" format. Subscription rate: $10 for 4 issues; sample copy $3.

☐Received 300 poetry mss. in 1982; accepted 30. Pays 1 or 2 free copies. Copyright reverts to author. Contact: G. Everett, Editor. Send 6 poems, each no longer than 2 pages. No simultaneous submissions; photocopies acceptable. Decision in 12 weeks.

☐Street Press Chapbook Series (sample publication: Bonnie Gordon, *Childhood in Reno*) pays 10% of the press run in free copies and royalties after costs are met. Reads mss. of 16 to 48 pages. Decision in 20 weeks. As of October 1983, not presently accepting new work.

The Sun, 412 West Rosemary Street, Chapel Hill, NC 27514. (919) 942-5282. Founded 1974. Circulation: 10,000. Poetry that makes sense and enriches our common space. Poets recently published: Robert Bly, Christopher Bursk, David Citino, Jimmy Santiago Baca. Besides poetry, publishes fiction, articles, essays, interviews, and photography. Size: 40 pages in an 8″ by 11″ format. Subscription rate: $25 for 12 issues; sample copy $3.

☐Received 150 to 200 poetry mss. in 1982; accepted 20. Pays 2 free copies and a free subscription. Copyright reverts to author. Contact: Sy Safransky, Editor. Send 3 to 6 poems. No simultaneous submissions; photocopies acceptable. Decision in 2 weeks.

Sun Dog, 406 Williams Building, English Department, Florida State University, Tallahassee, FL 32306. (904) 644-1248. Founded 1980. Circulation: 2,000. Poetry in all forms. Poets recently published: Paul Mariani, Jared Carter, David Bottoms, David Kirby. Besides poetry, publishes fiction and essays. Size: 100 pages in a 6″ by 9″ format. Subscription rate: $6 for 2 issues; sample copy $3.50.

☐Received 1,000 poetry mss. in 1982; accepted 42. Pays 5 free copies. Copyright reverts to author. Sun Dog Award gives a prize of $100 for the best poem in each issue—when funds are available. Contact: Rick Lott and Allen Woodman, Poetry Editors. Send 3 to 5 poems. No simultaneous submissions; clear photocopies acceptable. Decision in 10 weeks.

Tar River Poetry, Department of English, East Carolina University, Greenville, NC 27834. (919) 757-6041. Founded 1965. Circulation: 1,000. Poetry that makes skillful use of figurative language; poetry in traditional or open forms, but no flat statement poetry. Poets recently published: Louis Simpson, Frederick Morgan, Susan Fromberg Schaeffer. Also publishes reviews. Size: 56 pages in a 6″ by 9″ format. Subscription rate: $5 for 2 issues; sample copy $2.50.

☐Received 5,000 poetry mss. in 1982; accepted 100. Pays 2 free copies. Copyright reverts to author. Contact: Peter Makuck, Editor. Send 5 poems or 7 pages. Manuscripts not read during the summer. No simultaneous or photocopied submissions. Decision in 4 to 7 weeks.

Taurus, Box 28, Gladstone, OR 97027. Founded 1981. Circulation: 450. Poetry on human concerns that makes fresh, energetic use of language. No rhymed verse or Republican attitudes. Poets recently published: Alexander Blain, David Charlton, Walter MacBain, Tony Moffeit. Publishes poetry only. Size: 56 pages in a 5½" by 8½" format. Subscription rate: $7 for 4 issues; sample copy $2.

☐Received "20,000" poetry mss. in 1982; accepted 220. Pays 1 free copy. Copyright reverts to author. Contact: Bruce Combs, Editor. Send 4 poems, each no longer than 30 lines. No simultaneous submissions; clear photocopies acceptable. Decision in 24 hours.

Telescope, Box 16129, Baltimore, MD 21218. (301) 771–4544. Founded 1981. Circulation: 500. Poetry of all kinds. Poets recently published: Michael Burkard, Christopher Buckley, Laura Jensen, Albert Goldbarth. Besides poetry, publishes fiction, essays, interviews, and reviews. Size: 120 pages in a 5¾" by 8¾" format. Subscription rate: $9 for 3 issues; sample copy $2.

☐Received 1,000 poetry mss. in 1982; accepted 80. Pays 50¢ per line and 2 free copies. Buys additional rights. Contact: Julia Wendell or Jack Stephens, Editors. Send no more than 10 poems. No simultaneous submissions; photocopies acceptable. Decision in 6 weeks.

☐Ha'Penny Book Contest provides an open competition for poetry, novellas, and short fiction. Will not be sponsored in 1984. Write for current information and details.

Tendril Magazine, Box 512, Green Harbor, MA 02041. (617) 837–8986. Founded 1978. Circulation: 2,000. Quality poetry of all kinds; primarily contemporary American free verse. Poets recently published: Denis Johnson, Linda Gregg, Lorie Graham, William Matthews. Also publishes short stories. Size: 200 pages in a 6" by 9" format. Subscription rate: $10 for 3 issues; sample copy $5.95.

☐Received 10,000 poetry mss. in 1982; accepted 400. Pays 2 free copies. Copyright reverts to author. Contact: George Murphy, Managing Editor. Send 2 to 5 poems. Manuscripts not read during July and August. No simultaneous submissions; photocopies acceptable. Decision in 1 to 5 weeks.

☐Will soon begin sponsoring month-long fellowships for writers—residencies for writers completing works. Write for details.

Texas Review, Sam Houston State University, Huntsville, TX 77341. (409) 294–1429. Founded 1976. Circulation: 500. A variety of kinds of quality poetry. Poets recently published: Donald Justice, William Stafford, Fred Chappell, John Stone. Besides poetry, publishes fiction, articles, and interviews. Size: 140 pages in a 6" by 9" format. Subscription rate: $4 for 2 issues; sample copy $2.

☐Received 6,000 poetry mss. in 1982; accepted 70. Pays 1 or 2 free copies. Copyright reverts to author. Contact: Paul Ruffin, Editor. Send 3 to 4 poems, each no more than 30 lines. No simultaneous or photocopied submissions. Decision in 4 weeks.

The Three Penny Review, Box 9131, Berkeley, CA 94709. (415) 849–4545. Founded 1980. Circulation: 10,000. Formal and narrative poetry under 40 lines, or anything that is very good. Poets recently published: Thom Gunn, Howard Nemerov, Donald Davie. Brenda Hillman. Besides poetry, publishes fiction, critical essays, interviews, reviews, and political essays. Size: 28 pages in an 11″ by 17″ tabloid format. Subscription rate: $8 for 4 issues; sample copy $3.
☐Received 1,200 to 1,500 poetry mss. in 1982; accepted 10 from the unsolicited ones. Pays $25 to $50 per poem right now, but future payment uncertain. Also pays up to 10 free copies if author pays postage. Copyright reverts to author. Contact: Wendy Lesser, Editor. Send no more than 5 poems. No simultaneous submissions; photocopies acceptable. Decision in 8 weeks.

Thunder Mountain Review, Box 600574, Houston, TX 77260. Founded 1975. Circulation: 500 to 1,000. Contemporary experimental poetry. Poets recently published: Michael Waters, Ed Ochester, Andrew Glaze. Besides poetry, publishes prose poetry, interviews, and criticism. Size: 64 pages in an 8½″ by 5½″ format. Subscription rate: $6 for 1 issue; sample copy $6.
☐Received 1,000 to 1,500 poetry mss. in 1982; accepted between 25 and 45. Pays 2 free copies. Buys rights to republish. Contact: Steven Ford Brown, Editor. Send 5 to 8 poems. No simultaneous submissions; photocopies acceptable. Decision in 4 weeks.
☐Thunder City Press Chapbook Series (sample publication: Michael Waters, *The Stories in the Light)* pays free copies. Reads poetry mss. of any kind and length. Decision in 4 weeks.

Translation, Translation Center, 307–A Mathematics Building, Columbia University, New York, NY 10027. (212) 280–2305. Founded 1973. Circulation: 1,600 to 2,500. Publishes only new translations of important, contemporary foreign poetry not yet published in the U. S. Poets recently published: Lindolf Bell, Friederike Mayrocker, Sylven Poler, Sibanananda Das. Size: 220 to 280 pages in a 6″ by 9″ format. Subscription rate: $15 for 2 issues; sample copy $8, back issues $3.50.
☐Pays 2 free copies. Copyright reverts to author. Contact: Diane G. H. Cook, Managing Editor. Send no more than 5 translations, along with the originals and autobiographical material. No simultaneous submissions. Photocopies acceptable. Decision in 2 to 6 months.

TriQuarterly, 1735 Benson Avenue, Evanston, IL 60202. (312) 492–3490. Founded 1964. Circulation: 4,500. Excellent and serious poetry, aesthetically informed and weighty with concerns of moment, not trivial narcissistic accounts. Poets recently published: Thomas McGrath, Theodore Weiss, Linda Pastan, William Matthews. Besides poetry, publishes short fiction, essays, reviews, and graphic work. Size: 224 pages in a 6″ by 9″ format. Subscription rate: $16 for 3 issues; sample copy $2.

☐Received "thousands" of poetry mss. in 1982; accepted about 60. Pays about 50¢ a line on publication and 2 free copies. Copyright reverts to author. Contact: Reginald Gibbons, Editor. Send 3 poems. No simultaneous submissions; photocopies acceptable. Repeated submissions by nonsubscribers are not viewed positively. Decision in 8 weeks.

University of Portland Review, 5000 North Williamette Boulevard, Portland, OR 97203. (503) 283–7144. Founded 1948. Circulation: 1,000. Poetry that makes a significant statement about the contemporary scene. Poets recently published: Erland Anderson, Joan Yeagley, Richard Robbins. Besides poetry, publishes short stories, articles, and book reviews. Size: 52 pages in a 6″ by 9″ format. Subscription rate: $1 for 2 issues; sample copy 50¢. ☐Received 100 poetry mss. in 1982; accepted 30. Pays 5 free copies. Copyright reverts to author. Contact: Dr. Thompson M. Faller, Editor-in-Chief. Send any number of poems. No simultaneous or photocopied submissions. Decision in 12 to 24 weeks.

University of Windsor Review, Department of English, University of Windsor, Windsor, Ontario, N9B 3P4 Canada. (313) 863–0967. Founded 1965. Circulation: 700. Quality poetry of all kinds. Poets recently published: Dave Smith, Peter Wild, Hollis Summers, Tom Wayman. Besides poetry, publishes fiction, critical articles, reviews, and photography. Size: 125 pages in a 9″ by 6″ format. Subscription rate: $10 for 2 issues; sample copy $5. ☐Received 500 poetry mss. in 1982; accepted 15. Pays $10 per poem and 2 free copies. Copyright reverts to author. Contact: John Ditsky, Poetry Editor. Send 5 to 10 poems. No simultaneous or photocopied submissions. Decision in 1 week.

the unspeakable visions of the individual, Box 439, California, PA 15419. (412) 938–8956. Founded 1971. Circulation: 2,000. Beat poetry. Poets recently published: Allen Ginsberg, Michael McClure, Jack Kerouac, Gregory Corso. Besides poetry, publishes interviews, letters, and fiction. Size: 176 pages, usually in a 5½″ by 8½″ format. Subscription rate: $10 for 1 issue; sample copy $3. ☐Received 600 poetry mss. in 1982; accepted 20. Pays 2 free copies. Copyright reverts to author. Contact: Arthur and Kit Knight, Editors. Send 4 poems. No simultaneous or photocopied submissions. Decision in 4 weeks.

Virginia Quarterly Review, One West Range, Charlottesville, VA 22903. (804) 924–3124. Founded 1925. Circulation: 4,500. High-quality poetry of all kinds. Poets recently published: Louis Simpson, Dabney Stuart, Eleanor Ross Taylor, Joyce Carol Oates. Besides poetry, publishes short stories, essays, and book reviews. Size: 216 pages in a 6¾″ by 10″ format. Subscription rate: $10 for 4 issues; sample copy $3. ☐Received 10,000 mss. in 1982; accepted 77. Pays $1 per line and 1 free copy. Copyright reverts to author. Emily Clark Balch Prize awards $500 for the best poem or poems published in the magazine in a calendar year. Contact: Gregory S. Orr, Poetry Editor. Send no more than 10 poems. Manuscripts not read during July and August. Simultaneous and photocopied submissions acceptable. Decision in 8 weeks.

Visions: The International Magazine of Illustrated Poetry, 4705 South 8th Road, Arlington, VA 22204. (703) 521–0142. Founded 1979. Circulation: 500. Modern poetry with strong images, tight craftsmanship, and spare but powerful construction. Also translations of modern poetry. Poets recently published: Philip Dacey, Katharyn Machal Aal, Elisavietta Ritchie, Aaron Kramer. Besides poetry, publishes reviews by staff editor and black-and-white illustrations. Size: 44 pages in a 5¼" by 8¼" format. Subscription rate: $7 for 3 issues; sample copy $2 ($2.50 for latest issue).
□Received more than 1,600 poetry mss. in 1982; accepted 100. Pays 1 free copy; cash if grant money is available. Copyright reverts to author. Contact: Bradley R. Strahan, Editor-in-Chief; Shirley G. Sullivan, Associate Editor. Send 3 to 8 poems. No simultaneous submissions; photocopies acceptable. Decision usually in 2 weeks.
□Black Buzzard Illustrated Poetry Chapbook Series, founded in 1980, publishes mss. of 16 to 32 pages. Sample publication: Aaron Kramer, *In Wicked Times*. Pays free copies. Decision in 6 weeks. Query first: as of September 1983, publishing books by solicitation only.

Wascana Review, English Department, University of Regina, Regina, Saskatchewan, S4S 0A2 Canada. (306) 584–4298. Founded 1966. Circulation: about 500. Short poems of high literary value. Poets recently published: John V. Hicks, Norman Nathan, Joan Fern Shaw, Maura Eichner. Besides poetry, publishes short stories and literary criticism. Size: 80 pages in a 9¼" by 6" format. Subscription rate: $5 for 2 issues ($5.50 outside Canada); sample copy $2.50.
□Received several hundred poetry mss. in 1982; accepted 35. Pays $10 per page and free copies. Buys first publication rights. Contact: Dr. H. Dillow, Poetry Editor. Send any number of poems. Simultaneous submissions acceptable; no photocopies. Decision in 2 months.

Washington Review, Box 50132, Washington, DC 20004. (202) 638–0515. Year founded not given. Circulation: 2,000. Poems by poets who have some awareness that other people have written poetry before they did. Poets recently published: Ted Berrigan, Maxine Clair, Annabel Levitt, Jean Day. Besides poetry, publishes reviews and articles on visual and performing arts, books, film, and video—the arts in D. C. primarily. Size: 40 pages in a 16" by 11¼" format. Subscription rate: $10 for 6 issues; sample copy free with $1 postage.
□Received 2,500 poetry mss. in 1982; accepted 30. Pays 5 free copies. Copyright reverts to author. Contact: Doug Lang, Poetry Editor. Send 5 to 8 poems. Simultaneous and photocopied submissions acceptable. Decision in 8 weeks.

Waves, 79 Denham Drive, Thornhill, Ontario L4J 1P2, Canada. (416) 889–6703. Founded 1972. Circulation: 1,000. Poetry whose language and technique are as important as its content. Poets recently published: Margaret Atwood, Allen Ginsberg, Tom Shapcott, Mary di Michele. Besides poetry, publishes short fiction, excerpts from books, interviews, reviews, articles, and black-and-white graphics. Size: 100 pages in a 5″ by 8″ format. Subscription rate: $8 for 3 (or 4) issues; sample copy $2. (Note: a $1.00 charge on foreign checks makes small checks from the U.S. unacceptable.)
☐Received 700 to 800 poetry mss. in 1982; number accepted not given. Pays $5 per page and 1 free copy. Copyright reverts to author. Contact: Poetry Editor. Send 3 to 8 poems, from haiku length to 500 lines. No simultaneous submissions; clear photocopies acceptable. Decision in 4 to 6 weeks.

Webster Review, Webster University, Webster Groves, MO 63119. (314) 432–2657. Founded 1974. Circulation: 500. Translations of modern and contemporary poems and original work of high quality. Does not encourage work by beginners and students. Poets recently published: Rolf Jacobsen (Norwegian), Zui Ma'ir (Hebrew), Diane Tanzi. Besides poetry, publishes fiction, essays, and interviews. Size: 104 pages in a 5½″ by 8½″ format. Subscription rate: $5 for 2 issues; sample copy free.
☐Received 800 poetry mss. in 1982; accepted 60. Pays 2 or more free copies; when funds are available, pays $10 to $25 per poem. Copyright reverts to author. Poetry contests held irregularly, depending on grant funds. Contact: Pamela Hadas and/or Jerred Metz, Poetry Editors. Send 3 to 5 poems. Simultaneous and photocopied submissions acceptable. Decision in 6 weeks.

Western Humanities Review, University of Utah, Salt Lake City, UT 84112. (801) 581–6070 or 581–6168. Founded 1947. Circulation: 1,100. Poetry of high literary quality for a highly educated audience. Poems of many kinds, preferably short. Poets recently published: Mary Oliver, William Stafford, David Wagoner, Michael McFee. Besides poetry, publishes fiction, articles in the humanities, and book and film reviews. Size: 100 pages in a 6¾″ by 10″ format. Subscription rate: $15 for 4 issues; sample copy $4.
☐Received 2,000 poetry mss. in 1982; accepted 15. Pays $50 per poem and 2 free copies. Copyright reverts to author. Contact: Jack Garlington, Editor. Send no more than 5 poems, each no longer than 1 page. Simultaneous and photocopied submissions acceptable. Decision in 4 weeks.

Wind Magazine, Route 1, Box 809 K, Pikeville, KY 41501. (606) 631–1129. Founded 1971. Circulation: 550. Poetry from a variety of schools, without a preference for any one in particular. Interested in beginners who have something to say. Poets recently published: David Citino, Walter Bargan, Charles Semones. Besides poetry, publishes short stories, reviews of small press books, and some how-to articles. Size: 98 pages in an 8½″ by 5½″ format. Subscription rate: $5 for 3 issues; sample copy $1.50.

☐Received 5,125 poetry mss. in 1982; accepted 175. No payment. Copyright reverts to author. Contact: Quentin R. Howard, Poetry Editor. Send 5 poems. No simultaneous submissions; photocopies discouraged. Decision in 3 weeks.

Woman Poet, P. O. Box 60550, Reno, NV 89506. (702) 972–1671. Founded 1980. Circulation: 5,000. Top-quality poetry of any length. No particular political leanings or thematic bent. Poets recently published: Audre Lorde, June Jordan, Marie Ponsot, Ann Stanford. Besides poetry, publishes interviews, critical essays, and some biographical material for each of the three featured poets in each volume. Size: 100 to 130 pages in an 8" by 9½" format. Subscription rate: $14 for two annual volumes, $26 for 4 annual volumes; sample copy $7.50, plus $1 handling.
☐Received 600 poetry mss. in 1982; accepted 40. Pays in free copies, upon publication. Copyright reverts to author. Contact: Elaine Dallman, Executive Editor. Send 5 poems of any length. No simultaneous submissions; photocopies acceptable. Query, with SASE, for dates during which mss. are read. Decision in 4 to 8 weeks.

The Wormwood Review, Box 8840, Stockton, CA 95208–0840. (209) 466–8231. Founded 1959. Circulation: 700. Poetry in any style, and prose poetry reflecting the temper and depth of the present human scene. Poets recently published: Charles Bukowski, Ronald Koertge, Gerald Locklin, Lyn Lifshin. Besides poetry, publishes fables and short-short stories. Size: 40 to 44 pages in a 5½" by 8¼" format. Subscription rate: $6 for 4 issues; sample copy $3.
☐Received over 4,000 poetry mss. in 1982; accepted more than 300. Pays 3 to 25 free copies or the cash equivalent if so specified in a cover letter. Copyright reverts to author. Contact: Marvin Malone, Editor. Send 4 to 6 poems of any length. No simultaneous submissions; photocopies acceptable. Decision in 4 to 8 weeks.
☐Wormwood Poets Chapbook Series pays 25 to 30 free copies or their cash equivalent. Sample publication: Wilma Elizabeth McDaniel, *Flowers in a Tin Can*. Reads mss. of any length for a chapbook of 40 to 44 pages. Decision in 4 to 8 weeks.

The Wree-View of Women, 130 East 16th Street, New York, NY 10003. (212) 473–6111. Founded 1976. Circulation: 15,000. Poetry on issues of concern to women. Poets recently published: Loretta Benjamin, Elsem Lubetsky, Janice Mirikatini. Besides poetry, publishes news articles, analyses, and stories. Size: 12 pages in a tabloid format. Subscription rate: $5 for 6 issues; sample copy 75¢.
☐Received 40 to 50 poetry mss. in 1982; accepted 10. Pays free copies—as many as requested. Copyright reverts to author. Contact: Norma Spector, Editor. Send 1 to 2 poems, each no longer than 40 lines. Simultaneous and photocopied submissions acceptable. Decision in 8 weeks.

Writers Forum, University of Colorado at Colorado Springs, Austin Bluffs Parkway, Box 7150, Colorado Springs, CO 80933-7150. (303) 599-4023. Founded 1974. Circulation: 1,000. Poetry in which feeling and form work together, in which diction is articulated beyond prosiness. Especially interested in writers from the western states. Poets recently published: Fred Chappell, Gladys Swan, Reynolds Price, Reg Saner. Also publishes fiction. Size: 240 pages in a 5½" by 8½" format. Subscription rate: $8.95 for 1 issue; sample copy $5.95 to $8.95.
☐Pays in free copies. Copyright reverts to author. Contact: Dr. Virginia McCabe, Poetry Editor. Send 2 copies of 3 to 5 poems and 2 copies of a cover letter giving autobiographical information. Decision in 3 to 5 weeks.

Xanadu, Box 773, Huntington, NY 11743. Founded 1975. Circulation: 500 to 750. Poetry that is well focused and finely crafted, with keen perceptions and fresh images. No verbosity or worn-out language and abstractions. Poets recently published: Christopher Burke, Margot Treitel, Wallace Whatley, Norma Westwood. Also publishes art. Size: 68 pages in a 5½" by 7" format. Subscription rate: $3.50 for 1 issue; sample copy $2.50.
☐Received 1,500 poetry mss. in 1982; accepted 50. Pays 3 free copies and $5 per poem when funds are available. Buys additional rights for use in an anthology. Contact: Lois V. Walker *et al.*, Editors. Send 4 or 5 poems, each no longer than 100 lines. No simultaneous submissions. Photocopies acceptable. Decision in 8 to 10 weeks.

Yankee, Dublin, NH 03444. (603) 563-8111. Founded 1935. Circulation: 900,000. High-quality contemporary poetry, either traditional or free verse. Poets recently published: Josephine Jacobsen, Renée McQuilkin, William Stafford, Raymond Roseliep. Besides poetry, publishes fiction and feature articles of interest to New Englanders. Size: 125 to 200 pages in a 5¾" by 9" format. Subscription rate: $14 for 12 issues; sample copy $1.50.
☐Received about 25,000 poetry mss. in 1982; accepted 50. Buys all rights if author agrees; if not, buys first rights only. Pays $35 for all rights, $25 for first rights, and free copies. Contact: Jean Burden, Poetry Editor. Send any number of poems, each under 35 lines. No simultaneous submissions. Photocopies acceptable. Decision in 2 weeks.
☐Prizes ranging from $50 to $150 are awarded for the 3 best poems published in the year. The judge is always a prominent New England poet, acting independently of the editors.

A SELECTIVE INDEX TO MAGAZINES

What follows is not a comprehensive index, but a convenient cross-reference to entries classifiable into important categories.

Magazines Publishing Poetry in Specific Genres or Modes

Beat Poetry
*the unspeakable visions of the
  individual*
Haiku
Modern Haiku
Humor
Gryphon
Lettres from Limerick
Light Year
Pig Iron
Plainsong
Poultry
Smoke Signals

Narrative
The Devil's Millhopper
G. W. Review
Poet Lore
Sibyl-Child
The Three Penny Review
Religious
America
Science Fiction/Fantasy
Owlflight
Surrealist
Panjandrum Poetry Journal

Magazines Open to Poetry in Traditional Forms

Blue Unicorn
Chariton Review
Chelsea
Crab Creek Review
Good Housekeeping
The Hollins Critic
Kavitha
Lettres from Limerick
Negative Capability
New CollAge
the new renaissance
Outerbridge

The Pikestaff Forum
Plains Poetry Journal
Poem
Poetry
Portland Review
Pulpsmith
Seven
Stone Country
Southwest Review
Tar River Review
The Three Penny Review
Writers Forum

Magazines Publishing Translations

Bitterroot
Chelsea
Colorado State Review
Field
The Greenfield Review
International Poetry Review
Modern Poetry in Translation

Poet Lore
Pulp
Sibyl-Child
Translation
Visions
Webster Review

Magazines Publishing Poetry of Regional Interest

Appalachia
Laurel Review
California (Northwest)
Ridge Review

New England
New England Sampler
Yankee
Western States
Writers Forum

Magazines Publishing Poetry of Ethnic Interest

Black American
Overtone Series
Irish-American
Adrift
Jewish-American
Jewish Currents

Native American
Blue Moon Press
*Many Smokes Earth Awareness
  Magazine*

Magazines Publishing Poetry of Interest to Women

The Centennial Review
Family Circle
Feminist Studies
Helicon Nine
Kalliope

Primavera
Room of One's Own
Sing Heavenly Muse!
Woman Poet
Wree-View of Women

Magazines Publishing Poetry on Social and Political Issues

Maize
Many Smokes Earth Awareness
 Magazine
the minnesota review

North Country Anvil
Not Man Apart
San Fernando Poetry Journal
SEZ

Magazines Actively Seeking New Poets

Bitterroot
Passaic Review
Wind

Magazines Publishing Poetry Only

Blue Unicorn
Light Year
The Lyric

Orpheus
Poem
Seven

Magazines That Pay Cash for Poetry

Adrift
America
The American Poetry Review
The American Scholar
Antaeus
Antioch Review
The Atlantic Monthly
Bitterroot
The Bloomsbury Review
Boston Review
California Quarterly
Carolina Quarterly
Cedar Rock
The Chariton Review
The Chowder Review
Cimarron Review
Commonweal
Confrontation
Corona
Cosmopolitan
The Country Poet
Croton Review
Earthwise Publications
Family Circle
The Fiddlehead
Field
The Georgia Review

Good Housekeeping
Hanging Loose
The Hollins Critic
Indiana Review
Light Year
Malahat Review
Michigan Quarterly Review
Mid-American Review
Midway Review
Midwest Poetry Review
Modern Maturity
MSS Magazine
New Mexico Humanities Review
the new renaissance
The New Republic
New Yorker
Open Places
Orpheus
Owlflight
Paris Review
Partisan Review
Phantasm
Pig Iron
Plainsong
Poetry
Poetry Canada
PRISM international

Pulpsmith
Room of One's Own
Seven
The Sewanee River
Shenandoah
Sing Heavenly Muse!
The Southern Review
Southwest Review
Telescope

The Three Penny Review
TriQuarterly
University of Windsor Review
Virginia Quarterly Review
Wascana Review
Waves
Western Humanities Review
Wormwood Review
Yankee

SUPPLEMENTARY LISTINGS

The following list includes magazines that made no response to *The Poet's Marketplace* questionnaire; those whose response implied that they were less likely to be responsive to unsolicited manuscripts than the magazines described in the entries above; and those whose circulation is under 500 copies.

Although not a complete record of periodicals publishing poetry, the list offers more than 250 additional markets, arranged alphabetically by state, with Canadian addresses at the end. In approaching these magazines, you should first send a query letter and SASE for their needs, policies, guidelines, and the price of a sample copy. Concentrate your efforts in your geographical region, and study the samples carefully.

Alaska

Thomas Sexton, Poetry Editor, **Alaska Quarterly Review,** Department of English, University of Alaska, Anchorage 99504

Arizona

James Hepworth, Editor, **Blue Moon News,** English Department, University of Arizona, Tucson 85721

Michael Cuddihy, Editor, **Ironwood,** Box 40907, Tucson 85717

James Cervantes, Editor, **Porch,** 5310 East Taylor, Phoenix 85008

S. Schwartz, Editor, **Sonora Review,** Department of English, University of Arizona, Tucson 85721

L. Evers, Editor, **Sun Tracks,** Department of English, University of Arizona, Tucson 85721

Arkansas

Dennis Vannatta, Editor, **Crazyhorse,** English Department, University of Arkansas, Little Rock 72204

California

Robin Shectman, Editor, **The Altadena Review,** Box 212, Altadena 91001

Editors, **Antenna,** Box 16074, San Diego 92116

Robert Dorsett and Loretta Ko, Editors, **The Atavist,** Box 5643, Berkeley 94705

James Schamus, Editor, **Berkeley Poetry Review,** Office of Student Affairs, 103 Sproul Hall, University of California, Berkeley 94720

John Parker, Poetry Editor, **Forms,** Box 3379, San Francisco 94119

G. Young, Editor, **Greenhouse Review,** 3965 Bonny Doon Road, Santa Cruz 95060

Alfred Durand Garcia, Editor, **Heirs,** 2868 Mission Street, San Francisco 94110

L. F. Burnham, Editor, **High Performance,** 240 South Broadway, 5th Floor, Los Angeles 90012

N. Moser, Editor, **Illuminations,** 2110 9th Street, Apt. B, Berkeley 94710

H. W. Lond, Editor, **Intermedia,** Box 27670, Los Angeles 90027

L. Lacey, Editor, **Intimate Talk,** Box 489, Berkeley 94701

J. McBride & P. Vangelisti, Editors, **Invisible City,** Box 2853, San Francisco 94126

K. Chantikian, Editor, **Kosmos,** 381 Arlington Street, San Francisco 94131

T. Person, Editor, **Laughing Bear,** Box 23478, San Jose 95153

R. Campbell, Editor, **Night Light Magazine,** 216 East Victoria Street, Santa Barbara 93101

J. A. Powell *et al.*, Editors, **Occident,** 103 Sproul Hall, University of California, Berkeley 94720

L. Adams & M. De Baca, Editors, **Pacific Review,** English Office, San Diego State University, San Diego 92182

S. Mayhew & A. Erick, Editors, **Pentalpha Journal,** Box 861, Lakeport 95453

M. Rudman, Poetry Editor, **Pequod,** 536 Hill Street, San Francisco 94114

Alan Engebretsen, Editor, **Poetic Justice,** 8220 Royford Drive, Los Angeles 90045

H. Friedland, Editor, **Poetry/LA,** Peggor Press, Box 84271, Los Angeles 90073

A. Whitcher, Editor, **Poetry Magazine,** 1218 North Dalton, Azusa 91702

R. Radetsky & L. Lowe, Editors, **Quarry West,** Porter College, University of California, Santa Cruz 95064

I. Reed & A. Young, Editors, **Quilt,** 2140 Shattuck Avenue, Room 311, Berkeley 94704

M. Brewer, Editor, **The Record Sun,** Box 528, Topanga 90290

M. Osaki, Editor, **Rolling Thunder,** Box 9024, Berkeley 94709

M. Ward, Editor, **Sequoia,** Storke Publications Building, Stanford 94305

S. Vincent, Editor, **Shocks,** 45 Sheridan Street, San Francisco 94103

Editor, **Sulphur,** Box 228–77, California Institute of Technology, Pasadena 91125

B. Watten, Editor, **This,** 2020 9th Avenue, Oakland 94606

C. Monks, Editor, **Towards,** 17417 Vintage Street, Northridge 91325

L. Hejinian, Editor, **Tuumba,** 2639 Russell Street, Berkeley 94705

T. Janisse, Editor, **Volcano Review,** 142 Sutter Creek Canyon, Volcano 95689

Vortex, % Boyhearst Enterprises, Box 11622, San Francisco 94101

Colorado

Laurel J. Kallenbach, Editor, **Colorado-North Review,** University Center, University of Northern Colorado, Greeley 80639

Continental Drift, English Department, Box 226, Hellems 101, University of Colorado, Boulder 80309

K. George, Editor, **Frontiers,** Women's Studies, University of Colorado, Boulder 80309

Editors, **Pendragon,** 2969 Baseline Road, Boulder 80303

Jennifer and Edward Dorn, Editors, **Rolling Stock,** Campus Box 226, University of Colorado, Boulder 80309

Connecticut

R. A. Speers & J. C. White, Editors, **Connecticut Poetry Review,** Box 3783, Amity Station, New Haven 06525

J. Shaffer, Editor, **Connecticut Quarterly,** Box 68, Enfield 06082

Roger Ladd Memmott, Editor, **Eureka Review,** 90 Harrison Avenue, New Canaan 06840

M. Owen, Editor, **Telephone,** 109 Dunk Rock Road, Guilford 06437

Kai Erikson, Editor, **Yale Review,** 1902 A Yale Station, New Haven 06520

Delaware

T. Persun & J. M. Jankus, Editors, **Goblets,** Box 6236, Wilmington 19804

Robert Hogan, Editor, **Journal of Irish Literature,** Box 361, Newark 19711

Poetry Editor, **Mythos,** 22 Press, Box 6236, Wilmington 19804

District of Columbia

D. Bandow, Editor, **Inquiry Magazine,** Johnson Press, 1320 G Street S. E., Washington 20003

D. Baldwin, President, **Word Works,** Box 42164, Washington 20015

Florida

English Department, **Panhandler,** University of West Florida, Pensacola 32504

Georgia

W. S. Newman, Editor, **De Kalb Literary Arts Journal,** De Kalb College, 555 North Indian Creek Drive, Clarkston 30021

C. Kefalas, Editor, **New Arts Review,** Box 887, Athens 30603

Hawaii

Barbara Fulberson, Editor, **Hawaii Review,** Department of English, University of Hawaii, 1733 Donaghho Road, Honolulu 96822

Idaho

Linda Hutton, Editor, **Rhyme Time,** Box 2377, Coeur d'Alene 83814

Illinois

Jim McCurry, Editor, **Delirium,** Box 341, Wataga 61488

John Guzlowski, Editor, **Karamu,** Department of English, Eastern Illinois University, Charleston 61920

Indiana

F. Stefanile, Editor, **Sparrow Poverty Pamphlets,** Sparrow Press, 103 Waldron Street, West Lafayette 47906

R. Addleman *et al.,* Editors, **Veridian,** Box 2324, Bloomington 47402

Iowa

David Hamilton, Editor, **Iowa Review,** EPB 308, University of Iowa, Iowa City 52242

Peter Cooley, Poetry Editor, **North American Review,** University of Northern Iowa, Cedar Falls 50613

Kansas

A. G. Sobin, Editor, **The Ark Review,** Box 14, Wichita State University, Wichita 67208

Michael Heffernan, Poetry Editor, **Midwest Quarterly,** Pittsburg State University, Pittsburg 66762

English Department, **Touchstone,** Kansas State University, Manhattan 66506

Kentucky

Editor, **Bluegrass Literary Review,** Midway College, Midway 40347

S. J. Naslund, Editor, **Louisville Review,** English Department, University of Louisville, 315 Bingham Humanities, Louisville 40292

Q. R. Howard, Editor,**Wind Literary Journal,** RFD Route 1, Box 809 K, Pikeville 41501

Louisiana

Alice Moser Claudel, Editor, **New Laurel Review,** Box 1083, Chalmette 70044

John Biguenet, Poetry Editor, **New Orleans Review,** Loyola University, New Orleans 70118

D. Kronenwetter, Editor, **Southern Agitator,** Box 52467, New Orleans 70152

Editor, **The Southwestern Review,** English Department, University of Southwestern Louisiana, Lafayette 70504

Maryland

Robert Randolph Medcalf, Jr., Editor, **Apogee/Lyrical Ways,** Box 171, Baltimore 21203

P. Bartlett & B. Reynolds, Editors, **Hard Crabs,** Maryland Writers Council, Mt. Royal & Charles Street, Room 213, Baltimore 21201

Douglas Messerli, Editor, **Sun and Moon,** 4330 Hartwick Road #418, College Park 20740

L. Markert & S. Matanle, Editors, **Welter,** English Department, University of Baltimore, Baltimore 21201

Hal Roth, Editor, **Wind Chimes,** Box 601, Glen Burnie 21061

Massachusetts

Editors, **Acorn,** 185 Merriam Street, Weston 02193

David Low, Poetry Editor, **The American Literary Review,** 21 Woodman Street, Jamaica Plain 02130

Paul Kurt Ackermann, Editor, **Boston University Journal,** 704 Commonwealth Avenue, Boston 02215

J. Kelly and T. Glannon, Editors, **Gargoyle,** 40 St. John Street, Jamaica Plain 02130

P. Balakian *et al.*, Editors, **Graham House Review,** Phillips Academy, Andover 01810

P. Estey & J. Radoslovich, Editors, **Maenad,** Box 738, Gloucester 01930

John Hicks & Robert Tucker, Editors, **Massachusetts Review,** Memorial Hall, University of Massachusetts, Amherst 01002

Jeffrey Faude, Poetry Editor, **Nantucket Review,** Box 1234, Nantucket 02554

Nicholas Bromell, Editor, **New Boston Review,** 10–B Mount Auburn Street, Cambridge 02138

R. Okun & P. Greene, Editors, **New Roots,** Box 548, Greenfield 01302

DeWitt Henry *et al.*, Editors, **Ploughshares,** Box 529, Cambridge 02139

C. Keyes, Editor, **Soundings/East,** English Department, Salem State College, Salem 01970

Ned Griffin, Editor, **The Third Wind,** 10 Beech Street Extension, Hamilton 01982

Michigan

G. Dye *et al.*, Editors, **Moving Out,** 4866 3rd & Warren, Wayne State University, Detroit 48202

Alvin Aubert, Editor, **Obsidian,** Department of English, Wayne State University, Detroit 48202

Martin Grossman, Editor, **Skywriting,** 511 Campbell Street, Kalamazoo 49007

Minnesota

W. Elliott, Editor, **Loonfeather,** Bemidji Arts Center, 5th and Bemidji, Bemidji 56601

E. Buchwald, Editor, **Milkweed Chronicle,** Box 24303, Minneapolis 55424

J. Madson, Editor, **Truly Fine Press,** Box 891, Bemidji 56601

Mississippi

Frederick Barthelme, Editor, **Mississippi Review,** Southern Station Box 5144, Hattiesburg 39406

Missouri

D. Perkins, Editor, **Chouteau Review,** Box 10016, Kansas City 64111

Dan Jaffe, Poetry Editor, **Focus/Midwest,** 8606 Olive, St. Louis 63132

Speer Morgan, Editor, **Missouri Review,** Department of English, 231 Arts &

Science, University of Missouri–Columbia, Columbia 65211

Jan Castro, Editor, **River Styx,** 7420 Cornell Avenue, St. Louis 63130

J. Cox, Editor, **West Plains Gazette,** Box 469, West Plains 65775

New Hampshire

M. Gordon *et al.* Editors, **The Four Zoas Journal of Poetry and Letters,** 30 Main Street, Box 111, Ashuelot 03441

Jim Schley, Poetry Editor, **New England Review,** Box 170, Hanover 03755

Jill S. Jean, Editor, **Northern New England Review,** Box 825, Franklin Pierce College, Rindge 03461

C. A. Noon, Poetry Editor, **Penumbra,** Box 794, Portsmouth 03801

Editors, **Stand,** 45 Old Peterborough Road, Jaffrey 03452

New Jersey

Geoffrey Sill, Editor, **The Mickle Street Review,** 46 Centre Street, Haddon-field 08033

V. Scheinmann, Editor, **New Directions for Women,** 223 Old Hook Road, Westwood 07675

Raymond J. Smith, Editor, **Ontario Review,** 9 Honey Brook Drive, Princeton 08540

J. Amadeo, Editor, **Vega,** 252 North 16th Street, Bloomfield 07003

G. D. Kaliss, Editor, **West End Magazine,** 31 Montague Place, Montclair 07042

William Higginson and Penny Harter, Editors, **Xtras,** Box 219, Fanwood 07023

New Mexico

Editor, **New America,** Humanities Room 324, University of New Mexico, Albuquerque 87131

M. Kamei, Editor, **Plumbers Ink,** Box 233, Cerillos 87010

New York

Brian Swann, Poetry Editor, **The Amicus Journal,** 122 East 42nd Street, New York 10168

Bernhard Frank, Editor, **Buckle,** English Department, State University College, Buffalo 14222

Deborah Gimelson, Editor, **Columbia,** 404 Dodge, Columbia University, New York 10027

Bradford Morrow, Editor, **Conjunctions,** 33 West 9th Street, New York 10011

Robert Bertholf, Editor, **Credences,** 420 Capen Hall, State University of New York, Buffalo 14260

E. Jackson, Managing Editor, **Freedomways,** Freedomways Associates, Inc., 799 Broadway, Suite 542, New York 10003

M. Burnside & A. Kelly, Editors, **Gnome Baker,** Box 337, Great River 11739

Ben Sonnenberg and Elizabeth Pochoda, Editors, **Grand Street,** 50 Riverside Drive, New York 10024

G. Sheldon & A. Treichler, Editors, **The Grapevine Weekly,** 114 West State Street, Ithaca 14850

K. Kulikowski, Editor, **Gusto Magazine,** Box 1009, Bronx 10465

S. Mernit and R. Ratner, Editors, **Hand Book,** 50 Spring Street, Apt. #2, New York 10012

Editors, **Heresies,** Box 766, Canal Street Station, New York 10013

W. Perras *et al.*, Editors, **The High Rock Review,** Box 614, Saratoga Springs 12866

Paula Dietz & Frederick Morgan, Editors, **Hudson Review,** 684 Park Avenue, New York 10021

M. Hejna, Editor, **Inside/Out,** GPO Box 1185, New York 10116

A. DeLoach, Editor, **Intrepid,** Box 110 Central Park Station, Buffalo 14215

R. Yaffe, Editor, **Israel Horizons,** 150 Fifth Avenue, Room 1002, New York 10011

B. Early, Editor, **Junction Mag,** English Department, Brooklyn College, Bedford Avenue & Avenue H, Brooklyn 11210

C. Bovoso, Editor, **Letters Magazine,** Box 786, New York 10008

Dennis Cooper, Editor, **Little Caesar,** Box 1960, New York 10185

R. Steinke *et al.*, Editors, **Long Pond Review,** English Department, Suffolk Community College, Selden 11784

A. Menard & J. Bradley, Editors, **Main Trend,** Box 344 Cooper Station, New York 10003

Poetry Editor, **McCall's Magazine,** 230 Park Avenue, New York 10169

J. Carmichael, Poetry Editor, **Midstream,** 515 Park Avenue, New York 10022

Poetry Editor, **Ms.,** 119 West 40th Street, New York 10018

Grace Schulman, Poetry Editor, **The Nation,** 72 Fifth Avenue, New York 10011

Rob Baker, Editor, **Parabola,** 150 Fifth Avenue, New York 10011

L. Harss *et al.*, Editors, **Review,** Saybrook Press, 680 Park Avenue, New York 10021

Robert Boyers, Editor, **Salmagundi,** Skidmore College, Saratoga Springs 12866

K. Daniels & R. Jones, Editors, **Scandinavian Review,** 127 East 73rd Street, New York 10021

J. Crenner *et al.*, Editors, **Seneca Review,** Hobart and William Smith Colleges, Geneva 14456

John Friedman and Irving Gottesman, Editors, **Shantih,** Box 125 Bay Ridge Station, Brooklyn 11220

H. Greenberg *et al.*, Editors, **Some,** 309 West 104th Street, Apt. 9 D, New York 10025

V. Scott & J. Murray, Editors, **Sunbury,** Box 274, Jerome Avenue Station, Bronx 10468

Ellen Marie Bissert, Editor, **13th Moon,** Drawer F, Inwood Station, New York 10034

M. Crawford, Editor, **Time Capsule,** General P. O. Box 1185, New York 10116

B. Mayer & L. Warsh, Editors, **United Artists,** 172 East 4th Street, 9-B, New York 10009

Michael Andre, Poetry Editor, **Unmuzzled Ox,** 105 Hudson Street, #311, New York 10013

F. & H. Ruggieri, Editors, **Uroboros,** 111 North 10th Street, Olean 14760

A. Kramer *et al.*, Editors, **West Hills Review,** 246 Walt Whitman Road, Huntington Station 11746

J. Ornstein *et al.*, Editors, **Win Magazine,** 326 Livingston Street, 3rd Floor, Brooklyn 11217

S. Frank, Editor, **Women's Studies Quarterly,** Box 334, Old Westbury 11568

St. Mark's Poetry Project, **The World,** Second Avenue and 10th Street, New York 10003

North Carolina

Editor, **The Davidson Miscellany,** Box 696, Davidson 28036

Nina A. Wicker, Editor, **Manna,** Route 8, Box 368, Sanford 27330

Bob Hall, Managing Editor, **Southern Exposure,** Box 531, Durham 27702

Robert Waters Grey, Editor, **Southern Poetry Review,** English Department,

University of North Carolina, Charlotte 28223

North Dakota

Joan Eades & Linda Ohlsen, Editors, **Bloodroot,** Box 891, Grand Forks 58201

Robert Lewis, Editor, **North Dakota Quarterly,** Box 8237, University of North Dakota, Grand Forks 58202

Ohio

D. Wiebe & J. Bertolino, Editors, **Cincinnati Poetry Review,** Department of English (069), University of Cincinnati, Cincinnati 45221

D. Citino, Editor, **Cornfield Review,** Ohio State University–Marion Campus, 1465 Mount Vernon Avenue, Marion 43302

David Fratus, Editor, **Hiram Poetry Review,** Box 162, Hiram 44234

Ronald Sharp & Frederick Turner, Editors, **Kenyon Review,** Kenyon College, Gambier 43022

Lupe Gonzalez, Editor, **Live Writers!,** Box 8182, Cincinnati 45208

R. Foley, Editor, **The New Kent Quarterly,** 239 Student Center, Kent State University, Kent 44240

Wayne Dodd, Editor, **Ohio Review,** Ellis Hall, Ohio University, Athens 45701

Oregon

The Insurgent Sociologist, Department of Sociology, University of Oregon, Eugene 97403

R. Stanek, Editor, **Total Abandon,** Box 40502, Portland 97240

Pennsylvania

John C. Kleis, Editor, **Four Quarters,** La Salle College, Olney Avenue & 20th Street, Philadelphia 19141

D. Bartel *et al.*, Editors, **Gramercy Review,** 5536 Bryant Street, Pittsburgh 15206

D. Walter & D. Ernsberger, Editors, **Individual Liberty,** Box 1147, Warminster 18974

A. Pride *et al.*, Editors, **Motheroot Journal,** 214 Dewey Street, Pittsburgh 15218

Editor, **Painted Bride Quarterly,** 230 Vine Street, Philadelphia 19106

Gil Ott, Editor, **Paper Air,** 825 Morris Road, Blue Bell 19422

J. Mc Manis, Editor, **Pivot,** 221 South Barnard Street, State College 16801

Richard O'Connell, Editor, **Poetry Newsletter,** Department of English, Temple University, Philadelphia 19122

Pat Petrosky, Editor, **Slow Loris Reader,** 923 Highview Street, Pittsburgh 15206

Karl Patten & Robert Taylor, Editors, **West Branch,** English Department, Bucknell University, Lewisburg 17837

Rhode Island

Miles Parker, Editor, **Northeast Journal,** Box 235 Annex Station, Providence 02901

South Carolina

W. Johnston, Editor, **Pawnleys Island Perspective,** Box 1260, Pawnleys Island 29585

Editor, **The Struggling Writer,** Box 16315, Greenville 29606

South Dakota

Brother Benet Tvedten, O. S. B., Editor, **Blue Cloud Quarterly,** Marvin 57251

John R. Milton, Editor, **South Dakota Review,** Box 111 University Exchange, Vermillion 57069

Tennessee

Charles Stanfill, Editor, **Old Hickory Review,** Box 1178, Jackson 38301

Richard Jackson, Editor, **Poetry Miscellany,** English Department, University of Tennessee, Chattanooga 37402

Texas

A. Zu-Bolton *et al.,* Editors, **Hoo-Doo,** Box 1141, Galveston 77553

Loris Essary & Mark Loeffler, Editors, **Interstate,** Box 7068 University Station, Austin 78712

J. Haining, Editor, **Lucky Heart Books,** 320 Meadow Lea Drive, Austin 78745

Seth Wade, Editor, **Pan-American Review,** 1101 Tori Lane, Edinburg 78539

Nicolas Kanellos, Editor, **Revista Chicano-Riqueña,** University of Houston, Houston 77004

Dorey Schmidt, Editor, **Riversedge,** Box 1547, Edinburg 78539

J. Haining, Editor, **Salt Lick,** 320 Meadow Lea Drive, Austin 78745

J. Craven, Editor, **Separate Doors,** 911 W T Station, Canyon 79016

Charles R. Embry, Editor, **Sulphur River Poetry Review,** Box 3044, East Texas Station, Commerce 75428

Thomas M. Cranfill, Editor, **Texas Quarterly,** Box 7517 University Station, Austin 78712

Utah

D. Baker, Editor, **Quarterly West,** 312 Olpin Union, University of Utah, Salt Lake City 84112

Virginia

Edward Lynskey, Editor, **Crop Dust,** Route 2, Box 392, Bealeton 22712

Editor, **The Hague Review,** Box 385, Norfolk 23501

Tom O'Grady, Poetry Editor, **Hampden-Sydney Poetry Review,** Box 126, Hampden-Sydney 23943

Editorial Board, **New Virginia Review,** Box 12192, Richmond 23241

J. W. Harchick, Editor, **Phoebe,** George Mason University, 4400 University Drive, Fairfax 22030

R. Jones & K. Daniels, Editors, **Poetry East,** Star Route 1, Box 50, Earlysville 22936

Washington

Editors, **Catalyst,** Box 12067, Seattle 98102

S. Hackett, Editor, **Jeopardy,** Western Washington University, Humanities 350 WWU, Bellingham 98225

David Wagoner, Editor, **Poetry Northwest,** 4045 Brooklyn Avenue N. E., University of Washington, Seattle 98105

William Dunlop, Editor, **The Seattle Review,** Padelford Hall GN-30, University of Washington, Seattle 98195

Bill O'Daly, Editor, **Willow Springs,** Box 1063, Eastern Washington University, Cheney 99004

West Virginia

John McKernan, Editor, **The Little Review,** English Department, Marshall University, Box 205, Huntington 25701

Wisconsin

Editors, **Bread & Roses,** Box 1230, Madison 53701

T. Kubiak, Editor, **Cream City Review,** Box 413, English Department, Curtin Hall, University of Wisconsin, Milwaukee 53201

Mark Bruner, Editor, **Jump River Review,** Route 1, Box 10, Prentice 54556

J. Westburg, Editor, **North American Mentor Magazine,** 1745 Madison Street, Fennimore 53809

Dorothy Dalton, Editor, **Poetry Scope,** 1125 Valley Road, Menasha 54952

T. Scott Plutchak, Editor, **Wisconsin Review,** Box 276, Dempsey Hall, University of Wisconsin, Oshkosh 54901

Canada

Leona Gom, Editor, **Event,** Kwantlen College, Box 9030, Surrey, British Columbia V3T 5H8

D. Doss, Editor, **The Indian Voice,** 102–423 West Broadway, Vancouver, British Columbia V5Y 1R4

F. Tierney & W. Clever, Editors, **Journal of Canadian Poetry,** Box 5147 Station F, Ottawa, Ontario K2C 3H4

Douglas Smith, Poetry Editor, **Northern Light,** English Department, University of Manitoba, Winnipeg, Manitoba R3T 2N2

L. Filyer, Managing Editor, **This Magazine,** 70 The Esplanade, 3rd Floor, Toronto, Ontario M5E 1R2

5 | THE CHAPBOOK MARKET

With commercial publishing companies publishing fewer and fewer books of poetry, one alternative for a poetry collection is a chapbook—a slim volume of poetry of twenty-five pages or so, published by a small press. Though they vary greatly in production quality, chapbooks are ideal formats for closely unified sequences of poems, and can promote your reputation by getting a coherent body of your work into print. After publication in a chapbook, writers may find that grant agencies and major publishers give their future work a closer reading.

A chapbook publication hardly "establishes" a poet, however. A writer may still feel unpublished. With competition for review space so keen, chapbooks are usually ignored in the media. Nor do bookstores and libraries like to carry them: their usual folded format makes them difficult or impossible to stock or catalog. Also, there is a chance that being published in a chapbook may disqualify a poet for some major presses' first-book competitions.

Writing in *Coda* of June/July 1983, Allen Barnett found the future of chapbooks uncertain. On the one hand, they do not sell many copies, since they cost almost as much as a full-length paperback. On the other hand, they may thrive in the future as major publishers continue to publish less and less poetry. To poets, the advantage of publishing in a chapbook seems to be largely psychological. It's a way to mitigate the despair about ever getting published by a major press, and a device to build your confidence by getting a collection of your work to the public.

The chapbook publishers listed below include both small press publishers and literary magazine publishers whose chapbook series emerge from their magazines. In the latter case, poets often need to have published their work in the magazine before they can be considered for a collection.

One other source that you should check for chapbook publishers is *Small Press Record of Books in Print*, edited by Len Fulton and Ellen Ferber (12th ed., Paradise, CA: Dustbooks, 1983), which includes author, title, publisher, and subject indexes. The subject index for poetry gives the author and book title, so you can see where writers you're familiar with get published. Also, you can check the publishers' index for the names of authors they publish.

American Studies Press, Inc./Marilu Books, 13511 Palmwood Lane, Tampa, FL 33624. (813) 961–7200, 974–2857. Founded 1977. Publishes in paperback only. Special interest in Americana and American feminism. Sample publications: Thomas Wilkerson, *Boaz*; Phyllis McEwen, *Hystery, and Other Tools for Women*; Enid Shomer, *The Startle Effect*.
☐No advances; pays royalties of 10% on actual cash received after printing costs are met. Copyrights in ASP's name, but author has full right to grant permission for use upon notification, and ASP will not grant permission without author's confirmation. ASP maintains final decision on format. Authors are encouraged to help in promotion and sales. Contact: Donald R. Harkness, President and Editor-in-Chief. Send query letter and samples; if approved, mss. of 30 to 40 pages will be read. Prefers poems of one page or less. Decision in 2 weeks.

Andrew Mountain Press, Box 14353, Hartford, CT 06114. Founded 1980. Publishes in paperback only. Short imagistic poetry. Sample publications: George Ella Lyon, *Mountain*; Tony Magistrale, *Salvation on the Installment Plan*.
☐The Broadside Series Poetry Contest prize is $25 and 10 free copies. Contact: Candace Hall, Poetry Editor. Send original, unpublished poems with a reading fee of $1 for each poem submitted.
☐Lamont Hall Chapbook Series prize is publication of a 400- to 500-copy edition and 35 free copies, with later printings to be negotiated. Poems will also be eligible for publication in *Yet Another Small Magazine*, the house's poetry journal. Send samples; if approved, send a 20 to 24 page ms. of original poetry that has not been previously published in chapbook or book form. Enclose SASE, a $3 entry fee, a list of acknowledgments for individual poems, and biographical information. Decision in 4 weeks. Write for current deadlines on both series.

Beloit Poetry Journal Chapbooks—See *Beloit Poetry Journal*, Chapter 4.

Black Buzzard Illustrated Poetry Chapbook Series—See *Visions*, Chapter 4.

Black Market Press Chapbook Series—See *Smoke Signals*, Chapter 4. Black Warrior Chapbook Series—See *The Black Warrior Review*, Chapter 4.

Black Willow Chapbook Series—See *Black Willow*, Chapter 4.

Burning Deck—See Chapter 7 for address.

Cardinal Press, 76 North Yorktown, Tulsa, OK 74110. (918) 583-3651. Founded 1979. Publishes in paperback only. Original poetry of special interest to women and the counter-culture; avant-garde and free verse. Sample publications: Terry Hauptman, *Rattle*; Lynn Savitt, *No Apologies*; Betty Shipley, *Called Up Yonder.*
☐Pays in free copies: 10% of press run. Contact: Mary McAnally, Editor and Publisher. Send query letter and samples; if approved, a ms. of 5 to 6 poems will be read. Decision in 1 to 3 weeks.

Cedar Rock Press Chapbook Series—See *Cedar Rock*, Chapter 4.

Cerulean Press Chapbook Series—See *San Fernando Poetry Journal*, Chapter 4.

Chowder Chapbooks—See *The Chowder Review*, Chapter 4.

Confluence Press Chapbook Series—See *The Slackwater Review*, Chapter 4.

Devil's Millhopper Chapbook Series—See *The Devil's Millhopper*, Chapter 4.

Earth Series Chapbooks—See *Earthwise Publications*, Chapter 4.

T. S. Eliot Chapbook Competition—See *Earthwise Publications*, Chapter 4.

Forest Library Chapbook Series—See *Poet Papers*, Chapter 6.

Greenfield Review Press Chapbook Series—See *The Greenfield Review*, Chapter 4.

Hollow Spring Poetry Series—See *Hollow Spring Review of Poetry*, Chapter 4.

Konglomerati Press, Konglomerati Florida Foundation for Literature and the Book Arts, Inc., Box 5001, Gulfport, FL 33737. (813) 323-0386. Founded 1971. Publishes in both hardcover and paperback. Contemporary poetry in all forms. Sample publications: Richard Eberhart, *Florida Poems*; Lucky Jacobs, *Our Eyes, Like Walls.*

☐Pays in free copies. Contact: Richard Mathews or Barbara Russ, Poetry Editors. Send complete ms. of 20 poems. Decision in 6 to 8 weeks.

Light Year Chapbook Series—See *Light Year*, Chapter 4.

Limberlost Press Chapbooks—See *The Limberlost Review*, Chapter 4.

Maize Chapbook Series—See *Maize*, Chapter 4.

Midway Review Chapbook Series—See *Midway Review*, Chapter 4.

Midwest Arts & Literature Chapbooks—See *Midwest Arts & Literature*, Chapter 4.

National Looking Glass Poetry Chapbook Competition—See *Pudding Magazine*, Chapter 4.

Nightsun Books—See *Nightsun*, Chapter 4.

Overtone Series Chapbooks—See *Overtone Series*, Chapter 4.

Owl Creek Press Chapbook Series—See *The Montana Review*, Chapter 4.

Panjandrum Books Chapbook Series—See *Panjandrum Poetry Journal*, Chapter 4.

Perivale Press Chapbook Series—See *Perivale Press*, Chapter 6.

Phantasm Supplements Chapbook Series—See *Phantasm*, Chapter 4.

Pikestaff Poetry Chapbooks—See *The Pikestaff Forum*, Chapter 4.

Pteranodon Chapbook Series—See *Pteranodon*, Chapter 4.

Pudding Publications Chapbook Series—See *Pudding Magazine*, Chapter 4.

Pulp Chapbook Series—See *Pulp*, Chapter 4.

Red Weather Press, Box 1104, Eau Claire, WI 54701. Founded 1976. Publishes in paperback only. Open to all kinds of poetry. Sample publications: J. D. Whitney, *Mother*; Martha Mihalyi, *Bloodflowers*; D. C. Johnson, *Much Toil, Much Blame*.
☐No advances; pays royalties of 50% of actual cash received on second and subsequent printings. Contact: Bruce Taylor, Poetry Editor. Send a complete ms. of 30 to 40 pages with a brief autobiographical statement, a SASE, and a $5 reading fee, for which you will receive two copies of recent chapbooks. Decision within 3 months.

Riverstone International Poetry Chapbook Competition—See Chapter 8.

Second Coming Press Chapbook Series—See *Second Coming Press*, Chapter 4.

Shadow Press, U.S.A. Chapbook Series—See *SEZ*, Chapter 4.

Sibyl-Child Chapbook Series—See *Sibyl-Child*, Chapter 4.

Signpost Press Poetry Chapbook Competition—See *The Bellingham Review*, Chapter 4.

Silverfish Review Chapbooks—See *Silverfish Review*, Chapter 4.

Sparrow Press, 103 Waldron Street, West Lafayette, IN 47906. Founded 1954. Publishes in paperback only. Poetry in the modernist tradition with an intense care for language and aesthetic pattern, and a genuine commitment to life. No sloppy confessionalism, muddy prose chopped into lines, or writing that expects ideology to take the place of intelligent language and rhythm. Sample publications: William Zaranka, *A Mirror Driven Through Nature*; Sister Maura, *What We Women Know*; Ralph J. Mills, Jr., *March Light*; Raymond Roseliep, *Flute over Walden: Thoreauhaiku*.
☐Pays advance of $25 and 20% of profit after costs. Contact: Felix Stefanile, Editor. Send complete ms. of 20 to 30 poems for the Sparrow Poverty Pamphlets series, 40 to 50 poems for Vagrom Chap Books, during April and May only. Decision in 6 weeks.

State Street Press, 67 State Street, Pittsford, NY 14534. (716) 586-0154. Founded 1981. Publishes in paperback only. Poems that hold together as a collection; open to a variety of styles. Sample publications: Stephen Corey, *Fighting Death*; Nancy Simpson, *Across Water*; Christopher Bursk, *Making Wings*.
☐State Street Press Chapbook Series gives free copies and pays 40% of author's sales. Contact: Judith Kitchen, Poetry Editor. Send complete ms. of 18 to 22 pages, single-spaced, with no identification on the title page or in the text. In a sealed envelope include a page with the title and writer's name and address, and an acknowledgments page for any previously published material. Decision in 8 weeks. Write for current deadlines.

Stone Country Press Chapbooks—See *Stone Country*, Chapter 4.

Street Press Chapbook Series—See *Street Magazine*, Chapter 4.

Stronghold Press Chapbook Series—See *Plains Poetry Journal*, Chapter 4.

tadbooks—See *Orpheus*, Chapter 4.

Thunder City Press Chapbook Series—See *Thunder Mountain Review*, Chapter 4.

Unique Graphics—See *Owlflight*, Chapter 4.

The Word Works, Inc., Box 42164, Washington, DC 20015. Founded 1974. Publishes in paperback only. Well-crafted poetry; open to experimental work. Sample publications: Grace Cavalieri, *Creature Comforts*; Robert Sargent, *Aspects of a Southern Story.*
☐No payment. Contact: Deirdra Baldwin, Karren Alenier, Robert Sargent, or J. H. Beall, Editors. Send query letter and samples; if approved, a 5-page ms. will be read. Decision in 12 weeks.
☐Offers the Washington Prize, a $1000 award for a single poem of 12 to 24 lines by an American poet. Entries accepted from September 1 to November 1; write for details.

Wormwood Poets Chapbook Series—See *The Wormwood Review,* Chapter 4.

Zephyr Press—See Chapter 6.

A SELECTIVE INDEX TO CHAPBOOK PUBLISHERS

What follows is not a comprehensive index, but a convenient cross-reference to entries classifiable into important categories.

Americana
American Studies Press

Beat and Post-Beat Poetry
Second Coming Press

Black American
Overtone Series

Experimental
Black Market Press
Cardinal Press
Pudding Publications
The Word Works, Inc.

Feminist
American Studies Press
Cardinal Press

Imagistic
Andrew Mountain Press

Modernist
Sparrow Press

Multi-Cultural
The Greenfield Review Press

Politically and Socially Conscious
Cerulean Press
Maize
Shadow Press, U. S. A.

Traditional
Stronghold Press

6 | THE BOOK MARKET

Despite the difficulty of getting a book of poetry published, poetry books do continue to appear. Some observers say that more are being published now than ever before—mostly by the hundreds of small independent presses and the university presses. Some trade houses also continue to publish poetry, but there is little incentive for the large publishers to bring out poetry books. Printings are necessarily small, sales chronically slow, and profits rare. A few trade presses continue to publish poetry, mainly because they have the patience to await future sales while poets establish the quality of their work over the course of years. Because of the prestige associated with publication there, they attract a disproportionate number of manuscripts. Many people recommend that poets concentrate on the small presses, however, arguing that they represent the future of poetry publishing.

One factor influencing what poet gets published where is the existence of poets' networks, sometimes paranoiacally described as "the Poetry Mafia." You'll often notice that the same people who receive grants are running the creative writing workshops, judging contests, and recommending manuscripts to publishers. They print each other's work in their magazines, and take turns granting and receiving the visiting professorships and awards.

The institutionalization of poetry on campuses and a few

well-known centers has become a fact of life. Although this is partly a reaction to the general public's indifference to poetry, it sometimes encourages an insular mentality and a tendency to become a closed shop composed of teachers, students, and friends. This is displayed in poetry reviews, which often reflect an uncritical boosterism, a reflex of praise for someone in the clan. Since poetry books also suffer from too few reviews (and reviews that appear too late to help sales), these booster reviews further damage the sales of poetry. Readers know that they can't *all* be good books.

It is easy, however, to exaggerate the power of poets' networks. There is really no "Poetry Mafia"; there *is* a literary establishment that dispenses money, information, and helpful reviews. The networks represent no centralized conspiracy, only a number of groups organized on a variety of bases: regional, academic, religious, ethnic, political, and feminist, among others.

Reasonably free from outside influence, naturally wanting to preserve their independent judgment, poetry book publishers are still primarily committed to excellence. In most places, one can submit a poetry manuscript without any special recommendation and have it judged on its own merits. The publishers listed below are all prepared to read unsolicited manuscripts—provided you adhere to their guidelines on submissions. Where no phone number is listed, this indicates the publisher's preference that all correspondence be in writing.

Atlantic Monthly Press, 8 Arlington Street, Boston, MA 02116. (617) 536–9500. Founded 1857. Publishes in both hardcover and paperback. Poetry by established poets who have published in the *Atlantic Monthly* magazine. Two books a year, usually planned one or more years in advance. Sample publications: George Starbuck, *The Argot Merchant Disaster*; Mary Oliver, *American Primitive*; William Matthews, *A Happy Childhood*.
☐Pays advances and variable royalties, based on list price. Contact: Peter Davison, Senior Editor. Send query letter only. No decision time given.

August House, 1010 West Third Street, Little Rock, AR 72201. Founded 1979. Publishes in both hardcover and paperback. Poetry by Arkansans or poets accustomed to publication in periodicals. Sample publications: Jack Butler, *The Kid Who Wanted To Be A Spaceman*; Red Hawk, *Journey of the Medicine Man*.
☐No advances; pays royalties based on actual cash received. Contact: Ted Parkhurst, Executive Director. Send complete ms. of 60 to 100 poems with

SASE; individual poems can range from 1 to 4 pages. Don't phone. Decision in 10 weeks.

The Basilisk Press, Box 71, Fredonia, NY 14063. (716) 934–4199. Founded 1970. Publishes in paperback only. No particular type, style, or school of poetry is sought, but professionalism is expected; the poet must have studied the work of major poets of the past and present and practiced his craft. Sample publications: Lyn Lifshin, *Blue Dust, New Mexico*; Toni Zimmerman, *Entering Another Country*; Thomas M. Disch, *The Right Way to Figure Plumbing*.
☐Pays in free copies only. Books copyrighted for author. Contact: David Lunde, Editor; Marilyn Henris, Associate Editor. Send query letter and samples; if approved, ms. of 50 to 80 pages will be read. Decision in 4 weeks. (As of August 1983 not accepting manuscripts until current backlog ends.)

The Bellevue Press, 60 Schubert Street, Binghampton, NY 13905. (607) 729–0819. Founded 1973. Publishes in both hardcover and paperback. Open to all styles of poetry; shorter works are used more often. Sample publications: Harriet Zinnes, *The Book of Ten*; Barbara Unger, *The Man Who Burned Money*; Stephen Sandy, *Flight of Steps*.
☐No advances; usually pays 10% of edition, $10 for broadside poems, and $5 for poems used as postcards. Contact: Gil Williams, Deborah Hollander Williams, Poetry Editors. Send query letter and samples. Do not send translations or books already published for reprint. Decision in 6 weeks. Expect delays between acceptance and publication.

The Bieler Press, Box 3856, St. Paul, MN 55165. (612) 292–9936. Founded 1975. Publishes in both hardcover and paperback. No specific preferences for poems' form or content. Sample publications: David Romtvedt, *Moon*; Lewis Turco, *The Compleat Melancholick*; Ted Kooser, *The Blizzard Voices*.
☐No advances; pays royalties of 10% based on cash received. Contact: Gerald Lange, Publisher. Send query letter and samples. Decision in 1 week.

Blue Heron Press, Box 1326, Alliston, Ontario, L0M 1A0 Canada. (705) 435–5965. Founded 1979. Publishes in paperback only. Inspirational and/or hard-hitting, no-holds-barred poetry with the subject and the work combining to create a whole. Sample publications: W. F. Westcott, *Being*; W. F. Westcott, *Small Things*.
☐No advances; pays royalties of 10% based on actual cash received. Contact: W. F. Westcott, Publisher. Send query and samples with SASE. Decision in 12 weeks.

Blue Moon Press, Inc., English Department, University of Arizona, Tucson, AZ 85716. (602) 881–1981. Founded 1975. Publishes in paperback only. Poetry by Native Americans and contemporary writers from western America. Sample publication: Peter Wild, *Bitter-roots*.

☐Pays in free copies. Contact: Jim Hepworth, President. Send query letter. Decision in 8 weeks.

BOA Editions, Ltd., 92 Park Avenue, Brockport, NY 14420. (716) 637-3844. Founded 1976. Publishes in both hardcover and paperback. Poetry of the highest artistic and professional quality. No self-publishing poets. Sample publications: Joseph Stroud, *Signatures*; Peter Makuck, *Where We Live*; Louis Simpson, *Where We Live: Poems 1949-1983*.
☐Pays outright grants of $500 to $3,000. Contact: A. Poulin, Jr., Editor/Publisher. Send query letter; if approved, ms. of 60 to 70 pages will be read. Decision in 8 to 10 weeks.

George Braziller, Inc., 1 Park Avenue, New York, NY 10016. (212) 889-0909. Founded 1955. Publishes in both hardcover and paperback. Serious contemporary verse. Sample publications: Rika Lesser, *Etruscan Things*; Charles Simic, *Austerities*; J. D. McClatchy, *Scenes from Another Life*.
☐Pays advances and royalties of 6% to 10% based on list price. Contact: Richard Howard, Keith Goldsmith, Poetry Editors. Send query letter; if approved, ms. of 45 to 60 pages will be read. Decision in 6 weeks.

Carpenter Press, Route 4, Pomeroy, OH 45769. Founded 1973. Publishes in paperback only. Open to all types of poetry. Sample publications: Steve Kowit, *Lurid Confessions*; Jane Teller, *Love Poem for a Bank Robber*; Ron Davis, *Women and Horses*.
☐No advances; pays royalties of 10% of sales after production costs are met. Will probably publish unsolicited work only through competitions. Contact: Robert Fox, Publisher and Editor. Send query letter. Decision in 6 weeks.

Chantry Press, Box 144, Midland Park, NJ 07432. (201) 423-5882. Founded 1981. Publishes in paperback only. High-quality free verse. Sample publications: Maria Gillan, *Flowers from the Tree of Night*; Laura Boss, *Stripping*; Ruth Lisa Schecter, *Speedway*.
☐No advances; pays royalties of 15% after costs are met. Contact: D. Patrick, Editor. Send samples; if approved, ms. of 40 pages will be read. No submissions from June through September. Decision in 12 weeks.

Cleveland State University Poetry Center, Cleveland State University, Cleveland, OH 44115. (216) 687-3986. Founded 1970. Publishes in paperback only. Serious or light poetry. Sample publications: Lynn Luria Sukenick, *Houdini, Houdini*; Thylias Moss, *Hosiery Seams on a Bowlegged Woman*; Mark Jarman, *North Sea*.
☐No advances; pays 10% of actual cash received. Contact: Alberta T. Turner, Director. Send query letter and samples; if approved, ms. of 50 to 75 pages will be read between January 1 and March 1, if accompanied by a $5 reading fee. Clean photocopies and multiple submissions acceptable if director is notified. Decision in June.

Cooper Canyon Press, Box 271, Port Townsend, WA 98368. (206) 385–4925. Founded 1973. Both hardcover and paperback. Sample publications: Red Pine, *The Collected Songs of Cold Mountain*; Olga Broumas, *Pastoral Jazz*; Madeline De Frees, *Magpie on the Gallows*.
□Sometimes pays advances; pays royalties of 7% to 10% on a variable basis. No unsolicited manuscripts. Contact: Sam Hamill, Poetry Editor. Send query letter. No decision time given.

Copper Beech Press, Box 1852, Brown University, Providence, RI 02912. (401) 863–2393. Founded 1973. Publishes in paperback only. No specific requirements for poems' form or content. Sample publications: Keith Waldrop, *The Ruins of Providence*; Randy Blasing, *The Particles*.
□Pays 50 free copies. Contact: Randy Blasing, Edwin Honig, Poetry Editors. Send samples; if approved, ms. of 48 to 64 pages will be read. Decision in 3 to 4 weeks.

CSS Publications, Box 23, Iowa Falls, IA 50126. (515) 243–6407. Founded 1977. Primarily paperback. Publishes an annual anthology of poetry of all kinds and styles on an announced theme. Sample publications: *The Rhyme and Reason of Curt Sytsma*; *The Whisper of Dreams*; *Profiles Cut from the Wave*.
□Winners of the annual contest for publication in the anthology divide $100; each poet published receives a free copy of the book and additional copies at a reduced rate. Contact: Rebecca S. Bell, Editor and Co-Publisher. Submit unpublished poems, preferably short (up to 36 lines) by March 15, together with a reading fee of $2 per poem. Winning poets are notified in July; others, in September. Query for current information.

Curbstone Press, 321 Jackson Street, Willamantic, CT 06226. Founded 1975. Primarily paperback. Lyrical, political, and socially conscious poetry. Sample publications: James Scully, *Apollo Helmet*; Henrik Nordbrandt, *God's House*; Joan Joffe Hall, *The Rift Zone*.
□Pays 10% of press run in free copies. Contact: Alexander Taylor, Poetry Editor. Send samples; if approved, ms. of 40 to 60 pages sent with SASE will be read. No calls or in-person delivery of mss. Decision in 8 weeks.

Curbstone Publishing Company, Box 7445 U. T. Station, Austin, TX 78712. (512) 327–9706 (Work) or (512) 444–9463 (Home). Founded 1978. Both hardcover and paperback. Excellent poetry in any style. Sample publications: Geraldine Clinton Little, *Hakugai*; Freida Werden, *Philosophy Woman at Men's Rodeo*.
□No advances; pays royalties of 10% based on actual cash received. Offers Curbstone Award for the best manuscript, including poetry and fiction. Contact: Kathy Sheppard, R. D. Taylor, Poetry Editors. Send query letter and samples; if approved, ms. of 60 to 100 pages will be read. Decision in 8 weeks. (Not actively seeking poetry manuscripts through 1984.)

Dooryard Press, Box 221, Story, WY 82842. (307) 683-2937. Founded 1980. Both hardcover and paperback. Excellent poetry. Sample publications: Richard Hugo, *Sea Lanes Out*; Lee Bassett, *Gauguin and Food*; Ripley Schemm, *Mapping My Father*.
□No advances; pays in free books, 10% of run. Contact: Tom Rea, Editor. Send query letter and samples with SASE. Decision in 4 to 6 weeks.

East River Anthology, 75 Gates Avenue, Montclair, NJ 07042. Founded 1975. Publishes in paperback only. Special-issue anthologies on a theme. Sample publications: Jan Barry and W. D. Ehrhart, eds., *Demilitarized Zones*; Jan Barry, ed., *Peace Is Our Profession*.
□Pays in free copies only. Contact: Jan Barry, Poetry Editor. Send samples with SASE only after announcement of anthology in progress appears in *Coda* and other publications. Decision time varies.

The Ecco Press, 18 West 30th Street, New York, NY 10001. (212) 685-8240. Founded 1970. Both hardcover and paperback. Sample publications: Sandra McPherson, *Patron Happiness*; Jon Anderson, *The Milky Way*; Stanley Plumly, *Summer Celestial*.
□Pays advances; pays royalties of 10% on hardcover books, based on list price. Contact: Daniel Halpern, Poetry Editor. Send samples; if approved, ms. of 65 to 80 pages will be read. Decision in 6 weeks. Publication at least a year after acceptance.

Field Translation Series—See Chapter 4.

Front Street Publishers, 232 Elizabeth Street, New York, NY 10012. Founded 1978. Both hardcover and paperback. Poetry in open or closed forms, unsentimental. Accepts no sentimental or religious verse by well-meaning people with three or more names. Sample publications: Howard Winn, *Four Picture Sequence*; Margaret Ryan, *Filling in a Life*; Claudia Seaman, *Untitled*.
□No advances; pays in free copies only. Contact: Howard Winn, Editor. Send query letter; if approved, ms. of 48 to 94 pages will be read. Winners of yearly competition earn publication, a reading with a $350 honorarium, and 25 free copies of the book. Write for deadlines. Decision time not given.

The Future Press, Box 73, Canal Street, New York, NY 10013. Founded 1977. Publishes in hardcover, paperback, and other formats. Only the most innovative, experimental poetry—what nobody else would do. Sample publications: Ian Tarman, *First Principles*; Richard Kostelanetz, *Illuminations*; Bob Heman, *The Journey*.
□Pays in free copies. Contact: Richard Kostelanetz, Poetry Editor. Send query letter; if approved, send ms. Decision in 8 weeks.

Gay Sunshine Press, Box 40397, San Francisco, CA 94140. (415) 824-3184. Founded 1970. Publishes in paperback only. Poetry on gay themes

themes by poets whose work has appeared extensively in literary magazines. Sample publications: Jean Genet, *Treasures of the Night: Collected Poems*; Jim Everhard, *Cute and Other Poems*; Allen Ginsberg and Peter Orlovsky, *Straight Hearts' Delight: Selected Love Poems and Letters*.

☐No advances; pays royalties of 7% to 10% based on list price. Contact: Winston Leyland, Editor. Send query letter with SASE; if approved, ms. of 100 to 150 pages will be read. Decision in 8 weeks. Allow at least a year between acceptance and publication.

Graywolf Press, Box 142, Port Townsend, WA 98368. (206) 385-1160. Founded 1974. Both hardcover and paperback. Accomplished, striving, first-rate poetry with the special quality of voice that makes the work distinctive. Nearly all manuscripts are solicited. Sample publications: Linda Gregg, *Too Bright To See*; A. Poulin, Jr., trans., *Orchards: French Poetry of Rainer Maria Rilke*; William Stafford, *Smoke's Way: Poems from Limited Editions 1968-1981*.

☐Pays advances; pays royalties of 7½% to 12% on list price or actual cash received. Contact: Scott Walker, Editor. Send query letter and samples. Decision in 1 week.

Ha' Penny Book Contest—See *Telescope*, Chapter 4.

Harper & Row, Publishers, 10 East 53rd Street, New York, NY 10022. Founded 1817. Both hardcover and paperback. Expert poetry. Sample publications: Herbert Morris, *Peru*; Donald Revell, *From the Abandoned Cities*.

☐Pays advances only in certain cases; pays royalties based on list price of 10% to 5,000 copies sold; 12½% to 10,000 copies sold, and 15% thereafter. Contact: Frances Lindley, Senior Editor. Send no more than 10 sample poems. Decision in 6 to 8 weeks.

Holt, Rinehart and Winston, 521 Fifth Avenue, New York, NY 10175. Founded 1866. Both hardcover and paperback. Poetry from a fairly wide range of aesthetic camps, but no light verse. Sample publications: Louis Erdrich, *Jacklight*; John Yau, *Corpse and Mirror*; Arthur Vogelsang, *A Planet*.

☐Pays advances; pays royalties based on list price. Contact: Judy Karasik, Poetry Editor. Send query letter and 5 to 15 samples, double-spaced, with SASE; if approved, ms. of about 80 pages or more will be read. Do not phone. Decision time not given.

Houghton Mifflin New Poetry Series, 2 Park Street, Boston MA 02108. (617) 725-5907. Series founded 1975. Both hardcover and paperback. Significant and original poetry that merits major attention. Manuscripts chosen periodically on basis of open competition. Accepts poetry outside of the series only from solicited poets or poets already established with the house. Sample publications: Reginald Gibbons, *The Ruined Motel*; Maria Flook, *Reckless Wedding*; Tom Sleigh, *After One*.

☐Pays advances; pays royalties of 10% of list for hardcover books, 10% of net for paperback books. Contact: Laura Nash, New Poetry Series Coordinator. Send 5 samples by August 31; if approved, complete ms. will be read if submitted by September 30. Decision on sample in 2 weeks. Winning manuscripts submitted during the May 1–September 30 competition will be published in the fall of the following year.

Illuminati, 8812 Pico Boulevard, Suite 204, Los Angeles, CA 90035. (213) 271-1460. Founded 1978. Both hardcover and paperback. Contemporary English-language poetry. Sample publications: Greg Kuzma, *A Horse of a Different Color*; Lyn Lifshin, *Naked Charm*; Herbert Morris, *Afghanistan*.
☐Pays advances; pays royalties of 10% to 15% on list price. Contact: P. Schneidre. Send complete ms. with acknowledgments of places where poems were previously published. Decision in one week.

Ithaca House, 108 North Plain Street, Ithaca, NY 14850. (607) 272-1233. Founded 1970. Publishes in paperback only. High-quality work—no trend, style, or philosophy excluded. Sample publications: Carol Frost, *The Fearful Child*; Roy Marz, *The Island-Maker*; Deborah Tall, *Ninth Life*.
☐No payment. Contact: John Latta, Chris Henkel, Poetry Editors. Send samples; if approved, ms. of 50 to 70 pages will be read. Decision in 3 weeks on samples; in 2 months on manuscripts.

Alice James Books, Alice James Poetry Cooperative, Inc., 138 Mount Auburn Street, Cambridge, MA 12138. (617) 354-1408. Founded 1973. Both hardcover and paperback. High-quality poetry by writers living in New England, especially women. Sample publications: Celia Gilbert, *Bonfire*; Erica Funkhouser, *Natural Affinities*.
☐Alice James is a shared-work cooperative. Authors whose manuscripts are selected are required to join the cooperative and participate in decision-making, book production, and office tasks. Contact: Catherine Hawkes, Administrative Director. Send complete ms. of 60 to 70 pages, paginated, with a table of contents, during announced reading periods only. Decision in 8 weeks.

Alfred A. Knopf: The Knopf Poetry Series, 201 East 50th Street, New York, NY 10022. (212) 751-2600. Series founded 1980. Both hardcover and paperback. No specific requirements for poems' form or content. Sample publications: Amy Clampitt, *The Kingfisher*; Brad Leithauser, *Hundreds of Fireflies*; Katha Pollitt, *Antarctic Traveller*.
☐Pays advances; pays royalties of 10% on hardcover books, 7½% on paperback books, based on list price. Contact: Alice Quinn, Poetry Editor. Send samples; if approved, ms. of 40 to 100 pages will be read. Submit about 10 months before expected publication. Decision in 12 weeks.

L'Epervier Press, 762 Hayes #15, Seattle, WA 98109. Founded 1977. Both hardcover and paperback. Sample publications: Jack Myers, *I'm Amazed*

That You're Still Singing; Lorrie Goldensohn, *The Tether*; Robert Herz, *Stream*.

☐No payment. Contact: Bob McNamara, Poetry Editor. Send query letter and samples; if approved, ms. of about 56 pages will be read. Decision in 28 weeks.

Light Year, Bits Press—See Chapter 4.

Lotus Press, Inc., Box 21607, Detroit, MI 48221. (313) 861–1280. Founded 1972. Publishes mostly in paperback. Poetry of literary merit, especially by Black Americans. Sample publications: Gayl Jones, *The Hermit-Woman*; Dudley Randall, *A Litany of Friends*; James A. Emanuel, *The Broken Bowl*.

☐Pays in free copies. Contact: Naomi Andrews, Poetry Editor. Send samples; if approved, ms. of 64 to 80 pages will be read. Decision in 6 weeks.

Louisiana University Press, Baton Rouge, LA 70803. Year of founding not given. Both hardcover and paperback. Good poetry. Sample publications: Lisel Mueller, *The Need To Hold Still*; Betty Adcock, *Nettles*; James Applewhite, *Foreseeing the Journey*.

☐No advances; royalties range from zero to 10% of net sales. Contact: Beverly Jarrett, Executive Editor. Send query letter; if approved, ms. of about 50 pages will be read. Simultaneous submissions are encouraged, provided that the editor is kept informed of review elsewhere. Decision within a year.

Lynx House Press, Box 800, Amherst, MA 01004. (413) 665–3604. Founded 1975. Both hardcover and paperback. Publishes first books of poetry by writers with substantial journal publication. Emphasis on quality, not genre. Sample publications: Jenne Andrews, *Reunion*; Patricia Goedicke, *The Dog That Was Barking Yesterday*; Walt Curtis, *Poems for Alice Bluelight*; William Ryan, *Eating the Heart of the Enemy*.

☐Pays in free copies: 10% of press run. Contact: Chris Howell, Poetry Editor. Send complete ms. of 48 to 64 pages. Decision in 8 weeks. Publication a year or two after acceptance.

McPherson & Co., Box 638, New Paltz, NY 12561. Founded 1974. Both hardcover and paperback. Interested only in highly unconventional poetry; publishes poetry rarely. Sample publications: Robert Kelly, *The Book of Persephone*; Novalis, *Hymns to the Night*, trans. Dick Higgins.

☐Sometimes pays advances; pays royalties of 10% to 12% based on list price. Contact: Bruce R. McPherson, Publisher. Send query letter and samples with SASE. Decision in 2 to 12 weeks.

Modern Poetry in Translation, Comparative Literature, University of Iowa, Iowa City, IA 52242. Founded 1965. Publishes in paperback only. Translations of poetry, mostly modern. Sample publication: *Modern Poetry in Translation: 1983*.

☐No payment. Contact: Daniel Weissbort, Editor. Send complete ms. of 10 poems with a copy of the original. Accepted manuscripts are published in an annual volume of poetry in translation and articles about translation. Decision in 12 weeks.

Momentum Press, 512 Hill Street #4, Santa Monica, CA 90405. Founded 1974. Publishes in paperback only. Primarily poetry from the Southern California area. Sample publications: Dick Barnes, *A Lake on the Earth*; Alicia Ostriker, *The Mother/Child Papers*.
☐Contact: Bill Mohr, Poetry Editor. (As of September 1983, not reviewing poetry manuscripts.)

The National Poetry Series—See Chapter 8.

The New Poets Series, Inc., 541 Piccadilly Road, Baltimore, MD 21204. (301) 321–2863. Founded 1970. Publishes in paperback only. Poetic excellence is the only hard-and-fast requirement. Preference to Maryland poets. Sample publications: Donald Richardson, *Knocking Them Dead*; Lynne Dowell, *The Vinegar Year*; Jan M. Sherrill, *Blind Leading the Blind*; Hugh Burgess, *Dwell With These Distances*.
☐No payment. Poets must not have published a previous collection, and must obtain reprint permissions from magazines where individual poems appeared. Contact: Clarinda Harriss Lott, Editor/Director. Send samples; if approved, ms. no longer than 50 pages will be read. Decision in 6 weeks. Occasional contests.

New Rivers Press, Inc., 1602 Selby Avenue, St. Paul, MN 55104. (612) 645–6324. Founded 1968. Publishes in paperback only. Poetry of exceptional quality, including many first books and translations. Eclectic in choices; beholden to no particular school. Sample publications: Pete Green, *Deposition*; Sharon Chmielarz, *Different Arrangements*; Yvette Nelson, *We'll Come When It Rains*.
☐No advances; pays 100 free copies for the first printing, royalties of 15% of list price for second and subsequent printings. Contact: C. W. Truesdale, Editor/Publisher. Send samples or complete ms. of 40 to 60 pages. The Minnesota Voices Project, an annual competition, pays $500, plus 15% royalties on second and subsequent printings. The competition is open to writers from Minnesota, Wisconsin, Iowa, and North and South Dakota. Submit by March 1. Decision by mid-July and publication by November 1.

W. W. Norton & Company, Inc., 500 Fifth Avenue, New York, NY 10110. Founded 1925. Both hardcover and paperback. Quality literary poetry; no light or inspirational verse. Considers only poets whose work has been published in quality literary magazines. Sample publications: Ellen Bryant Voigt, *The Forces of Plenty*; Norman Dubie, *Selected and New Poems*.
☐No advances; pays royalties of 10% based on publisher's invoice list price.

Contact: Kathy Anderson, Poetry Editor. Send query letter with 15-poem sample, list of places where the sample poems have been published, list of grants or awards received, and list of poetry readings given, with the dates and locations. If samples approved, ms. will be read between January 1 and February 15 or June 1 and July 15. Decision in 16 weeks. Simultaneous submissions acceptable if editor is notified.

Pacific Poetry Series—See Chapter 8.

Panjandrum Books, 11321 Iowa Avenue, Suite 1, Los Angeles, CA 90025. (213) 477-8771. Founded 1971. Publishes in paperback only. Surrealist and experimental poetry. Sample publications: Bernard Bador, *Sea Urchin Hari-Kiri*; Lennart Bruce, *The Broker*; *Four Texts by Antonin Artaud*, trans. Clayton Eshleman and Norman Chase.
□Pays royalties of 8% to 10% based on list price. Contact: Dennis Koran, Editor. Send samples with a brief biographical sketch; if approved, a ms. no longer than 80 pages will be read. Decision in 6 weeks.

Paycock Press, Box 3567, Washington, DC 20007. (202) 333-1544. Founded 1976. Poetry that makes adventurous and/or imaginative use of language; that effects an intelligent and imaginative marriage of style and subject. Sample publications: Tina Fulker, *Jukebox*; Harrison Fisher, *Blank Like Me*; George Myers, Jr., *Natural History*.
□Pays 10% of the press run in free copies with promise of a 50-50 split on all earnings after the press breaks even. Contact: Richard Myers Peabody, Jr., Publisher/Editor-in-Chief. Send query letter; if approved, send ms. of 50 to 125 pages. Decision in 4 weeks.

The Penumbra Press, Route 1, Box 12, Lisbon, IA 52293. (319) 455-2182. Founded 1972. Publishes in both hardcover and paperback in "fine press" editions of 200 to 250 copies, all handprinted and handbound, usually with original prints as illustrations. Prices range from $25 to $75 per book. Contemporary American poetry and translations. Especially interested in suites of poems or related sequences. Sample publications: David St. John, *The Man in the Yellow Gloves*; Brenda Hillman, *Coffee, 3 A. M.*; Debora Greger, *Cartography*.
□No advances; pays royalties of 10% in books, cash, or a combination, based on list price. Contact: Bonnie and George O'Connell, Editors. Send samples; if approved, ms. no longer than 50 pages will be read. Decision in 6 to 8 weeks. Occasional competitions.

Perivale Press, 13830 Erwin Street, Van Nuys, CA 91401. (213) 785-4671. Founded 1968. Publishes in paperback only. Poetry modern in tone and viewpoint. Sample publications: R. L. Barth, *Forced-Marching to the Styx*; Lawrence P. Spingarn, *The Dark Playground*.
□No advances; pays royalties of 10% based on list price. Contact: Lawrence

P. Spingarn, Publisher. Send query letter and 1 or 2 samples with SASE; if approved, ms. of about 48 pages will be read. Decision in 4 weeks.

☐For Perivale Press Chapbook Series award contest, send a $5 reading fee with a 20-page manuscript. But query first with SASE.

Petronium Press, 1255 Nuuanu Avenue, 1813, Honolulu, HI 96817. Founded 1975. Both hardcover and paperback. High-quality contemporary poetry; no light verse. Prefers writers from Hawaii. Sample publications: Michael McPherson, *Singing with the Owls*; Marjorie Edel, *The Place Your Body Is*; *Talk Story: An Anthology of Hawaii's Local Writers*; special editions of Merwin, Stafford, Logan, and others.

☐No advances; pays royalties of 10% based on actual cash received, or an amount negotiated with the author. Accepts few unsolicited manuscripts. Contact: Frank Stewart, Poetry Editor. Send query letter. Decision in 4 weeks.

Poet Papers, Box 528, Topanga, CA 90290. Founded 1970. Publishes in paperback only. Poetry of all kinds, preferably short, with photographs and graphics as well. Sample publications: G. Laimons Juris, *American Refugee Poet*, and *New Years: Return of the Life Force*.

☐Pays 10 free copies of first printing; 25% of all sales if there is a second printing. No submissions from September to February. Contact: Poetry Editor. Send query letter; if approved, ms. of at least 30 pages will be read for a fee of $2.50. Decision within the year.

☐Forest Library Chapbook Series pays 10 free copies of a published manuscript of any length. Decision in 2 years.

Princeton University Press: Princeton Series of Contemporary Poets; Lockert Library of Poetry in Translation, 41 William Street, Princeton NJ 08540. (609) 452-5775, 4884, 4883. Founded 1975. Both hardcover and paperback. Serious, contemporary poetry; not religious. Translations in bilingual editions; translations that stand up as poetry in English. Sample publications in PSCP: Robert Pinsky, *Sadness and Happiness*; Grace Schulman, *Burn Down the Icons*; Susan Stewart, *Yellow Stars and Ice*. Sample Lockert translations: C. P. Cavafy, *Collected Poems*, trans. by Edmund Keeley and Philip Sherrard and ed. by George Savidis; Osip Mandelstam, *Stone*, trans. by Robert Tracy.

☐No advances; probably no royalties on first run of cloth editions; royalties of 5% on paperback books (simultaneous editions) based on list price. Contact: Marjorie Sherwood for original poetry; Robert E. Brown for translations. For the poetry series, send a complete ms. of at least 64 pages. double-spaced, with your name on the title page only, by the deadlines at the end of June and December. For translations, send complete ms. with the originals and an introduction, by the deadlines at the end of February and August. Decision in 8 to 10 weeks after the deadlines.

Quarterly Review of Literature Contemporary Poetry Series, 26 Haslet Avenue, Princeton, NJ 08540. (609) 452-4703. Founded 1943. Both hardcover and paperback. High-quality poetry. Poets published: Jo Chong-lu, Jane Flanders, Christopher Bursk, Wistawa Szymborska.
☐Pays Betty Colladay Award of $1,000 for each ms. chosen. Contact: T. or R. Weiss, Editors. Send ms. of 50 to 80 pages during October or May. Manuscript can be a group of connected poems, a selection of miscellaneous poems, a poetic play, a translation of poetry, or a long poem of more than 30 pages. Send only one ms. during the reading period. Writers are requested to subscribe to the series (at $15 for 2 volumes) when they submit their work. Decision in 6 to 8 weeks.

Random House/Vintage, 201 East 50th Street, New York, NY 10022. (212) 572-2120. Founded 1925. Both hardcover and paperback. Poetry by major contemporary American and foreign poets. Sample publications: Frank Bidart, *The Sacrifice*; C. K. Williams, *Tar*; Bill Knott, *Becos*.
☐Pays advances; pays royalties of 10% for hardcover books, 7½% for paperback books, based on list price. Contact: Wendy Garrett, Editorial Offices. Send samples; if approved, ms. under 100 pages will be read. Decision in 8 weeks.

Saturday Press, Inc., Box 884, Upper Montclair, NJ 07043. Founded 1975. Publishes in paperback only. Mostly but not exclusively women's poetry. Sample publications: Charlotte Mandel, Maxine Silverman, and Rachel Hadas, eds., *Saturday's Women*; Colette Inez, *Eight Minutes from the Sun*; Ghita Orth, *The Music of What Happens*.
☐Pays in free copies or a small grant. Offers Eileen W. Barnes Award for a first book of poetry by a woman over 40. Contact: Charlotte Mandel, Editor. Send query letter with SASE. No decision time given.

Shameless Hussy Press, Box 3092, Berkeley, CA 94703. (415) 548-7800. Founded 1969. Publishes in paperback only. Open to any good work; has published "minority" poetry, women's poetry, and children's books by children. Sample publications: Barbara Noda, *Strawberries*; Mitsuye Yamada, *Camp Notes*; Alta, *Song of the Wife/Song of the Mistress*.
☐No advances; pays 100 free copies of book. Contact: Alta. Send complete ms. of 60 to 200 pages with SASE. Decision in 15 weeks.

The Smith, 5 Beekman Street, New York, NY 10038. Founded 1964. Both hardcover and paperback. Particularly interested in story-poems, sonnets, and lyrics; open to poets published in *Pulpsmith Magazine*. Sample publications: Ken McKlaren, *Yes with Variations*; Jared Smith, *Song of the Blood*; Celia Watson Strome, *The Drum and the Melody*.
☐Pays advances; pays royalties of about $500. Contact: Joe Lazarus, Poetry Editor. Send sample of 5 poems. Decision in 3 to 6 weeks.

Station Hill Press, Station Hill Road, Barrytown, NY 12507. (914) 758–5840. Founded 1978. Both hardcover and paperback. Technically and conceptually innovative poetry. Sample publications: Armand Schwerner, *Sounds of the River Naranjana*; Charles Simic, *Weather Forecast*; Charles Stein, *Parts and Other Parts*.
☐No advances; pays 10% royalties in books. Contact: George Quasha, Michael Coffey, Editors. Send samples; if approved, send ms. of about 60 pages, typed double-spaced on 8½" by 11" sheets. Write for deadlines. Decision in 8 weeks.

The Struggling Writer, Box 16315, Greenville, SC 29606. Founded 1981. Publishes in paperback only. Poetry of all kinds. Poets published: Craig Neuman and Michelle Spivey.
☐No advances; pays royalties of 10% and free copies. Contact: J. F. Lowe, Editor. Send complete book-length ms. of at least 40 poems. No simultaneous submissions. Provides critique of poems at the rate of $10 per lot of 10. Decision in 8 weeks.

Sun & Moon Press, Contemporary Literature Series, 4330 Hartwick Road, College Park, MD 20740. (301) 864–6921. Founded 1976. Both hardcover and paperback. Contemporary poetry with an emphasis on "language" and experimental work. Sample publications: Clark Coolidge, *Solution Passage*; Charles Bernstein, *Shade*; James Wine, *Longwalks*.
☐Pays 10% of sales and 10 copies. Contact: Douglas Messerli, Editor. Send complete ms. of at least 70 pages. Decision in 9 weeks.

The Toothpaste Press, Box 546, West Branch, IA 52358. (319) 643–2604. Founded 1970. Both hardcover and paperback. No particular kind of poetry sought. Sample publications: Anselm Hollo, *No Complaints*; Ron Padgett, *How To Be a Woodpecker*; Barbara Moraff, *The Telephone Company Repairman Poems*.
☐Pays advances; pays royalties of 10% based on list price. Contact: Allan Kornblum, Editor. Send samples; if approved, ms. of about 48 pages will be read. Decision in 2 weeks. (As of August 1983, not accepting unsolicited manuscripts until publishing backlog ends.)

University of Alabama Press, Box 2877, University, AL 35486. (205) 348–5065. Founded 1945. Both hardcover and paperback. No specific requirements on poems' form or content. Sample publications: Alberta Turner, *A Belfry of Knees*; Marieve Rugo, *Fields of Vision*; Brian Swann, *The Middle of the Journey*; Mary Ruefle, *Memling's Veil*.
☐No advances; pays royalties of 10% of receipts after sale of a stipulated quantity. Contact: Thomas Rabbitt, Poetry Editor. Send complete ms. of 48 to 75 single-spaced pages, with table of contents, acknowledgments, and SASE, between September 1 and November 30 annually. Poems submitted must not have been published previously, except individually or in a limited

edition of 500 or fewer copies. Simultaneous submissions acceptable if editor is notified. Decision before January 30.

University of Arkansas Press, Fayetteville, AR 72701. (501) 575–3246. Founded 1980. Both hardcover and paperback. Interested in poetry that is not coy about its first, literal meaning and dramatic situation and still calls the reader into a deeper confrontation with its full import. Open to all approaches, but longs to see first-rate, hard-edged poetry by poets who can handle rhyme and the measures. Sample publications: John Ciardi, *Selected Poems*; George Garrett, *Collected Poems*; Debra Bruce, *Pure Daughter*; Ronald Koertge, *Life on the Edge of the Continent*.
☐No advances; pays royalties of 10% based on actual cash received. Contact: Miller Williams, Director. Send query letter and samples; if approved, ms. of about 53 poems or pages will be read. The manuscript should be clean, double-spaced, unbound on non-ring-holed white bond. The ms. should be typed in pica or elite only, and should contain no handwritten corrections. A photocopy is acceptable for screening purposes, but must be replaced by ribbon copy if the ms. is accepted. Decision in 8 weeks.

University of Georgia Press, Athens, GA 30602. (404) 542–2830. Founded 1938. Both hardcover and paperback. Mature, excellent poetry. Sample publications: Dannie Abse, *One-Legged on Ice*; Brendan Galvin, *Winter Oysters*; John Engels, *Weather Fear: New and Selected Poems*.
☐No advances; pays standard royalties on actual cash received. Manuscripts are received in the months of January and September. Contact: Paul Zimmer, Director. Poets with at least one full-length publication with this or any other press should submit ms. of 48 to 75 pages by the end of January each year. First-book poets who have no book-length publications except chapbooks should submit ms. of the same length by the end of September each year. With all submissions include a $5 handling fee. Decision in 15 weeks.

University of Massachusetts Press, Juniper Prize. For manuscripts: University of Massachusetts Press, c/o Mail Room, University of Massachusetts, Amherst, MA 01003. For inquiries and correspondence: Juniper Prize, University of Massachusetts Press, Box 429, Amherst, MA 01004. (413) 545–2217. Founded 1964. Both hardcover and paperback. No translations, books by more than one author, or poems previously published in books. Sample publications: Marc Hudson, *Afterlight*; Jane Flanders, *The Students of Snow*; David Brendan Hopes, *The Glacier's Daughters*.
☐Offers publication and a cash prize for an original ms. that does not have to be a poet's first work. Prize award of $1,000 (or $500 in the event of a tie) in lieu of royalties on the first print run. Pays royalties based on list price in subsequent printings. Contact: Juniper Prize. Send complete ms. of about 60 pages (50 to 60 poems) with SASE and $7 entry fee by October 1. Decision in April or May; publication in following fall or winter.

University of Missouri Press—See Breakthrough Series and Devins Award for Poetry, Chapter 8.

University of Utah Press, 101 USB, Salt Lake City, UT 84112. (801) 581–3338. Founded 1949. Publishes in paperback only. Original poetry. Sample publications: Carole Oles, *Quarry*; R. H. W. Dillard, *The Greeting: New and Selected Poems*; Brewster Ghiselin, *Windrose*.
☐No advances; pays royalties of 10% based on actual cash received. Contact: Acquisitions Editor, Poetry. Send query letter; if approved, ms. of at least 60 pages with SASE will be read during the month of March. Decision by following September. Multiple submissions acceptable if editor is notified.

Utah State University Press, Utah State University, UMC 95, Logan, Utah 84322. (801) 750–1362. Founded 1969. Both hardcover and paperback. Prefers poetry from western and southwestern writers. Sample publications: Kenneth Brewer, *To Remember What Is Lost*; Keith Wilson, *Stone Roses*.
☐No advances; pays 10% of cash receipts after first 500 copies have sold. Contact: Linda E. Speth, Press Director. Send query letter and samples; manuscripts should be submitted only during the month of August. Simultaneous submissions discouraged.

Viking Penguin, Inc., The Viking Press and Penguin Books, 40 West 23rd Street, New York, NY 10010. (212) 807–7300. Founded 1923. Both hardcover and paperback. No particular kinds of poetry sought; no sample publications given.
☐Pays advances; pays standard royalties based on list price. Contact: Poetry Editor. Send samples with SASE. Decision in 6 to 8 weeks.

Wake-Brook House, 990 Northwest 53rd Street, Fort Lauderdale, FL 33309. (305) 776–5884. Founded 1946. Publishes in hardcover only. Good poetry; no stream of consciousness, far-out verse, or explicit sex. Sample publications: Kendall E. Lappin, trans., *Baudelaire Revisited*; Sophia Lisa Benjamin, *Mosaic Trilogy*; Janemarie Luecke, *The Rape of the Sabine Women*.
☐No advances; pays royalties of 10% on the first 1,000 copies, 15% thereafter, based on list price. Contact: Edwin P. Geauque, Director. Send samples and summary of your background. Especially interested in teachers, lecturers, and others who are active in public life and can make public appearances to promote their books. Decision in 4 weeks.

Wampeter Press, Box 512, Green Harbor, MA 02041. (617) 834–4137. Founded 1978. Publishes primarily in paperback. Serious contemporary poetry; no light verse, "experimental" writing of any kind, or work that might be labeled "confessional." Sample publications: Judith Steinbergh, *Lillian Bloom: A Separation*; Don Johnson, *Reeling in the Dark*; Martha McFerren, *Get Me Out of Here*.

☐No advances; pays royalties of 8% to 10% based on actual cash received. Contact: George E. Murphy, Jr., Director. Send samples; if approved, ms. of 64 to 72 pages will be read. Decision in 8 weeks.

John Weatherhill, Inc., 6 East 39th Street, New York, NY 10016. (212) 686–2857. Founded 1964. Both hardcover and paperback. Translations of Asian poetry, usually with commentary. No original poetry. Sample publications: Benjamin Hoff, *The Way of Life: At the Heart of the Tao Te Ching*; John Stevens, trans., *Mountain Tasting: Zen Haiku by Santoka Taneda*; Hiroaki Sato, *One Hundred Frogs: From Renga to Haiku in English*.
☐Pays advances; usually pays royalties of 10% based on list price. Contact: Ms. Miriam Yamaguchi, John Weatherhill, Inc., 7-6-13 Roppongi, Minato-ku, Tokyo 106 Japan. Send query letter first; if approved, follow with sample translations. Decision in 6 to 8 weeks. Allow 12 months from receipt of all materials to U. S. publication date.

Wingbow Press, 2940 Seventh Street, Berkeley, CA 94710. (415) 549–3030. Founded 1972. Publishes primarily in paperback. Good, strong poems, but not inspirational. Traditional or modern. Sample publications: Leslie Simon, *High Desire*; Edward Dorn, *Hello La Jolla*; John Brandi, *That Back Road In*.
☐Pays advances; pays royalties of 7% to 8½% based on list price. Contact: Randy Fingland or Bill Merryman, Editors. Send query letter and samples; if approved, a ms. of about 120 pages will be read. Decision in 4 to 6 weeks.

The Yale Series of Younger Poets—See Chapter 8.

Zephyr Press, 13 Robinson Street, Somerville, MA 02145. (617) 628–9726. Founded 1981. Both hardcover and paperback. All types of poetry except haiku and light verse. No racist, sexist, or right-wing content. Sample publications: Sue Standing, *Amphibious Weather*; Miriam Sagan, title to be announced.
☐No advances; pays royalties of 10% of first edition's press run, in free books; pays 20% of second edition's net sales, in cash. Contact: Miriam Sagan, Poetry Editor. Send complete ms. of 30 to 40 poems for chapbook, 40 to 80 poems for full book size. Include SASE and $12 reading fee; send photocopy with letter-size SASE if you don't want the ms. returned. Multiple submissions acceptable if editor is notified. Decision in 8 weeks.

A SELECTIVE INDEX TO BOOK PUBLISHERS

What follows is not a comprehensive index, but a convenient cross-reference to entries classifiable into important categories.

Publishers of Poetry with a Specialized Content

Black American
Lotus Press, Inc.

Homosexual
Gay Sunshine Press

Experimental
Sun & Moon Press
Feminist
American Studies Press, Inc.
Alice James Books
Saturday Press, Inc.
Shameless Hussy Press

Humorous
Light Year, Bits Press
Political
Curbstone Press
Surrealist
Panjandrum Books

Publishers of Translations

Field Translation Series
Modern Poetry in Translation
Penumbra Press

Princeton University Press
John Weatherhill, Inc.

Publishers with Regional Preferences or Requirements

Arkansas
August House
California (Southern)
Momentum Press
Hawaii
Petronium Press

Maryland
The New Poets Series
New England
Alice James Books

Publishers Offering Prizes and Awards

Andrew Mountain Press
Carpenter Press
CSS Publications
Curbstone Publishing Company
Front Street Publishers
Houghton Mifflin New Poetry Series

New Rivers Press, Inc.
Quarterly Review of Literature
  Contemporary Poetry Series
Saturday Press, Inc.
University of Massachusetts Press
The Word Works

SUPPLEMENTARY LISTINGS

The following list includes book publishers who either made no reponse to *The Poet's Marketplace* questionnaire, or whose response implied that they were less likely to read new manuscripts than the publishers described in the entries above.

Although not a complete record of all poetry publishers, the list offers more than 120 additional markets, arranged alphabetically by state, with Canadian addresses at the end. (Naturally, these entries include some chapbook publishers, too.) In approaching these publishers, you should first send a query letter and SASE for their needs, policies, and guidelines.

Omissions from this list fall into three categories: publishers who expressly asked not to be listed, publishers who do not read unsolicited manuscripts, and those listed in *Literary Market Place* as poetry publishers who do not, in fact, publish poetry.

California

Michael Davidson, Editor, **Archive for New Poetry,** University of California, San Diego, C–075, La Jolla 92093

John Martin, President, **Black Sparrow Press,** Box 3993, Santa Barbara 93105

Melissa Mytinger, Editor, **Christopher's Books,** 390 62nd Street, Oakland 94618

Lawrence Ferlinghetti, Editor, **City Lights Books, Inc.,** 261 Columbus Avenue, San Francisco 94133

Geoffrey Young, Editor, **The Figures,** 2016 Cedar, Berkeley 94709

William Greenwood, Editor, **Green Horse Press,** 471 Carr Avenue, Aromas 95004

Harold Darling, Editor, **The Green Tiger Press,** 7458 La Jolla Boulevard, La Jolla 92037

Paul O. Proehl, Editor, **Guide of Tutors Press of International College,** 1019 Gayley Avenue, Suite 105, Los Angeles 90024

Ted Yukawa, President, **Heian International, Inc.,** Box 2402, South San Francisco 94080

Arlene Steibel, Editor, **Henry E. Huntington Library and Art Gallery,** 1151 Oxford Road, San Marino 91108

Robert Miles, Editor, **Miles & Weir Ltd.,** Box 1906, San Pedro 90733

F. Rice, Editor, **Moving Parts Press,** 419-A Maple Street, Santa Cruz 95060

Erasmus Newborn, Editor, **Mudborn Press,** 209 West De la Guerra, Santa Barbara 93101

George Erikson, Managing Editor, **Ross-Erikson Publishers,** 629 State Street, Santa Barbara 93109

Colorado

A. Blackburn, Editor, **Writers Forum,** University of Colorado, Colorado Springs 80907

Connecticut

Editor, **Black Swan Books Ltd.,** Box 327, Redding Ridge 06876

Jeanette Hopkins, Director, **Wesleyan University Press,** 110 Mount Vernon Street, Middletown 06457

District of Columbia

Frank Di Federico, Editor-in-Chief, **Decatur House Press Ltd.,** 2122 Decatur Place N. W., Washington 20008

G. Jacobik *et al.*, Editors, **Washington Writers Publishing House,** Box 50068, Washington 20004

Florida

Donald R. Harkness, President, **American Studies Press, Inc.,** 13511 Palmwood Lane, Tampa 33624

Illinois

Kenneth Northrop, President, **Garrard Publishing Company,** 1607 North Market Street, Champaign 61820

Luci Shaw, Editor, **Harold Shaw Publishers,** Box 567, 388 Gundersen Drive, Wheaton 60187

Morton Weisman, Editor, **The Swallow Press, Inc.,** 811 West Junior Terrace, Chicago 60613

Indiana

R. Max Rees, Chairman, **Friends United Press,** 101 Quaker Hill Drive, Richmond 47374

Kentucky

Jonathan Greene, President, **Gnomon Press,** Box 106, Frankfort 40602

Jonathan Williams, Editor, **The Jargon Society,** Box 106, Frankfort 40602

Maine

Richard Millett, Editor-in-Chief, **The Merriam-Eddy Company, Inc.,** Box 25, South Waterford 04081

Maryland

P. Mc Caffrey, Editor, **The Charles Street Press,** Box 4692, Baltimore 21212

Poetry Editor, **Dryad Press,** 15 Sherman Avenue, Takoma Park 20912

A. Richter, Editorial Director, **Johns Hopkins University Press,** Baltimore 21218

Massachusetts

Gary Metras, Editor, **Adastra Press,** 101 Strong Street, Easthampton 01027

Philip W. Zuckerman, President, **Apple-wood Books,** Box 2870, Cambridge 02139

Dan Valenti, Editor, **Cellarway Press,** 824 East Street, Pittsfield 01201

Leslie Zheutlin, Editor, **Charles River Books, Inc.,** One Thompson Square, Charlestown 02129

Carl Kay & John Kristensen, Editors, **Firefly Press,** 607 Franklin Street, Cambridge 02139

Mark Saxton, Director, **Gambit,** 27 North Main Street, Meeting House Green, Ipswich 01938

William B. Goodman, Editoral Director, **David R. Godine Publisher, Inc.,** 306 Dartmouth Street, Boston 02116

Winthrop Hodges, Executive Editor, **Little, Brown & Company,** 34 Beacon Street, Boston 02106

W. Ferguson & N. King, Editors, **Metacom Press,** 31 Beaver Street, Worcester 01603

D. Wellman, Editor, **O. Ars Press,** Box 179, Cambridge 02101

Michael Mc Curdy, Editor, **Penmaen Press Ltd.,** RD 2, Box 145, Great Barrington 01230

J. Randall, Editor, **Pym-Randall Press,** 73 Cohasset Street, Roslindale 02131

Michigan

Ellendea Proffer, President, **Ardis Publishers,** 2901 Heatherway, Ann Arbor 48104

Leonard Kniffel, Editor, **Fallen Angel,** 1981 West Mc Nichols C-1, Highland Park 48203

Minnesota

Paul Feroe, Editor, **Ally Press,** Box 30340, St. Paul 55175

Mississippi

Barney McKee, Director, **University Press of Mississippi,** 3825 Ridgewood Road, Jackson 39211

Missouri

Anthony Summers & James Finnegan, Editors, **Cornerstone Press,** Box 28048, St. Louis 63119

Warren H. Green, Editor, **Fireside Books,** 8356 Olive Boulevard, St. Louis 63132

Nebraska

Editor, **Black Oak Press,** Box 4663, University Place Station, Lincoln 68504

Nevada

William Fox, Editor, **West Coast Poetry Review Press,** 1335 Dartmouth Drive, Reno 89509

New Hampshire

William L. Bauhan, Publisher, Dublin 03444

Marion Boyars, President, **Marion Boyars Publishers, Inc.,** 99 Main Street, Salem 03079

Gene A. Clark, Editor, **The Golden Quill Press,** Francestown 03043

Frances T. Rutter, President, **Tompson & Rutter, Inc.,** Box 297, Grantham 03753

New Jersey

J. Barry & W. D. Ehrhart, Editors, **East River Anthology,** 75 Gates Avenue, Montclair, 07042

W. Eshelman, Editor, **Scarecrow Press,** Box 656, Metuchen 08840

New Mexico

James Clois, President, **The Sunstone Press,** Box 2321, Santa Fe 87501

New York

Jack Antreassian, Editor, **Ashod Press,** Box 1147, Madison Square Station, New York 10159

Carl Brown, President, **AUM Publications,** Box 32433, Jamaica 11431

Editor, **Backstreet Editions, Inc.,** Box 555, Port Jefferson 11777

Stephen Zarlenga, President, **Books in Focus,** 160 East 38th Street, New York 10016

Richard W. Seaver, V. P. and Publisher, General Books, **CBS Educational and Professional Publishing,** 383 Madison Avenue, New York 10017

Elaine & John Gill, Editors, **The Crossing Press,** 17 West Main Street, Box 640, Trumansburg 14886

Theodore W. Macri & Philip Pochoda, Editorial Group Directors, **Doubleday & Company, Inc.,** 245 Park Avenue, New York 10167

David & Phillis Gershator, Editors, **Downtown Poets Co-op,** Box 1720, Brooklyn 11202

Robert Giroux, Chairman, Editorial Board, **Farrar, Straus & Giroux, Inc.,** 19 Union Square West, New York 10003

Joe David Bellamy, Editor, **Fiction International,** St. Lawrence University, Canton 13617

Christine Valentine, Editorial Director, **The Franklin Library,** 800 Third Avenue, New York 10022

Ron Padgett *et al.*, Editors, **Full Court Press, Inc.,** 138–140 Watts Street, New York, 10013

C. Bennett, Editor, **Gull Books,** 657 East 26th Street, #4–S, Brooklyn 11210

Robert Hershorn *et al.*, Co-Editors, **Hanging Loose Press,** 231 Wyckoff Street, Brooklyn 11217

Jeff Wright, Editor, **Hard Press,** 340 East 11th Street, New York 10003

Harry Barba, Editor, **Harian Creative Press-Books,** 47 Hyde Boulevard, Ballston Spa 12020

Robin Prising & William Leo Cookley, Editors, **Helikon Press,** 120 West 71st Street, New York 10023

Arthur W. Wang, Editor, **Hill and Wang,** 19 Union Square West, New York 10003

Lita Hornick, Editor, **Kulchur Foundation,** 888 Park Avenue, New York 10021

Pedro Yanes, President, **Las Americas Publishing Company, Inc.,** 37–A Union Square West, New York 10003

Bonnie E. Nelson, Editor, **Lintel,** Box 34, St. George 10301

D. Anthony English, Humanities Editor-in-Chief, **Macmillan Publishing Company, Inc.,** 866 Third Avenue, New York 10022

James Laughlin, President, **New Directions Publishing Corporation,** 80 Eighth Avenue, New York 10011

Sarah Brown Weitzman, Publisher, **New York Contemporary Press,** Box 670, New York 10021

Herbert J. Addison, Executive Editor, **Oxford University Press,** 200 Madison Avenue, New York 10016

Judith Shepard, Editor, **The Permanent Press,** RD 2, Noyac Road, Sagaponack 11963

Daniel Weissbort, Poetry Editor, **Persea Books, Inc.,** 225 Lafayette Street, New York 10012

Nick Beilenson, Editor, **Peter Pauper Press,** 135 West 50th Street, New York 10020

Joanna & Warren Gunderson, Editors, **Red Dust, Inc.,** Box 630, Gracie Station, New York 10028

S. Miller & K. Botnick, Editors, **Red Ozier Press,** Box 101, Old Chelsea Station, New York 10113

Stanley Moss, Editor, **The Sheep Meadow Press/Flying Point Books,** %
Persea Books, 225 Lafayette Street, New York 10012

J. Kitchen *et al.*, Editors, **State Street Press,** Box 252, Pittsford 14534

Paul Zweig, Editor, **State University of New York Press,** State University
Plaza, Albany, 12246

Wieland Schulz-Keil & Ann Hemingway, Editors, **Urizen Books, Inc.,** 66 West
Broadway, New York 10007

North Carolina

Editor, **Carolina Wren Press,** 300 Barclay Road, Chapel Hill 27514

Teo Savory, Editor, **Unicorn Press, Inc.,** Box 3307, Greensboro 27402

Editor, **Wake Forest University Press,** Winston-Salem 27109

Ohio

Editor, **Ashland Poetry Press,** Ashland College, Ashland 44805

Virgil Smith, Editor, **Catcher Press,** 215 West Elm, Kent 44240

Editor, **Raincrow Press**, 153 Maple Street, Rossford, 43460

Oregon

James Andersen, Executive Editor, **Breitenbush Publications,** Box 02137,
Portland 97202

Pennsylvania

H. K. Henisch, Editor, **The Carnation Press,** Box 101, State College 16801

Editor-in-Chief, **Concourse Press,** Box 28600, Overbrook Station, Philadelphia
19151

Muriel M. Berman, President, **Jewish Publication Society of America,** 1930
Chestnut Street, Philadelphia 19103

Judith Keith, President, **Tandem Press, Inc.,** Tannersville 18372

Frederick Hetzel, Director, **University of Pittsburgh Press,** 127 North
Bellefield Avenue, Pittsburgh 15260

Tennessee

David Spicer, Editor, **St. Luke's Press/Raccoon Books, Inc.,** Mid-Memphis
Tower, Suite 401, 1407 Union, Memphis 38104

Maxie D. Dunnam, Editorial Director, **The Upper Room,** Box 189, 1908 Grand
Avenue, Nashville 37202

Alice Cooper, Editor, **Winston-Derek Publishers, Inc.,** Box 90883, Pennywell Drive, Nashville 37209

Texas

Ryan Petty, Editor, **Cold Mountain Press,** % Provision House, Box 5487, Austin 78763

Cameron Northouse, Editor, **Pressworks Publishing, Inc.,** 2800 Routh Street, Suite 225, Dallas 75201

Virginia

D. L. Davis, Editor, **Briarfields Press,** Rt. 6, Box 327–B, Hartwood 22471

M. E. Mills, Director, **The University Press of Washington, D.C.,** University Press Building, Dellbrook Campus, CAS, Riverton 22651

Washington

Gwen Head, Editor, **Dragon Gate, Inc.,** 508 Lincoln Street, Port Townsend 98368

West Virginia

Ira Herman, Managing Editor, **Mountain State Press,** University of Charleston, 2300 MacCorkle Avenue S. E., Charleston 25304

Wisconsin

John Judson, Editor, **Center for Contemporary Poetry,** Murphy Library, University of Wisconsin, La Crosse 54601

Bruce Taylor, Editor, **Red Weather Press,** Box 1104, Eau Claire 54702

Ray Reiman, President, **Reiman Publications, Inc.,** Box 643, Milwaukee 53201

Canada

Bill Bissett, Editor, **Blewointmentpress,** Box 48870 Station Bentall, Vancouver, British Columbia

Stan Bevington *et al.*, Editors, **Coach House Press,** 401 Huron Street (Rear), Toronto, Ontario M5S 2G5

S. Mayne *et al.*, Editors, **Mosaic Press/Valley Editions,** Box 1032, Oakville, Ontario, L6J 5E9

7 | ALTERNATIVE MARKETS

Poets want to reach more people than the conventional markets allow. Having seen the enormous success of public arts such as film, theater, and dance, they have begun to seek other media besides books and magazines for their work, and, using their creativity, have found them. At the Cambridge Arts Council in Massachusetts, for example, Peter Payack has arranged for poets to have illustrated poems painted on the windows of stores and public buildings, has had poetry flashed on an electric signboard in Harvard Square, and even has had a plane light the sky with poetry flashed on a computerized grid of light bulbs. (Payack may be reached at 64 Highland Avenue, Cambridge, MA 02139.)

Other poets have explored ways of reintegrating poetry with drama, dance, and music. Many have participated in public poetry readings and in the state arts councils' Poets-in-the-Schools programs. (The main source of sponsors for readings and special poetry programs is Poets and Writers' *Sponsors List*, available for $3.50 from Poets and Writers, Inc., 201 West 54th Street, New York, NY 10019.)

Other developments have included poetry broadsides, posters, and placards, usually with fine graphics and artwork; poetry postcards and stamps; and poetry posters on buses. The listings that follow provide entries in each of these categories. Writers should send query letters before submitting work.

BROADSIDES, POSTERS, AND PLACARDS

American Artists in Exhibition, Inc., 799 Greenwich Street, New York, NY 10014. Literature posters that combine poetry with graphics and photographs. Featured poets: James Wright, Laura Gilpin, Siv Cedering Fox.

Basement Workshop, Inc., Basement Editions, 102 Third Avenue #2, New York, NY 10003. Illustrated poetry broadsides. Featured poets: Ntozake Shange, Jessica Hagedorn, Lawson Fusao Inada. Contact: John Woo.

The Bellevue Press, 60 Schubert Street, Binghampton, NY 13905. Broadsides in signed, limited, letterpress editions. Featured poets: Clayton Eshleman, Heather McHugh, William Stafford. Contact: Gil and Deborah Williams.

Bloomington Area Arts Council, Inc., The Old Library, 202 East 6th Street, Bloomington, IN 47401. Poetry billboards and broadsides featuring Indiana poets.

Burning Deck, 71 Elmgrove Avenue, Providence, RI 02906. Broadsides that combine poems with silkscreen portraits. Featured poets: Michael Benedikt, Michael Harper, Rochelle Owens. Not reading mss. in 1983–84. Contact: Keith and Rosmarie Waldrop.

Just Buffalo, Allentown Community Center, 111 Elmwood Avenue, Buffalo, NY 14201. Poetry and prose broadsides, silkscreened in signed or unsigned sets or single copies. Featured poets: Maureen Owen, Diane di Prima, Anselm Hollo. Contact: Debora and John Daley.

Luna Bisonte Productions, 137 Leland Avenue, Columbus, OH 43214. Poetry broadsides, postcards, and labels. Featured poets: Richard Kostelanetz, Al Ackerman, William Garrett. Contact: John Bennett.

Motherall Press, 3000 West Gambrell, Fort Worth, TX 76133. Illustrated poetry broadsides. Featured poets: William Burford, Simone Weil. Contact: William Burford.

Mudborn Press, 209 West De la Guerra, Santa Barbara, CA 93101. Poetry broadsides and postcards. Featured poets: L. S. Fallis, Paul Portuges. Contact: Sasha Newborn and Judyl Mudfoot.

Open Chord Press, Box 2528, Bath, OH 44210. Poetry broadsides and postcards. Featured poet: Steven Osterlund.

A Poem A Month Club, Inc., North Shore Books, Ltd., 8 Green Street, Huntington, NY 11743. Monthly series of signed, hand-set, letterpress broadsides. Featured poets: Stanley Kunitz, Galway Kinnell, June Jordan.

Poetry in Motion, 159 Ludlowville Road, Lansing, NY 14882. Poetry broadsheets, postcards, and greeting cards. Featured poets: David Rigsbee, Peter Frank, John Yau. Contact: David Lehman.

Poetry Place, 166 Kingsbury Lane, Tonawanda, NY 14150. Poetry placards by Buffalo poets for display in the Buffalo area. Contact: Mrs. Alice Stein.

South Solon Press, RFD 4 Box 168, Skowhegan, ME 04976. Poetry broadsheets in a variety of typefaces and papers. Featured poets: Miriam Dyak, Constance Hunting, Bern Porter.

Stone Press, 1790 Grand River, Okemos, MI 48864. Poetry posters designed to complement the poem. Featured poets: Richard Kostelanetz, William Stafford, Earle Birney. Contact: Albert Drake.

Thunder City Press, Box 11126, Birmingham, AL 35202. Poetry broadsides. Featured poets: Donald Hall, Robert Bly, Leonard Michaels. Contact: Steven Ford Brown.

Unicorn Folded Broadside Series, Unicorn Press, Box 3307, Greensboro, NC 27402. Poetry broadsides, handprinted and illustrated, folded and enclosed in a paper cover. Contact: Teo Savory.

the unspeakable visions of the individual, Box 439, California, PA 15419. Illustrated poetry broadsides, many of them printed on fine stock. Featured poets: Gregory Corso, Jack Kerouac. Contact: Arthur and Kit Knight.

Vehicle Editions, 238 Mott Street, New York, NY 10012. Poetry broadsides. Featured poets: Simon Schuchat, Annabel Levitt. Contact: Annabel Levitt.

Yanagi, Box 466, Bolinas, CA 94942. Poetry broadsides with artwork ranging from photographs and letterpress typography to comic strips. Featured poets: Frank O'Hara, Ed Sanders, Tom Clark. Contact: Louis Patler.

The Yellow Pages Poets, c/o My Back Pages, 1896 North High Street, Columbus, OH 43201. Poetry placards on billboards donated by a Columbus area advertising firm. Featured poets: Susan Merrit, Terry Hermenson, Galen Green.

POSTCARDS AND STAMPS

Artists' Postcards, 2 East 34th Street, New York, NY 10016. Featured poets: Tom Wolfe, Jonathan Williams, Dick Higgins.

BOA Editions, 92 Park Avenue, Brockport, NY 14420. Featured poets: W. D. Snodgrass, M. L. Rosenthal, Ralph J. Mills, Jr. Contact: A. Poulin, Jr.

Bridger Canyon Card Series, 521 South 6th, Bozeman, MT 59715. Featured poet: Linda Sellers Peavy.

Burning Deck—see address above.

CIE/Media Central, 628 Grand Avenue #307, St. Paul, MN 55105. Featured poets: Robert Bly, Ezra Pound, Emily Dickinson.

The Jargon Society, Highlands, NC 28741. Featured poet: Jonathan Williams.

Luna Bisonte Productions—see address above.

Match Books, 86 East 3rd Street, Apt. 4B, New York, NY 10003. Contact: Chuck Wachtel.

Mudborn Press—see address above.

Open Chord Press—see address above.

Piirto Press, 445 South Grove Street, Bowling Green, OH 43202. Featured poets: Carolyn Forché, Judith Lindenau, Anick O'Meara. Contact: Jane Navarre.

Post Me Poetry Stamp Series, Box 1132, Peter Stuyvesant Station, New York, NY 10009. Featured poets: Mark Melnicove, Carlo Pittore. Contact: Carlo Pittore.

Prescott Street Press, Box 40312, Postal Building, Portland, OR 97240. Featured poets: Sandra McPherson, Olga Broumas, Primus St. John. Contact: Vi Gale.

Seven Buffaloes Press, Box 249, Big Timber, MT 59011. Contact: Art Cuelho.

Spectacle Press, 49 Essex Street, Buffalo, NY 14213. Featured poets: Linda Lerner, Charles Fishman, Suzanne Johnson. Contact: Suzanne Johnson.

The Spirit That Moves Us, Box 1585, Iowa City, IA 52240. Contact Morty Sklar.

the unspeakable visions of the individual—see address above.

White Pine, 73 Putnam Street, Buffalo, NY 14213. Featured poets: Gary Snyder, John Logan, Maureen Owen, Lew Welch. Contact: Dennis Maloney and Steve Lewandowski.

POETRY POSTERS ON BUSES

Illinois Arts Council, 111 North Wabash, Chicago, IL 60602. Poetry placards by Illinois poets on buses and trains in Chicago and thirteen other cities. Featured poets: Michael Anania, Angela Jackson, Jim Haining. Contact: Jennifer Moyer.

Poetry In Public Places, 799 Greenwich Street, New York, NY 10014. Poetry placards on more than 2,000 buses throughout New York State. Featured poets: Larry Eigner, Leslie Silko, Paul Metcalf. Contact: Verna Gillis.

Poetry On The Buses, Inc., Box 26, Carnegie–Mellon University, Pittsburgh, PA 15213. Poetry placards on city buses throughout the U.S. Featured poets: Robert Creeley, Robert Bly, Lisel Mueller, Galway Kinnell. Contact: Francis Balter, Director.

The Poets' League of Greater Cleveland, Box 6055, Cleveland, OH 44101. Poetry by Ohio poets on buses throughout the State of Ohio. Contact: Scott Mason.

The Spirit That Moves Us, Box 1585, Iowa City, IA 52240. Poetry placards on Iowa City and Kent State University buses. Featured poets: Robert Bly, Anna Akhmatova. Contact: Morty Sklar.

8 | AWARDS AND CONTESTS

Awards and contests offer the poet some recognition and a little money for his labor. Given by publishers, associations, and a variety of organizations, they range from periodical publication and pocket money to sizeable cash awards and book publication. All those listed here are open to application; awards made at the giver's initiative lie outside the marketplace proper—if not always outside a writer's sphere of influence.

To update the following list, poets should regularly consult periodicals like *Coda*, *Small Press Review*, and the others cited in Chapter Three, and the current editions of the following books:

Awards, Honors, and Prizes, ed. Paul Wasserman and Gita Siegman. Vol. 1. Detroit: Gale, 1982.
☐The subject index for poetry on pp. 797–99 directs you to an extensive list of poetry awards. Entries on pp. 453–59 describe the awards offered by members of the National Federation of State Poetry Societies.

Literary and Library Prizes, ed. Olga S. Weber and Stephen J. Calvert. 10th ed. New York: R.R. Bowker, 1980.
☐Thirteen major poetry prize series are listed on pp. 357–87, in entries which not only describe the awards and give the deadlines, but also list the names and dates of previous winners. The entries include both prizes to be applied for and those awarded by nomination only.

The Academy of American Poets, 177 East 87th Street, New York, NY 10128. (212) 427–5665. Founded 1934.
☐The Walt Whitman Award entails a $1,000 cash prize and publication of the first book by an American poet who has not had a book published in a standard edition. The Academy also distributes 1,200 copies of the prize book to members and friends. U. S. citizens may submit a manuscript of 50 to 100 pages between September 15 and November 15. Send SASE for the necessary application form.
☐The Lamont Poetry Selection, awarded to insure the publication of a poet's second book, entails a cash prize of $1,000 to the poet and a contract to purchase 1,200 copies of the winning book from the publisher. Available to U. S. citizens only; the selection must result from a nomination by the publisher, on an entry form, by April 15.
☐The Harold Morton Landon Translation Award biennially gives a $1,000 prize for a published translation into English of poetry from any language. The translation may be of a book-length poem, a collection of poems, or a verse-drama. Available to U. S. citizens only, the award has a deadline of January 1.
☐College and University Poetry Prizes, available at 128 participating colleges, award $100 to winning student poets. Send SASE for details. Contact: Dorothy Ampagoomian.

The Jane Addams Children's Book Award, Jane Addams Peace Association, Inc., 777 United Nations Plaza (at 44th Street), New York, NY 10017. (212) 682–8830. Founded 1953.
☐Annually awards a hand-illuminated scroll for the children's book (for pre-school through high school ages) that best promotes the cause of peace, social justice, and world community. Books may be submitted by publishers. Query for current deadlines and details. Awarded each year on September 6. Contact: Annette Blank, 5477 Cedonia Avenue, Baltimore, MD 21206. (301) 488–6987.

All Seasons Poetry, Box 9314, Jacksonville, FL 32208. Founded 1982.
☐Awards cash, books, or copies of the winning poems made suitable for framing, and publishes the winners in a newsletter and/or anthology. Open to all styles and all subjects. Deadlines for the seasonal contests are January 31, April 30, July 31, and October 31. Awards are given on February 15, May 15, August 15, and November 15. Query for details on entries. Contact: Lou Capps.

The American Poetry Review—See Chapter 4.

Annual International Narrative Contest, Poets & Patrons, Inc., 13942 Keeler Avenue, Crestwood, IL 60445. Founded 1974.
☐Awards cash prizes of $10 and $25 for unpublished narrative poems in any form and on any subject, 40 lines or less. Deadline: September 1. Decision by October 15. Contact: Mary Mathison.

Apalachee Quarterly—See Chapter 4.

The Archer—See Chapter 4.

Arizona Quarterly—See Chapter 4.

Associated Writing Programs, Old Dominion University, Norfolk, VA 23508. (803) 440-3839. Founded 1967.
☐The AWP Award Series in Poetry entails a $1,000 cash prize for a book of poetry and guaranteed publication by the University Press of Virginia. The competition is open to all writers in English, regardless of their nationality or residence. Manuscripts must be at least 48 pages. In 1983, entries were due between October 1 and December 31. Send SASE for current deadlines and requirements.
☐The AWP Anniversary Awards in Poetry give cash prizes ranging from $150 to $1,500 for single poems. Poems must be submitted in duplicate, with the name and full address of the author on one copy only, and must be accompanied by an entry fee of $5 per poem. Send SASE for current deadlines and requirements. Contact: Gale Arnoux.

The Athenaeum Literary Award, the Athenaeum of Philadelphia, 219 South 6th Street, Philadelphia, PA 19106. (215) 925-2688. Founded 1950.
☐Awards a bronze medal for a literary work written by a Philadelphian. The book should be submitted during its year of publication, to be read by the committee during the following year. The deadline is December 31. The winner will be announced in April. Contact: Ellen L. Batty, Circulation Librarian.

Emily Clark Balch Prize—See *Virginia Quarterly Review*, Chapter 4.

The Banta Award, Wisconsin Library Association, 1922 University Avenue, Madison, WI 53705. (608) 231-1513. Founded 1973.
☐Annual award for an outstanding publication by a Wisconsin author during the previous year. Awards a plaque at the annual meeting in October and pays travel expenses. To be eligible, the book (poetry or other) must be more than 50 pages in length and contribute to the world of literature and ideas. Send SASE for more information and deadlines. Contact: Faith Miracle.

The Gordon Barber Memorial Award—See The Poetry Society of America, Chapter 10.

Eileen W. Barnes Award—See Saturday Press, Inc., Chapter 6.

Bitterroot—See Chapter 4.

The Irma Simonton Black Award, Bank Street College of Education, 610 West 112th Street, New York, NY 10025.
☐An annual award for a children's book (including poetry books for children), judged for the excellence of both text and illustration. Authors may ask publishers to submit their books, if appropriate for young children

from three to eight years old. Probable deadline: January 1984. Contact: Joan
Auclair.

Blue Unicorn Contests—See *Blue Unicorn*, Chapter 4.

The Oscar Blumenthal Prize—See *Poetry*, Chapter 4.

The Frederick Bock Prize—See *Poetry*, Chapter 4.

The Book of the Year for Children Medal, Canadian Library Association, 151 Sparks Street, Ottawa, Ontario K1P 5E3, Canada. (204) 985–6488.
Founded 1947.
☐Awards a medal for the outstanding children's book published during the
calendar year and written by a Canadian or a resident of Canada. While the
award is generally given to a work of fiction, it is open to books of poetry for
children. Deadline: Prior to January 1. Decision at the end of April. Contact:
Bessie C. Egan, Convener.

Breakthrough Series and **Devins Award For Poetry,** University of
Missouri Press, Box 7088, Columbia, MO 65205-7088. (314) 882-7641.
☐Breakthrough Series Competition awards publication for a poetry collec-
tion that supports from 64 to 104 printed pages in estimated print length.
Send ms., application form, and $10 entry fee between February 1 and
March 31. Send SASE for full information on the next competition in 1985.
☐Devins Award for Poetry gives $500 to Breakthrough poet whose collec-
tion is recognized as exceptional by the Editorial Committee. Next award in
1985. Contact: Susan E. McGregor.

The Broadside Series Poetry Contest—See Andrew Mountain Press,
Chapter 5.

Brodine Award—See *Connecticut River Review*, Chapter 4.

CAA Poetry Award, Canadian Authors Association, Suite 480, 151
Bloor Street West, Toronto, Ontario M5S 1T3, Canada. (416) 923-9360.
Founded 1921.
☐Awards $5,000 and a silver medal for a book of poetry written in English
by a Canadian writer. Nominations can be made by any individual or group.
Submit 5 copies of the book by December 31 of the year of publication.
Awards are announced in June. Contact: Gerald Nason or Debra Jackson.

The Melville Cane Award—See The Poetry Society of America Award,
Chapter 10.

Carpenter Press Competitions—See Carpenter Press, Chapter 6.

Sri Chinmoy Poetry Awards, The Committee for Spiritual Poetry, 86-16 Parsons Boulevard, Jamaica, NY 11432. (212) 523-3692. Founded 1977.
☐ Awards annual prizes ranging from $75 to $300 for "spiritual poetry"—that is, poetry which expresses our aspiration for a higher or deeper existence based on love, oneness, and the acceptance of life. The winners and 20 honorable mentions are also published in an anthology. The deadline is November 27 each year. The winners are announced on the following January 27. Contact: Justin Catz or Jonathan Roberts.

The Gertrude B. Clayton Memorial Award—See The Poetry Society of America, Chapter 10.

Betty Colladay Award—See *Quarterly Review of Literature Contemporary Poetry Series*, Chapter 6.

College and University Poetry Prizes—See The Academy of American Poets, above.

The Bernard F. Conners Prize for Poetry—See *Paris Review*, Chapter 4.

Hart Crane Memorial Poetry Contest—See *California Quarterly*, Chapter 4.

Croton Review—See Chapter 4.

CSS Publications Annual Contest—See CSS Publications, Chapter 6.

Curbstone Award—See Curbstone Publishing Company, Chapter 6.

The Gustav Davidson Memorial Award—See The Poetry Society of America, Chapter 10.

The Mary Carolyn Davies Memorial Award—See The Poetry Society of America, Chapter 10.

Deep South Writers' Contest, Box 44691-USL, Lafayette, LA 70504. (318) 231-6908. Founded 1967.
☐ Awards 3 cash prizes of $25 for unpublished poetry. Manuscripts, of no more than 6 poems, should be unsigned. The poet's name should appear only on a cover letter. Deadline: July 15. Awarded in late September. Contact: Dr. David Thibodaux.

Billee Murray Denny Poetry Award, Lincoln College, Lincoln, IL 62656. (217) 732-3155. Founded 1981.

☐Awards cash prizes of $1,000, $450, and $200, makes 15 honorable mentions, and arranges for publication of the 18 winning poems. Write for current guidelines and deadlines. Contact: Award Committee.

Marie-Louise D'Esternaux Poetry Scholarship, The Brooklyn Poetry Circle, 61 Pierrepont Street, Brooklyn, NY 11201. (212) 875–8736. Founded 1965.
☐Awards $50 for a poem under 24 lines written by a student 16 to 21 years old. Deadline: April 1. Send SASE for more details. Contact: Gabrielle Lederer.

Devins Award—See Breakthrough Series.

The Alice Fay DiCastagnola Award—See The Poetry Society of America, Chapter 10.

The Emily Dickinson Award—See The Poetry Society of America, Chapter 10.

"Discovery"/The Nation, % The Poetry Center of the 92nd Street Y, 1395 Lexington Avenue, New York, NY 10028. (212) 427–6000. Founded 1974.
☐Awards to the four finalists a cash prize of $100, a reading at The Poetry Center, and publication in *The Nation.* Open to poets who have not published a book of poems, including chapbooks and self-published books. Submit 4 sets of a 10-poem manuscript. Deadline: February 17, 1984. Query with SASE for full information. Contact: Director.

Earthwise Annual Summer Competition—See Earthwise Publications, Chapter 4.

T. S. Eliot Chapbook Competition—See Earthwise Publications, Chapter 4.

The English-Speaking Union Prize—See *Poetry,* Chapter 4.

Evangelical Christian Publishers Association, Box 2439, Vista, CA 92083. (619) 941–1636. Founded 1974.
☐The annual Gold Medallion Book Awards give a plaque and certificate for religious/inspirational poetry. Books published in the 12 months ending October 31 of each year are submitted by their publishers, who pay an entry fee. Awards are made in July of the following year. Contact: C. E. (Ted) Andrew, Executive Director.

Dorothy Canfield Fisher Children's Book Award, 138 Main Street, Montpelier, VT 05602. (802) 658–0238. Founded 1956.
☐Award for original book of poetry by an American poet suitable for children in grades 4 to 8. Anthologies not accepted. Books, copyrighted in the current publication year, must be submitted by January 1. Winner is invited to the award ceremony in Vermont in late May or early June, where he

or she will receive an illuminated scroll. Contact: Virginia Golodetz, Chairman.

Footwork—See Chapter 4.

The Consuelo Ford Award—See The Poetry Society of America, Chapter 10.

Front Street Publishers Annual Competition—See Front Street Publishers, Chapter 6.

The Jacob Glatstein Memorial Prize—See *Poetry*, Chapter 4.

Gold Medallion Book Awards—See Evangelical Christian Publishers Association, above.

Lamont Hall Chapbook Series Prize—See Andrew Mountain Press, Chapter 5.

Ha' Penny Book Contest—See *Telescope*, Chaper 4.

The Cecil Hemley Memorial Award—See The Poetry Society of America, Chapter 10.

Harold G. Henderson Memorial Award—See The Haiku Society of America, Chapter 10.

Hohenberg Award—See *Memphis State Review*, Chapter 4.

The Bess Hokin Prize—See *Poetry*, Chapter 4.

The Hollins Critic—See Chapter 4.

Houghton Mifflin New Poetry Series Competition—See Houghton Mifflin New Poetry Series, Chapter 6.

International Poetry Review—See Chapter 4.

The International Shakespearean Sonnet Contest, Poet's Club of Chicago, % Nolan Boiler Company, 8531 S. Vincennes, Chicago, IL 60620. (312) 994–4700. Founded c. 1948.
☐Awards cash prizes ranging from $10 to $75 for Shakespearean sonnets. Deadline: September 1. Decision by October 15. Send SASE for details. Contact: Anne Nolan.

Iowa Poetry Association, 1724 East 22nd Street, Des Moines, IA 50317. (515) 266–4280. Founded 1945.

☐Adult, college, and school poetry contests for Iowa residents offer cash prizes ranging from $2 to $25. Deadline is February 15 each year. Winners are notified the last week in April. Send SASE for full information. Contact: Virginia Blanck Moore, Editor.

Joseph Henry Jackson Award—See The San Francisco Foundation, below.

Japanese Literary Translation "Friendship Fund" Prize, Japan Society, Inc., 333 East 47th Street, New York, NY 10017. (212) 832–1155. Founded 1979.
☐Awards a prize of $1,000 for the best book-length translation of Japanese literature into English by a first-time American translator. Considers manuscripts and books published after January 1, 1981. Deadline for 1984: February 29, 1984. Decision in May or June. Send SASE for full information on future awards. Contact: Peter M. Grilli.

Jewish Currents—See Chapter 4.

Juniper Prize—See University of Massachusetts Press, Chapter 6.

Kansas Arts Commission Awards—See *Kansas Quarterly*, Chapter 4.

The Lamont Poetry Selection—See The Academy of American Poets, above.

The Harold Morton Landon Translation Award—See The Academy of American Poets, above.

The Levinson Prize—See *Poetry*, Chapter 4.

The Elias Lieberman Student Poetry Award—See The Poetry Society of America, Chapter 10.

The Literary Review—See Chapter 4.

Little Balkans Review—See Chapter 4.

Little Sister Awards—See *Midway Review*, Chapter 4.

The Lyric—See Chapter 4.

Manhattan Poetry Review—See Chapter 4.

The John Masefield Memorial Award—See The Poetry Society of America, Chapter 10.

The Lucille Medwick Memorial Award—See The Poetry Society of America, Chapter 10.

Merit Book Award—See The Haiku Society of America, Chapter 10.

Mid-American Review—See Chapter 4.

Midwest Poetry Review—See Chapter 4.

The Minnesota Voices Project—See New Rivers Press, Inc., Chapter 6.

Modern Haiku—See Chapter 4.

National Federation of State Poetry Societies Prize, National Federation of State Poetry Societies, Inc., 3520 State Route 56, Mechanicsburg, OH 43044. Founded 1959.
□Contest offers prizes ranging from $200 to $1,000 for a poem under 100 lines in any form and on any subject. Also publishes the winners in an anthology. The limit is 4 poems per contestant, and the entry fee is $5 per poem. The poems must be unpublished, not submitted for another contest, and not the winners of any contest with a prize value of $10 or more. Deadline is March 15. Write for details. Contact: Amy and Sam Zook, Contest Chairman and Clerk for Contest.

National Looking Glass Poetry Competition—See *Pudding Magazine*, Chapter 4.

National Poetry Competition, The Chester H. Jones Foundation, Box 43033, Cleveland, OH 44143. (216) 286–6310. Founded 1982.
□Awards cash prizes of $1,000, $500, and $250 for the three top winners and $50 for honorable mentions. The winners and runners-up will also be published in an anthology and receive a complimentary copy of it. Open to poets who live, work, or study in the U. S. or are American or Canadian citizens. Entrants may submit up to 10 unpublished poems, each under 32 lines, with an entry fee of $1 per poem. The writer's name should not appear on the manuscript, only on the entry form.
□Deadline: March 15, 1984. Write for current details and an entry form. Contact: William G. Ferris, Administrator.

The National Poetry Series, 18 West 30th Street, New York, NY 10001. (212) 686–3397. Founded 1978.
□Underwrites the publication of 5 books of poetry every year through participating trade publishers. Two of the 5 books are selected through an open competition. Manuscripts of 48 to 64 pages by U. S. citizens will be read between January 1 and February 15. The ms. must be unpublished (including in chapbook or self-published form), although individual poems may have appeared in periodicals. Enclose an entrance fee of $10, payable to The National Poetry Series, with a manuscript-size SASE. (A self-addressed, stamped postcard will ensure notification of the manuscript's receipt.) Decision in early May. Contact: Emmeline H. Vander Zwaag.

Negative Capability—See Chapter 4.

Pablo Neruda Prize for Poetry—See *Nimrod*, Chapter 4.

New England Sampler—See Chapter 4.

New Writers Awards, Great Lakes Colleges Association, 220 Collingswood, Suite 240, Ann Arbor, MI 48103. (317) 362–1400, Ext. 232. Founded 1968.
☐Awards an expenses-paid tour of the colleges in the Great Lakes Colleges Association, with guaranteed honoraria of $150 on each campus visited of the 12 total.
☐Annually given to the best *first* book of poetry submitted by a *publisher*. Publishers should send 4 copies of the galleys or printed book by February 29. The winner is announced in May. Contact: Donald W. Baker, Director, GLCA New Writers Awards, English Department, Wabash College, Crawfordsville, IN 47933.

Nit & Wit—See Chapter 4.

Northwest Review—See Chapter 4.

The Ohio Journal—See Chapter 4.

Owlflight—See Chapter 4.

Pacific Poetry Series, University of Hawaii Press, 2840 Kolowalu Street, Honolulu, HI 96822. (808) 948–8694. Founded 1983.
☐Awards book publication with standard royalties to a winning manuscript of 60 to 100 pages. Open to poets who have not previously published a volume of poetry and whose work adds significantly to the literature of the Pacific region. Write for complete contest rules. Entries accepted in March only; results announced in June. Contact: Stuart Kiang.

Passages North—See Chapter 4.

PEN American Center Awards, 47 Fifth Avenue, New York, NY 10003. (212) 255–1977. Founded 1922.
☐*Calouste Gulbenkian-PEN Translation Prize* awards $500 every other year for a distinguished translation from Portuguese into English published in the U. S. Submit 2 copies of the eligible book. No application form required. Deadline: December 31.
☐*PEN Southwest Houston Discovery Awards* provide $1,100 each to a poet and fiction-writer in order to encourage and support new literary talent in the Houston area. Winners will each give 4 public readings.

☐Applicants must have been residents of the Houston/Metro Area for at least six months and may not have had their work published in book form. Poets should submit 15 pages of poetry (in English or Spanish) to PEN/Southwest, Dept. of English, University of Houston, Houston, TX 77004. No manuscripts are returned. Deadline: January 15.

☐*PEN Translation Prize* awards $1,000 annually for a distinguished translation from any language into English published in the U. S. during the calendar year under consideration. Submit 2 copies of the eligible book. No application form required. Deadline: December 31.

☐*PEN Writing Awards for Prisoners* award a total of $525 annually and publication in *The Fortune News* to authors of the best poetry, fiction, and nonfiction received from prisoner-writers in the U. S. Inquire with SASE for application procedure. Manuscripts accepted from September 1 to March 1. Contact: John Morrone.

The Penumbra Press—See Chapter 6.

James D. Phelan Award—See The San Francisco Foundation.

Phillips Award—See *Stone Country*, Chapter 4.

Poet and Critic—See Chapter 4.

Poetry—See Chapter 4.

Poetry Canada Review—See Chapter 4.

The Poetry Center, San Francisco State University, 1600 Holloway Avenue, San Francisco, CA 94132. (415) 469-2227. Founded 1953.

☐The Poetry Center Book Award gives $500 and a reading at the Poetry Center to the author of an outstanding book. To be eligible, books must be published and copyrighted in the year of the award. Writers should submit 2 copies of the book and a $3 entry fee by December 31.

☐With the San Francisco Browning Society, co-sponsors a $100 award for the best dramatic monologue written by a student at San Francisco State. Deadline in early December.

☐With the Academy of American Poets, co-sponsors a contest for 3-poem mss. by San Francisco State students. Prize money determined by the Academy. Deadline in early April. Contact: Frances Phillips, Assistant Director.

The Poetry Society of America—See Chapter 10.

Poetry Society of Texas, 4244 Skillman, Dallas, TX 75206. (214) 827-0105. Founded 1921.

☐Offers varied cash prizes annually, with some awards open to non-

members. An entry fee is required. Write for current contest brochures in
November. Contact: Faye C. Adams.

Prairie Schooner—See Chapter 4.

Primavera—See Chapter 4.

PRISM international—See Chapter 4.

Pteranodon—See Chapter 4.

Pudding Magazine—See Chapter 4.

Pulitzer Prizes, 702 Journalism Building, Columbia University, New
York, NY 10027. (212) 280–3841, Ext. 42. Founded 1917.
☐Annually awards $1,000 for a distinguished volume of verse by an
American author first published during the year in book form and available
for purchase by the general public. Requires a completed entry form,
biography and photograph of the author, 4 copies of the book, and a $20
handling fee. Deadline is November 1. Contact: Robin Kuzen, Assistant Administrator.

Pulpsmith—See Chapter 4.

Pushcart Prizes, Pushcart Press, Box 380, Wainscott, NY 11975. (516)
324–9300. Founded 1976.
☐Awards publication in the annual *Pushcart* anthologies (*The Pushcart Prize:
Best of the Small Presses*), which reprint outstanding poetry from little
magazines and small presses. Also awards a free clothbound copy of the anthology.
☐Eligible poetry must be nominated by the editor of the magazine or press
by October 15. Contact: Bill Henderson.

Red Cedar Review—See Chapter 4.

Riverstone International Poetry Chapbook Competition, The
Poets of Foothills, 809 15th Street, Golden, CO 80401. (303) 279–3922.
Founded 1976.
☐Annually awards publication of one chapbook manuscript (16 to 24 pages)
plus $100 in cash. The 1983 deadline was October 1, and the date of the
award, December 31. Send SASE for the latest rules and entry form. Contact: Beth Finnell, Poetry Coordinator.

Dorothy Rosenberg Annual Poetry Award, Religious Arts Guild, 25
Beacon Street, Boston, MA 02108. (617) 742–2100. Founded 1971.
☐Awards 2 prizes of $50 and $25 annually for poems best dealing with "the

human spirit." Publishes winners in *U U World*, the Unitarian Universalist house newspaper, distributed to more than 130,000 members.
□Contact: Barbara M. Hutchins, Executary. 1984 Entries: ℅ Ellin Carter, 2535 Findley Avenue, Columbus, OH 43202. Send a maximum of 3 poems, unpublished and copyrighted, by March 31. No photocopies. Each page should have the designation *DRAPA* along with the writer's name and address. Decision in mid-June.

Sadakichi-Hartmann Prize—See *Smoke Signals*, Chapter 4.

The San Francisco Foundation, 500 Washington Street, 8th Floor, San Francisco, CA 94111. (415) 392-0600.
□The Joseph Henry Jackson Award, begun in 1956, and the James D. Phelan Award, begun in 1935, each award $2,000 to the author of an unpublished work-in-progress, including poetry manuscripts. For the 1984 awards, applicants must be between 20 and 35 years of age on January 15, 1984. Jackson Award contestants must be residents of Northern California or Nevada for three consecutive years immediately prior to January 15, 1984; Phelan Award contestants must have been born in California. Application forms and mss. are accepted only between November 1 and January 15. Winners will be announced on or before June 15.
□Eligible applicants may compete for both awards and in more than one genre, but may win only one award. Write for current information, deadlines, and forms. Contact: Susan Kelly, Assistant Coordinator.

Seaton Awards—See Kansas Quarterly, Chapter 4.

Seven—See Chapter 4.

The Shelley Memorial Award—See The Poetry Society of America, Chapter 10.

Signpost Press Poetry Chapbook Competition—See *Bellingham Review*, Chapter 4.

Silverfish Review—See Chapter 4.

Sing Heavenly Muse!—See Chapter 4.

Constance Lindsay Skinner Award—See Women's National Book Association, Chapter 10.

Mary Elinore Smith Poetry Prize—See *The American Scholar*, Chapter 4.

Elizabeth Matchett Stover Award—See *Southwest Review*, Chapter 4.

Jesse Stuart Contest—See *Seven*, Chapter 4.

Sun Dog Award—See *Sun Dog*, Chapter 4.

The Eunice Tietjens Prize—See *Poetry*, Chapter 4.

Towson State University Prize For Literature, Towson State University, Towson, MD 21204. (301) 321–2128. Founded 1980.
☐Awards annual prize of $1,000 for a published book of poetry or imaginative non-fiction by a Maryland resident under 40 years old. Award may be divided. Deadline in May each year; award presented in October. Send SASE for current information. Contact: Annette Chappell, Dean, College of Liberal Arts.

Translation Center Awards, The Translation Center, 307 A Mathematics Building, Columbia University, New York, NY 10027. (212) 280–2305.
☐Awards $500 to translators for an outstanding translation of a substantial part of a book-length literary work. The main criteria are excellence in the use of English and the merit of the original text as a work of literature. Preference is given to the first or second projects of younger translators, and to translations from the lesser-known languages. Generally, retranslations are discouraged.
☐Applicants must be U. S. citizens or permanent residents and must have a serious indication of interest from a publisher *before* applying. They should submit with the official application form no more than 30 pages of the translated work, together with the corresponding pages of the original foreign language text.
☐The deadline is January 15. Notification occurs on June 30. Contact: Awards Secretary.

Virginia Quarterly Review—See Chapter 4.

Voertman's Poetry Award, The Texas Institute of Letters, Box 8594, Waco TX 76714-8594. Founded 1936.
☐Awards a $200 prize for the best volume of poetry by a Texas writer. The poet or publisher should mail the book, with "T.I.L. Awards" on the envelope, along with evidence of the poet's Texas association. The deadline for 1983 books was January 15, 1984. Contact: Stephen Harrigan, *Texas Monthly*, Box 1569, Austin, TX 78767.

The Celia B. Wagner Award—See The Poetry Society of America, Chapter 10.

Washington Prize—See The Word Works, Inc., Chapter 5.

Webster Review—See Chapter 4.

The Walt Whitman Award—See The Academy of American Poets.

Richard Wilbur Prize for Translation—See American Literary Translators Association, Chapter 10.

The William Carlos Williams Award—See The Poetry Society of America, Chapter 10.

World Order of Narrative Poets, Box 2085, Dollar Ranch Station, Walnut Creek, CA 94595. Founded 1980.
☐Offers awards totaling $1,000 in 12 categories from experts in traditional forms and techniques, including rhyme royal, Shakespearean sonnet, ballad, sestina, villanelle, shaped poem, *terza rima*, sapphic, limerick, and blank verse dramatic monologue. Query with SASE for the contest rules. Deadline for 1984: February 15. Contact: Dr. Alfred Dorn, Box 174, Station A, Flushing, NY 11358.

James Wright Award—See *Mid-American Review,* Chapter 4.

Writer's Digest Writing Competition, Writer's Digest, 9933 Alliance Road, Cincinnati, OH 45242. Founded 1920.
☐Awards prizes for original, unpublished poetry of 16 lines or less on any subject. First-place prize is a Silver-Reed typewriter and an engraved commemorative plaque. Second-place prize is three reference books from Merriam-Webster: *The Third New International Dictionary, The Ninth New Collegiate Dictionary,* and *The Collegiate Thesaurus*—as well as an engraved plaque. The third-place winner receives a plaque, and winners of fourth-through one-hundredth place receive award certificates. In addition, the names of the one hundred winners are published in the October issue of *Writer's Digest* and in a booklet of winners, which also publishes the top two poems.
☐Entries must be postmarked by May 31, 1984. All winners will be notified by mail by September 30. Contact: Marcy Kanter.

The Yale Series of Younger Poets, Yale University Press, 92A Yale Station, New Haven CT 06520. (203) 432-4958. Founded 1922.
☐Awards publication with standard royalties for a ms. of 48 to 64 pages. $5 entry fee, payable to Yale University Press. Manuscripts accepted only in February. Decision by June. Send SASE for complete rules. Contact: Charles Grench.

Yankee—See Chapter 4.

A SELECTIVE INDEX TO CONTESTS AND AWARDS

What follows is not a comprehensive index, but a convenient cross-reference to entries classifiable into important categories.

Awards for Published Books of Poetry

The Academy of American Poets
June Addams Children's Book
   Award
Associated Writing Programs
Athenaeum
The Banta Award
The Irma Simonton Black Award
The Book of the Year for Children
   Medal
CAA Poetry Award
The Melville Cane Award
Dorothy Canfield Fisher Children's
   Book Award
Gold Medallion Book Awards
Calouste Gulbenkian-PEN
   Translation Prize

Japanese Literary Translation
   "Friendship Fund" Prize
Harold Morton Landon
   Translation Award
Merit Book Award
New Writers Awards
PEN Translation Prize
The Poetry Center
Pulitzer Prizes
Towson State University Prize for
   Literature
Voertman's Poetry Award
The William Carlos Williams
   Award

Awards for Book-Length Manuscripts

The Academy of American Poets
Associated Writing Programs
   Award Series
Eileen W. Barnes Award
Breakthrough Series
Carpenter Press Competitions
Curbstone Award
Devins Award
T. S. Eliot Chapbook Competition
Front Street Publishers
Lamont Hall Chapbook Series
   Prize
Ha' Penny Book Contest
Houghton Mifflin New Poetry
   Series Competition
Joseph Henry Jackson Award

Japanese Literary Translation
   "Friendship Fund" Prize
Juniper Prize
Lamont Poetry Selection
The Minnesota Voices Project
The National Poetry Series
Pacific Poetry Series
The Penumbra Press
James D. Phelan Award
Riverstone International Poetry
   Chapbook Competition
The San Francisco Foundation
Signpost Press Poetry Chapbook
   Competition
Translation Center Awards
Walt Whitman Award
The Yale Series of Younger Poets

Awards for Individual Poems or Small Groups of Poems

All Seasons Poetry
The American Poetry Review
Annual International Narrative
   Contest
Apalachee Quarterly
The Archer
Arizona Quarterly
Associated Writing Programs
   Anniversary Awards in
   Poetry
The Gordon Barber Memorial
   Award
Bitterroot
Blue Unicorn Contests

The Oscar Blumenthal Prize
The Frederick Bock Prize
The Broadside Series Poetry Contests
Brodine Award
Sri Chinmoy Poetry Awards
The Gertrude B. Clayton Memorial
   Award
The Bernard F. Conners Prize for
   Poetry
Hart Crane Memorial Poetry
   Contest
Croton Review
CSS Publications Annual Contest
The Gustav Davidson Memorial
   Award

The Mary Carolyn Davies Memorial
  Award
Deep South Writers' Contest
Billee Murray Denny Poetry Award
Marie-Louise D'Esternaux Poetry
  Scholarship
"Discovery"/The Nation
Alice Fay Di Castagnola Award
Earthwise Annual Summer
  Competition
The Emily Dickinson Award
The English-Speaking Union Prize
Footwork
The Consuelo Ford Award
The Jacob Glatstein Memorial Prize
The Cecil Hemley Memorial Award
Harold G. Henderson Award
Hohenberg Award
The Bess Hokin Award
The Hollins Critic
International Poetry Review
The International Shakespearean
  Sonnet Contest
Iowa Poetry Association
Jewish Currents
Kansas Quarterly
The Levinson Prize
The Literary Review
Little Balkans Review
Little Sister Awards
The Lyric
Manhattan Poetry Review
The Lucille Medwick Memorial
  Award
Mid-American Review
Midwest Poetry Review
Modern Haiku
National Federation of State Poetry
  Societies Prize

National Poetry Competition
Negative Capability
Pablo Neruda Prize for Poetry
New England Sampler
Nit & Wit
Northwest Review
The Ohio Journal
Owlflight
Pacific Poetry
Passages North
The Phillips Award
Poet and Critic
Poetry
Poetry Canada Review
Prairie Schooner
Primavera
PRISM international
Pteranodon
Pudding Magazine
Pulpsmith
Pushcart Prizes
Red Cedar Review
Dorothy Rosenberg Annual Poetry
  Award
Seaton Awards
Seven
Silverfish Review
Sing Heavenly Muse!
Mary Elinore Smith Poetry Prize
Elizabeth Matchett Stover Award
Sun Dog Award
The Eunice Tietjens Prize
Virginia Quarterly Review
Washington Prize
Webster Review
World Order of Narrative Poets
Writer's Digest Writing Competition
Yankee

Awards for Poetry Translations

Calouste Gulbenkian-PEN
  Translation Prize
Japanese Literary Translation
  "Friendship Fund" Prize

Harold Morton Landon Translation
  Award
PEN Translation Prize
Translation Center Awards
Richard Wilbur Prize for Translation

Regional Awards for Poetry

California
The San Francisco Foundation
Great Lakes Region
New Writers Awards

Iowa
Iowa Poetry Association
Maryland
Towson State University Prize
for Literature

Nevada
The San Francisco Foundation
Pacific Region
Pacific Poetry Series
Pennsylvania (Philadelphia)
The Athenaeum Literary Award
Southern States
Deep South Writers' Contest

Texas
PEN Southwest Houston Discovery
   Awards
Voertman's Poetry Award
Wisconsin
The Banta Award
Canada
The Book of the Year for Children
   Medal
CAA Poetry Award

Awards for Various Kinds of Poetry

Children's Poetry
Jane Addams Children's Book
   Award
The Irma Simonton Black
   Award
The Book of the Year for
   Children Medal
Dorothy Canfield Fisher
   Children's Book Award
Narrative Poetry
Annual International Narrative
   Contest
World Order of Narrative Poets
Prisoners' Poetry
PEN Writing Awards for Prisoners
Religious Poetry
Sri Chinmoy Poetry Awards

Evangelical Christian Publishers
   Association
Dorothy Rosenberg Annual Poetry
   Award
Seasonal Poetry
All Seasons Poetry
Sonnets
International Shakespearean Sonnet
   Contest
World Order of Narrative Poets
Students' Poetry
College and University Poetry Prizes
   (The Academy of American Poets)
Marie-Louise D'Esternaux Poetry
   Scholarship
The Poetry Center
Traditional Forms
World Order of Narrative Poets

SUPPLEMENTARY LISTINGS

The following list includes sources of poetry awards that made no response to *The Poet's Marketplace* questionnaire or whose response did not permit a full entry in the directory. You should send a query letter with SASE for information.

California

Gundar Strads, **American Book Award,** Before Columbus Foundation, 1446 Sixth Street, Suite D, Berkeley 94710

Borestone Mountain Poetry Awards, Box 653, Solana Beach 92075

Michael Brassington, **California Literature Medal Awards,** Commonwealth Club of California, Monadnock Arcade, 681 Market Street, San Francisco 94105

Duvall Hecht, **Golden Cassette Award,** Books on Tape, Inc., Box 7900, Newport Beach 92660

Claire J. Baker, **International Peace Poetry Contest,** 2451 Church Lane #47, San Pablo 94806

Cornel Lengyel, **Living Playwrights Award,** Dragon's Teeth Press, El Dorado National Forest, Georgetown 95634

Sue Alexander, **Society of Children's Book Writers,** Box 296, Mar Vista Station, Los Angeles 90066

Sylvia Cross, **Women's National Book Association Award,** Women's National Book Association, 19824 Septo Street, Chatsworth 91311

Connecticut

E. Whitbeck, Chairman, **Popular Choice Poetry Contest,** Vista Avenue, Danbury 06810

Delaware

Drew Cassidy, **International Reading Association,** Box 8139, 800 Barksdale Road, Newark 19711

Illinois

Mildred L. Batchelder Award, Association for Library Service to Children, 50 East Huron Street, Chicago 60611

Friends of American Writers, 55 Indian Hill Road, Winnetka 60093

Friends of Literature Award, 3415 Pratt, Lincolnwood 60645

Harriet Monroe Poetry Award, University of Chicago, Chicago 60637

M. Janderson, **John Newbery Medal,** Association for Library Service to Children, 50 East Huron Street, Chicago 60611

Eleanor B. North Award in Poetry, Sigma Tau Delta, Northern Illinois University, English Department, De Kalb 60115

Salute to the Arts Poetry Contest, Triton College, 2000 Fifth Avenue, Rider Grove 60171

Indiana

Ruth Davis, Contest Chairman, **Poets Study Club,** Maryvale 325, West Terre Haute 47885

Iowa

Walter F. Stromer, **Hephaestus Poetry Contest,** 410 Seventh Avenue South, Mt. Vernon 52314

Kansas

William Allen White Children's Book Award, Emporia State University Library, 1200 Commercial, Emporia 66801

Kentucky

James W. Proctor, **Kentucky State Poetry Contest,** 505 Southland Boulevard, Louisville 40214

Louisiana

Caddo Writing Society, Box 3157, Shreveport 71133-3157

Chris Thomas, **Louisiana Literary Award,** Box 131, Baton Rouge 70821

Red River Poetry Contest, Box 3157, Shreveport 71133

Massachusetts

Contest Director, **Arts Wayland Poetry Series,** 57 Washington Street, Natick 01760

Emerson-Thoreau Medal, American Academy of Arts and Sciences, Norton's Woods, 136 Irving Street, Cambridge 02138

Melcher Book Award, 25 Beacon Street, Boston 02108

Professor Guy Rotella, Chair, **Samuel French Morse Poetry Prize,** English Department, Northeastern University, Boston 02115

Ruth Berrien Fox, **New England Poetry Club,** 17 Clark Road, Wellesley Hills 02181

North River Poetry Collective, % Mary A. Barclay, 159 Onion Street, Rockland 02370

New Hampshire

Jeane Michie, **Sarah Josepha Hale Award,** Friends of the Richards Library, 58 North Main Street, Newport 03773

New Mexico

The Pan-American International Literary Award, Box 1505, Las Vegas 87701

New York

Joan Cunliffe, **American Book Awards,** Association of American Publishers, One Park Avenue, New York 10016

American-Scandinavian Foundation, 127 East 73rd Street, New York 10021

John Donovan, **Hans Christian Andersen Prize,** International Board on Books for Young People, % The Children's Book Council, 67 Irving Place, New York 10003

Nancy Abramowitz, **Beefeater Club Prize for Literature,** The Beefeater Foundation, 134 East 40th Street, New York 10016

Joseph O'Hare, **Campion Award,** Catholic Book Club, 106 West 56th Street, New York 10019

Clarence L. Holte Literary Prize, Twenty-first Century Foundation, 112 West 120th Street, New York 10027

James Marshall, **Lenore Marshall Prize for Poetry,** New Hope Foundation, 445 Park Avenue, New York 10022

Richard Locke, President, **National Book Critics Circle Awards,** Box 6000, Radio City Station, New York 10019

Hazel Karp, **National Foundation for Jewish Culture,** 122 East 42nd Street, Room 1512, New York 10017

National Jewish Book Awards, 15 East 26th Street, New York 10010

Dr. Dorothea Neale, **The New York Poetry Forum,** 30064 Albany Crescent, Apt. 54, Bronx 10463

Delmore Schwartz Memorial Poetry Award, N. Y. U. College of Arts and Sciences, New York University, New York 10003

Oscar Williams and Gene Derwood Award, Community Funds, Inc., 415 Madison Avenue, New York 10017

North Carolina

American Association of University Women Award, AAUW, North Carolina Division, North Carolina Literary & Historical Association, 109 East Jones Street, Raleigh 27611

Roanoke-Chowan Award, North Carolina Literary and Historical Association, 109 East Jones Street, Raleigh 27611

Ohio

Elliston Book Award, Department of English, University of Cincinnati, Cincinnati 45221

James Barry, Director, **Ohioana Book Awards,** Ohioana Library Association, 1105 Ohio Departments Building, 65 South Front Street, Columbus 43215

Carl Sandburg Award, International Platform Association, 2564 Berkshire Road, Cleveland Heights 44106

Oklahoma

Sequoyah Children's Book Award, Oklahoma Department of Libraries, 2500 North Lincoln, Oklahoma City 73105

South Carolina

Mrs. Elias E. Horry, **Poetry Society of Georgia Contests,** Route 3, Box 112, Ridgeland 29936.

Texas

Faye Carr Adams, **Poetry Society of Texas,** 4244 Skillman, Dallas 75206

Summerfield G. Roberts Award, The Sons of the Republic of Texas, 519 Hyannis Port North, Crosby 77532

Virginia

Mrs. Fred Martin, **Irene Leache Memorial Contest,** 1544 Cloncurry Road, Norfolk 23505

Washington

Mae Benne, **Pacific Northwest Young Reader's Choice Award,** Pacific Northwest Library Association, University of Washington School of Librarianship, 133 Suzzalo Library FM-30, Seattle 98195

West Virginia

Betty D. Grugin, WVPS Contest Chairman, **West Virginia Poetry Society,** 225 Simmons Drive, Ripley 25271

Canada

M. Claire Pierrard, **Canada Council,** Box 1047, 255 Albert Street, Ottawa, Ontario K1P 5V8

Joan Tutton, **CLA Book of the Year for Children Award,** Canadian Association of Children's Librarians, 151 Sparks Street, Ottawa, Ontario K1P 5E3

9 | GRANTS

For poets, a primary source for grants is the NEA and the state arts councils that it funds. Write for the guidelines to the NEA's Literature Program, and contact the arts council in your area for information. The addresses of the NEA and the state and territorial councils are as follows:

Frank Conroy, Literature Program Director, **National Endowment for the Arts,** 1100 Pennsylvania Avenue, N.W., Washington, DC 20506. (202) 682–5451

Mr. M. J. Zakrzewski, Executive Director, **Alabama State Council on the Arts and Humanities,** 114 North Hull Street, Montgomery, AL 36130. (205) 832–6758

Ms. Christine D'Arcy, Acting Director, **Alaska State Council on the Arts,** 619 Warehouse Avenue, Suite 220, Anchorage, AK 99501. (907) 279–1558

Ms. Matilda Lolotai, Executive Director, **American Samoa Council on Culture, Arts, and Humanities,** Box 1540, Office of the Governor, Pago Pago, American Samoa, 96799. 9–011–684–633–5613 or 9–011–684–633–4347

Mrs. Adrienne N. Hirsch, Executive Director, **Arizona Commission on the Arts and Humanities,** 2024 North Seventh Street, Suite 201, Phoenix, AZ 85006. (602) 255–5884

Ms. Carolyn Staley, Executive Director, **Arkansas Arts Council,** Continental Building, Suite 500, Main and Markham Streets, Little Rock, AK 72201. (501) 371–2539

Mrs. Marilyn Ryan, Executive Director, **California Arts Council** 1901 Broadway, Suite A, Sacramento, CA 95818. (916) 445–1530

Ms. Ellen Pierce, Executive Director, **Colorado Council on the Arts and Humanities,** Grant-Humphreys Mansion, 770 Pennsylvania Street, Denver, CO 80203. (303) 866–2617 or 2618

Mr. Gary Young, Executive Director, **Connecticut Commission on the Arts,** 340 Capitol Avenue, Hartford, CT 06106. (203) 566–4770

Dr. Ann Houseman, Administrator, **Delaware State Arts Council,** State Office Building, 820 North French Street, Wilmington, DE 19801. (302) 571–3540

Ms. Mildred E. Bautista, Executive Director, **District of Columbia Commission on the Arts and Humanities,** 420 Seventh Street, N. W., Second Floor, Washington, DC 20004. (202) 724–5613 or (202) 727–9332

Mr. Chris Doolin, Director, **Arts Council of Florida,** Division of Cultural Affairs, Department of State, The Capitol, Tallahassee, FL 32301. (904) 487–2980

Mr. Frank Ratka, Executive Director, **Georgia Council for the Arts and Humanities,** Suite 100, 2082 East Exchange Place, Tucker, GA 30084. (404) 656–3967

Ms. Annie Benavente Stone, Executive Director, **Guam Council on the Arts and Humanities,** Office of the Governor, Box 2950, Agana, Guam 96910. (477–9845)

Mrs. Sarah M. Richards, Executive Director, **Hawaii State Foundation on Culture and the Arts,** 335 Merchant Street, Room 202, Honolulu, HI 96813. (808) 548–4145

Ms. Joan Lolmaugh, Executive Director, **Idaho Commission on the Arts,** 304 West State Street, % Statehouse, Boise, ID 83720. (208) 334–2119

Mr. Carl J. Petrick, Executive Director, **Illinois Arts Council,** 111 North Wabash Avenue, Room 720, Chicago, IL 60602. (312) 793–6750

Mr. Thomas B. Schorgl, Executive Director, **Indiana Arts Commission,** Union Title Building, Suite 614, 155 East Market Street, Indianapolis, IN 46204. (317) 232–1268

Dr. Sam W. Grabarski, Executive Director, **Iowa State Arts Council,** State Capitol Building, Des Moines, IA 50319. (515) 281-4451

Mr. John A. Reed, Executive Director, **Kansas Arts Commission,** 112 West Sixth Street, Topeka, KS 66603. (913) 296-3335

Ms. Nash Cox, Director, **Kentucky Arts Council,** Berry Hill, Louisville Road, Frankfort, KY 40601. (502) 564-3757

Mr. Albert B. Head, Director, **Louisiana Department of Culture, Recreation, and Tourism,** Division of the Arts, Box 44247, Baton Rouge, LA 70804. (504) 925-3930

Mr. Alden C. Wilson, Executive Director, **Maine State Commission on the Arts and the Humanities,** 55 Capitol Street, State House Station 25, Augusta, ME 04333. (207) 289-2724

Mr. Hank Johnson, Executive Director, **Maryland State Arts Council,** 15 West Mulberry Street, Baltimore, MD 21201. (301) 685-6740

Ms. Anne Hawley, Executive Director, **Massachusetts Council on the Arts and Humanities,** 1 Ashburton Place, Room 2101, Boston, MA 02108. (617) 727-3668

Mr. E. Ray Scott, Executive Director, **Michigan Council for the Arts,** 1200 Sixth Avenue, Executive Plaza, Detroit, MI 48226. (313) 256-3735

Mr. G. James Olsen, Executive Director, **Minnesota State Arts Board,** 432 Summit Avenue, St. Paul, MN 55102. (612) 297-2603 or (800) 652-9747 (toll free within Minnesota)

Ms. Lida Rogers, Executive Director, **Mississippi Arts Commission,** 301 North Lamar Street (physical site), Box 1341 (mailing address), Jackson, MS 39205. (601) 354-7336

Mr. Rick Simoncelli, Executive Director, **Missouri State Council on the Arts,** Wainwright State Office Complex, 111 North Seventh Street, Suite 105, St. Louis, MO 63101. (314) 444-6845

Mr. David E. Nelson, Executive Director, **Montana Arts Council,** 1280 South Third Street West, Missoula, MT 59810. (406) 543-8286

Ms. Robin Tryloff, Executive Director, **Nebraska Arts Council,** 1313 Farnam-on-the-Mall, Omaha, NE 68102-1873. (402) 554-2122

Ms. Jacqueline Belmont, Executive Director, **Nevada State Council on the Arts,** 329 Flint Street, Reno, NV 89501. (702) 789-0225

Mr. Robert Hankins, Executive Director, **New Hampshire Commission on the Arts,** Phenix Hall, 40 North Main Street, Concord, NH 03301. (603) 271-2789

Mr. Jeffrey A. Kesper, Executive Director, **New Jersey State Council on the Arts,** 109 West State Street, Trenton, NJ 08608. (609) 292-6130

Mr. Bernard Blas Lopez, Executive Director, **New Mexico Arts Division,** 224 East Palace Avenue, Santa Fe, NM 87501. (505) 827-6490

Ms. Mary Hays, Executive Director, **New York State Council on the Arts,** 80 Centre Street, New York, NY 10013. (212) 587-4555

Miss Mary B. Regan, Executive Director, **North Carolina Arts Council,** North Carolina Department of Cultural Resources, Raleigh, NC 27611. (919) 733-2821

Ms. Donna M. Evenson, Executive Director, **North Dakota Council on the Arts,** Black Building, Suite 811, Fargo, ND 58102. (701) 237-8962

Ms. Ana Teregeyo, Director, and Ms. Kim Bailey, Program Consultant, **Commonwealth Council for Arts and Culture** (Northern Mariana Islands), Ferreira Building, Beach Road, Garapan, Saipan, Commonwealth of the Northern Mariana Islands 96950. Telephone 7230; *or* Ms. Linda Whitney, Commonwealth of the Northern Mariana Islands, 2121 "R" Street, N. W., Washington, DC 20008. (202) 328-3847

Dr. Wayne P. Lawson, Executive Director, **Ohio Arts Council,** 727 East Main Street, Columbus, OH 43205. (614) 466-2613

Mrs. Betty Price, Executive Director, **State Arts Council of Oklahoma,** Jim Thorpe Building, Room 640, 2101 North Lincoln Boulevard, Oklahoma City, OK 73105. (405) 521-2931

Mr. Peter Hero, Executive Director, **Oregon Arts Commission,** 835 Summer Street, N. E., Salem, OR 97301. (503) 378-3625

Ms. June Batten Arey, Executive Director, **Commonwealth of Pennsylvania Council on the Arts,** Room 216, Finance Building, Harrisburg, PA 17120. (717) 787-6883

Mr. Angel Avila, Acting Executive Director, **Institute of Puerto Rican Culture,** Apartado Postal 4184, San Juan, PR 00905. (809) 723-2115

Ms. Christina A. White, Executive Director, **Rhode Island State Coun-**

cil on the Arts, 312 Wickenden Street, Providence, RI 02903-4494. (401) 277-3880

Ms. Scott Sanders, Executive Director, **South Carolina Arts Commission,** 1800 Gervais Street, Columbia, SC 29201. (803) 758-3442

Mrs. Charlotte Carver, Executive Director, **South Dakota Arts Council,** 108 West Eleventh Street, Sioux Falls, SD 57102. (605) 339-6646

Mr. Arthur L. Keeble, Executive Director, **Tennessee Arts Commission,** 505 Deaderick Street, Suite 1700, Nashville, TN 37219. (615) 741-6395 (Mr. Keeble's office) or (615) 741-1701 (switchboard)

Mr. Richard Huff, Executive Director, **Texas Commission on the Arts,** Box 13406, Capitol Station, Austin, TX 78711. (512) 475-6593

Mrs. Ruth R. Draper, Director, **Utah Arts Council,** 617 East South Temple Street, Salt Lake City, UT 84102. (801) 533-5895 or 5896

Mrs. Ellen McCulloch-Lovell, Executive Director, **Vermont Council on the Arts, Inc.,** 136 State Street, Montpelier, VT 05602. (802) 828-3291

Ms. Peggy Baggett, Executive Director, **Virginia Commission for the Arts,** 400 East Grace Street, First Floor, Richmond, VA 23219. (804) 786-4492

Mr. Stephen J. Bostic, Executive Director, **Virgin Islands Council on the Arts,** Caravelle Arcade, Christiansted, St. Croix, U. S. Virgin Islands 00820. (809) 773-3075, Ext. 3; or Mr. John Jowers, Associate Director, Box 103, St. Thomas, U. S. Virgin Islands 00801. (809) 774-5984

Mr. Michael A. Croman, Executive Director, **Washington State Arts Commission,** Ninth and Columbia Building, Mail Stop GH-11, Olympia, WA 98504. (206) 753-3860

Mr. James B. Andrews, Executive Director, **West Virginia Department of Culture and History,** Arts and Humanities Division, Science & Culture Center, Capitol Complex, Charleston, WV 25305. (304) 348-0240

Mr. Marvin E. Weaver, Executive Director, **Wisconsin Arts Board,** 123 West Washington Avenue, Madison, WI 53702. (608) 266-0190

Mr. David J. Fraher, Executive Director, **Wyoming Council on the Arts,** Second Floor, Equality State Bank Building, Cheyenne, WY 82002. (307) 777-7742

In addition to public agencies, a number of private institutions and associations give grants for poetry. These, listed below, should also be queried—always with a SASE.

For information about obtaining grants, you might want to consult the following books:

Grants and Awards Available to American Writers. 12th ed. New York: PEN American Center, 1982. ($5.00 from PEN American Center, 47 Fifth Avenue, New York, NY 10003)
□The poetry subject index on page 88 directs you to 51 sources of poetry grants and awards, described in entries which give the address, a description, and the application deadlines.

Sponsors List. New York: Poets & Writers, 1982. ($3.95 from Poets & Writers, 201 West 54th Street, New York, NY 10019)
□A list of 641 organizations which sponsor readings and workshops in poetry and fiction, this can direct you to sites for poetry readings in your area.

Additional sources, available in libraries, include:

The Foundation Directory, ed. Loren Renz. 9th ed. New York: The Foundation Center, 1983.
□A "Language and Literature" index on page 751 directs you to private foundations which fund writers. Entries give the address and phone number of the contact person, a description of the purpose and activities of the foundation, and the application deadlines.

The Foundation Grants Index, ed. Marsha Levine and Elan Garonzik. 12th ed. New York: The Foundation Center, 1983.
□The subject index on page 567 directs you to foundation grants for poetry in categories like poetry associations, community programs, conferences, publications, radio programs, research, television programs, translation, use in psychiatric service, women's poetry, and workshops.

Grants and Aid to Individuals in the Arts, ed. Daniel Millsaps. 5th ed. Washington: Washington International Arts Letter, 1983.
□An index on page 246 directs you to the private-sector grants, prizes, and awards for writers in general described in the alphabetical listings. Those listings are supplemented by a list of the primary governmental sources on pp. 231–33 and a list of artists' retreats and residency programs on pp. 234–44.

Scholarships, Fellowships and Loans, ed. S. Norman Feingold and Marie Feingold. Vol. 7. Arlington: Bellman, 1982.

☐The Vocational Goals Index for poetry directs you to scholarships, fellowships, and grants available from the Poetry Society of America, NEA, and a few other groups.

Grants for the Arts, Virginia White. New York: Plenum Press, 1980.
☐A good introduction to the NEA, the state arts councils, and the Foundation Center, this lists information sources in the arts, state foundation directories, and, in appendices, the NEA state and jurisdictional agencies. It also gives advice on grant proposal writing from the planning to the post-application phases.

The following grant agencies, drawn from the preceding books and the periodicals cited in Chapter Three, include only those that accept applications, not those that make grants solely on their own initiative.

The Artists Foundation, Inc., 110 Broad Street, Boston, MA 02110. (617) 482–8100. Founded 1973.
☐The Artists Fellowship Program annually offers fifty $5,000 unrestricted grants in the categories of literary, performing, visual, and media arts. The applicant must be over 18 years of age, a Massachusetts resident, and not enrolled in any degree- or certificate-granting educational program of any kind.
☐Poets should submit two typed or clear photocopies (8½″ by 11″) of a maximum of 8 poems in two separate binders, securely fastened. The deadline always falls within the first week of October. Write for details. Contact: Susan Walton, Assistant Director of the Artists Fellowship Program.

The George Bennett Fellowship at Phillips Exeter Academy, Exeter, NH 03833. (603) 772–4311. Founded 1968.
☐Awards a $4,800 stipend plus room and board for one academic year to a writer at the outset of his or her professional career. The Fellow's only official duties are to be in residence at the Academy when school is in session and to work on a manuscript in progress, but he also is expected to be informally available to students interested in writing.
☐Applicants are judged primarily on the basis of a manuscript submitted (preferably the manuscript in progress). Preference is given to a writer of fiction: four poets have been selected in the first fifteen years of the Fellowship. Deadline for applications is early December for the following academic year; decisions are announced in March. For applications and full information, send SASE after September 1. Contact: Chairperson, Selection Committee, George Bennett Fellowship.

The Bush Foundation Fellowships for Artists, E-900 First National Bank Building, St. Paul, MN 55101. (612) 227–0891. Founded 1976.

☐Awards a stipend of $20,000 for 12 to 18 months, or $1,666 per month for 6 to 11 months, to Minnesota residents who are at least 25 years old. The application deadline is in early November; the fellowships are awarded in early March. Contact: Sally Dixon.

The Witter Bynner Foundation for Poetry, Inc., Box 2188, Santa Fe, NM 87504. (505) 988–3251. Founded 1972.
☐Awards about $75,000 worth of grants annually to non-profit organizations to advance the art of poetry. The four major areas of grant support include support for individual poets through existing non-profit institutions; the development of the poetry audience; poetry translation; and various uses of poetry, including its use in dramatic, educational, historical, or therapeutic programs. Support for poetry readings and publication projects occurs only if they are closely related to the four areas.
☐Official grant applications, submitted in triplicate with a tax-exempt ruling from the IRS, must be received by February 1. Send SASE for forms and current information. Contact: Ms. Jeton Brown, Executive Secretary.

Creative Artists Program Services, 250 West 57th Street, New York, NY 10107. (212) 247–6303. Founded 1970.
☐CAPS Poetry Fellowships grant $5,000 to $6,500 to poets from New York State to create new works or complete works in progress. (Matriculating students and past recipients are ineligible.)
☐Write for information and applications in the spring. The deadline is in June, and the award is given in the following spring. Contact: Isabelle Fernandez, Executive Director.

Dobie-Paisano Writing Fellowships, The Texas Institute of Letters, % Office of Graduate Studies, Main Building 101, The University of Texas at Austin, Austin, TX 78712. Founded 1936.
☐Grants a 6-month stipend of $5,000 and free lodging to Texas writers at the University of Texas at Austin. Send SASE for details and application form. Contact: Dr. Audrey Slate.

Fine Arts Work Center in Provincetown, 24 Pearl Street, Box 565, Provincetown, MA 02657. (617) 487–9960. Founded 1968.
☐Offers a 7-month residency program for writers from October 1 to May 1. The fellowships include monthly stipends, living space, and a distinguished resident and visiting staff. Query for details. Application deadline: February 1. Contact: Director.

General Electric Foundation Awards—See Coordinating Council of Literary Magazines, Chapter 10.

D. H. Lawrence Fellowship, Department of English, University of New Mexico, Albuquerque, NM 87131. (505) 277–6360. Founded 1956.

☐Awards the use of the facilities at the D. H. Lawrence Ranch in Taos, New Mexico, for the summer. Send SASE for full details. Contact: Prof. Lee Bartlett, Director, Creative Writing Program.

PEN American Center, 47 Fifth Avenue, New York, NY 10003. (212) 255-1977. Founded 1922. Contact: John Morrone.
☐Renato Poggioli Translation Award gives $3,000 annually to encourage a beginning and promising translator who is working on his first book-length translation from Italian into English. It is preferable, but not necessary, that the candidate spend the grant period in Italy. Letters of application should be accompanied by a curriculum vitae, a description of the candidate's Italian studies, a statement of purpose, and samples of the translation-in-progress with the original Italian text. Deadline: February 1.

The Mary Roberts Rinehart Fund, % English Department, George Mason University, Fairfax, VA 22030. (703) 323-2220.
☐Awards a grant of $2,500 every other year to writers nominated by established writers or editors. Deadline for the 1985 grant is November 1, 1985. The grant will be announced the following March. Contact: Richard Bausch, Director.

Tendril Fellowships—See *Tendril Magazine*, Chapter 4.

The Writers Community—See Chapter 10.

A SELECTIVE INDEX TO GRANTS
What follows is not a comprehensive index, but a convenient cross-reference to entries classifiable into important categories.

Fellowships

The George Bennett Fellowship
  at Phillips Exeter Academy
The Bush Foundation Fellowships
  for Artists
Dobie-Paisano Writing Fellowships

Fine Works Art Center
  in Provincetown
D. H. Lawrence Fellowship
Tendril Fellowships

Grant for Non-Profit Organizations
The Witter Bynner Foundation for Poetry, Inc.

Grant for Translation (Italian)
PEN American Center

Grants Restricted to State Residents

Massachusetts
The Artists Foundation, Inc.
Minnesota
The Bush Foundation Fellowships
  for Artists

New York
Creative Artists Program Services
Texas
Dobie-Paisano Writing Fellowships

SUPPLEMENTARY LISTINGS

The following list includes sources of poetry grants that made no response to *The Poet's Marketplace* questionnaire or whose response did not permit a full entry in the directory. Send a query letter with SASE for information.

California

Wallace E. Stegner Fellowships, Creative Writing Center, Department of English, Stanford University, Stanford 94305

District of Columbia

Joe Prince, **Poets-in-the-Schools,** Artists in the Schools Program, National Endowment for the Arts, Washington 20506

Illinois

McArthur Foundation, 140 South Dearborn Street, Chicago 60603

New York

Oscar Dystel Fellowship, New York University, Gallatin Division, 25 Waverly Place, New York 10011

Fellowships in Creative Writing, The Cornelia Ward Fellowship, Syracuse University, Graduate School Admissions, 206 Steele Hall, Syracuse 13210

D. Turnbaugh, Treasurer, **The Ludwig Vogelstein Foundation,** Box 537, New York 10013

Vermont

The Bread Loaf Writers' Conference Endowment Fund, Middlebury College, Middlebury 05753

Robert Frost Fellowship in Poetry, Bread Loaf Writers' Conference, Middlebury College, Middlebury 05753

Virginia

Henry Hoyns Fellowships, University of Virginia, Department of English, Charlottesville 22903

10 | WRITERS' AND POETS' ASSOCIATIONS

Although writers in general (and poets in particular) are notoriously independent individuals, not "joiners," they can enjoy and benefit from membership in writers' associations. These groups provide them with general information and news about markets, offer some sense of confidence and camaraderie in a largely indifferent world, and sometimes give tangible support through grants and awards.

The Academy of American Poets, 177 East 87th Street, New York, NY 10128. (212) 427–5665. Founded 1934. Services to members include scheduled readings in New York City, a monthly newsletter, and free copies of the two annual book prize selections.
□The Academy also offers a number of awards with cash prizes up to $1,000: The Walt Whitman Award, The Lamont Poetry Selection, The Harold Morton Landon Translation Award, and The College and University Poetry Prizes. (See Chapter 8 for details.)
□Memberships come in various categories: Contributing Memberships for $1 to $24; Associate Memberships for $25 to $99; Sustaining Memberships for $100 to $999. All members who contribute $30 or more will receive the annual book prize selections, and those who contribute at least $10 will receive the monthly newsletter, *Poetry Pilot*. Send SASE for additional information. Contact: Dorothy Ampagoomian.

American Literary Translators Association (ALTA), University of Texas at Dallas, Box 803688, Richardson, TX 75083–0688. (214) 690–2093. Founded 1978.

☐Services to members include a newsletter (six times a year); *Translation Review* (three times a year); an index on translators, writers, publishers, and grants; and an annual conference in October. Annual dues are $20.
☐With the University of Missouri Press, offers the Richard Wilbur Prize for translation every 2 years, starting in 1985. Query Prof. Margaret Sayers Peden, University of Missouri Press, 200 Lewis Hall, Columbia, MO 65211.
☐Eligible for membership are literary translators from any language into English. Contact: Dr. S. Gostautas.

Associated Writing Programs, Old Dominion University, Norfolk, VA 23508. (804) 440–3839. Founded 1967. Services to members include information services, publications (including the *AWP Newsletter*), competitions, news on publishing opportunities, advocacy, job placement services, residencies, and reading referrals.
☐The AWP Award Series in Poetry and the AWP Anniversary Awards in Poetry offer cash prizes of up to $1,500 for individual poems and book-length manuscripts. (See Chapter 8 for details.)
☐Membership is open to all writers of all genres. The annual dues are $25, with $5 extra for the Placement Service. Contact: Gale Arnoux.

The Authors Guild, Inc., 234 West 44th Street, New York, NY 10036. (212) 398–0838. Founded 1921. Serves the business and professional interests of writers in the areas of publishers' contracts and royalty statements, taxes, health and life insurance, freedom of expression, conglomeration in book publishing, and copyright law. Publishes the *Authors Guild Bulletin*, which gives news of its work in all of these areas, and others, and pamphlets on book contracts.
☐Membership open to any author who has had a book published by an established American publisher within seven years prior to application, or who has had three works, fiction or non-fiction, published by a magazine or magazines of general circulation within 18 months prior to application, or who has a professional standing that qualifies him, in the opinion of the Membership Committee, for membership. There is no initiation fee. Annual dues are $60. Contact: Jean Wynne.

The Authors League of America, Inc., 234 44th Street, New York, NY 10036. (212) 391–9198. Founded 1912. Works to promote the professional interests of authors and dramatists, procure satisfactory copyright legislation, guard freedom of expression, and support fair tax treatment for writers.
☐Membership restricted to members of The Authors Guild and The Dramatists Guild (212-398-9366). Contact: The Authors Guild, Inc. (212) 398–0838.

Beyond Baroque Foundation, Box 806, Venice, CA 90291. (213) 822–3006. Founded 1968. Services include readings, workshops, and Small Press Library borrowing privileges. Publishes *Magazine*, which contains

poetry and news on the literary scene in Southern California.
☐Membership obtained through a donation of $15. Contact: Any staff member.

Coordinating Council of Literary Magazines (CCLM), 2 Park Avenue, New York, NY 10016. (212) 481–5245. Founded 1967.
☐Offers annual Victoria Chen Haider Memorial Contest for college literary magazines, General Electric Foundation Awards for Younger Writers, and grants to magazines. Query for details.
☐Membership is open to any noncommercial literary magazine that has published for at least 1 year and printed at least 3 issues. Annual dues are $10. Services to members include a newsletter (CCLM News), exhibits of magazines at national conferences, access to resources and library, early announcements of awards and deadlines, ad brokering, and listing in *The CCLM Literary Magazine Directory*. Contact: Chael Graham, Projects Director.

Feminist Writers' Guild, Box 9396, Berkeley, CA 94709. (415) 524–3692. Founded 1977. Services include peer workshops, discussion groups, readings, and seminars. A triannual newsletter includes calls for material, self-help articles, descriptions of members' works, local chapter activities, and a directory of members.
☐Membership open to any feminist who takes her writing seriously. Contact: Laura Tow, Administrator.

Haiku Society of America, 11 Hillcrest Road, Mountain Lakes, NJ 07046. Founded 1968.
☐Awards include the Harold G. Henderson Memorial Award for the best unpublished haiku; the biannual Merit Book Award for excellence in published haiku, translations, and criticism; and the best-of-issue prize for publication in *Frogpond*.
☐Services to members include 4 issues of *Frogpond* a year, quarterly meetings in New York City, lectures, discussions, workshops, and readings. Membership dues are $15 annually. Contact: Ross Kremer, Box 609, Ringoes, NJ 08551.

International Women's Writing Guild, Box 810, Gracie Station, New York, NY 10028. (212) 737–7536. Founded 1976. Services to writers include the use of eleven New York literary agents who have agreed to read members' work; annual and semi-annual conferences; health insurance at group rates; and a supportive writing network. Publication: *Network* newsletter six times a year.
☐Membership requirements: a sincere connection to the written word. Contact: Hannelore Hahn.

National Federation of State Poetry Societies—See Chapter 8.

PEN American Center, 47 Fifth Avenue, New York, NY 10003. (212) 255-1977. Founded 1922. Services include health insurance, invitations to all PEN events (receptions, conferences, panels, etc.), Hertz discount, reciprocal hospitality in foreign PEN centers, and the quarterly *PENewsletter*. Publications include *Grants and Awards Available to American Writers*, 12th Edition, 1982/83 ($5).

☐Awards and grants include the PEN Translation Prize, Calouste Gulbenkian-PEN Translation Prize, Renato Poggioli Translation Award, PEN Writing Awards for Prisoners, and PEN/Southwest Houston Discovery Awards. See Chapters 8 and 9 for details.

☐Membership requirements: two published books of literary merit *or* two book-length literary translations (published) *or* seven years' service to literature as a book editor or literary agent-editor. Contact: John Morrone, Programs and Publications.

The Poetry Society of America, 15 Gramercy Park, New York, NY 10003. (212) 254-9628. Founded 1910.

☐Services to members include seminars and educational programs; poetry workshops; publications, including *The Poetry Review*, a semi-annual literary magazine, and a tri-annual newsletter; and access to the Van Voorhis Library, which houses over 6,000 volumes of poetry, criticism, and biography.

☐Contests, which now exceed $10,000 in annual cash prizes, are divided into two kinds: those open to PSA members only, and those open both to members and non-members. Those open to members only include The Gordon Barber Memorial Award ($200), The Gertrude B. Clayton Memorial Award ($250), The Gustav Davidson Memorial Award ($500), The Mary Carolyn Davies Memorial Award ($250), The Alice Fay DiCastagnola Award ($2,000), The Emily Dickinson Award ($100), The Consuelo Ford Award ($250), The Cecil Hemley Memorial Award ($300), and The Lucille Medwick Memorial Award ($500).

☐Contests open to non-members include three for individual poems: The Elias Lieberman Student Poetry Award ($100) for the best unpublished poem by a high school or preparatory school student; The Celia B. Wagner Award ($250) for the best poem worthy of the tradition of the art; and The John Masefield Memorial Award ($500) for a narrative poem. The Melville Cane Award ($500) goes in even-numbered years to a book of poems published in either of the two previous calendar years; in odd-numbered years it goes to a prose work on poetry or a poet. The William Carlos Williams Award, which awards the purchase of copies of the winning book for distribution to PSA members, goes to a book of poetry published by a small press, non-profit press, or university press. The Shelley Memorial Award, with a variable cash prize, is awarded to a living American poet by a jury of three poets. For details and deadlines on all the awards, send a SASE.

☐Membership is granted by the Governing Board after judging samples of published or unpublished poems submitted by the applicant or after review-

ing a list of poetry publications from a recognized poet. Associate membership is open to men and women of letters, educators, critics, editors, and
scholars. Dues are $20 annually. Contact: Rocio Aragon.

Poets & Writers, Inc., 201 West 54th Street, New York, NY 10019. (212)
757–1766. Founded 1970. Services include a nationwide information center
for writers, practical guidebooks for writers, fee payments for readings and
workshops, and *Coda: Poets and Writers Newsletter.*
☐Poets & Writers, Inc., is not a membership organization. Writers are listed
with Poets & Writers by virtue of their publications, detailed in *A Directory of
American Poets and Fiction Writers.*

Women's National Book Association, 19824 Septo Street,
Chatsworth, CA 91311. (213) 886–8448. Founded 1917. Local chapters offer
programs featuring speakers, workshops, and discussion groups. Some also
sponsor book-and-author luncheons and dinners and offer seminars on
aspects of publishing and the book industry. WNBA also publishes *The Book
Woman* three times a year, and offers the Constance Lindsay Skinner Award
biennially to a distinguished bookwoman for her extraordinary contribution
to the world of books.
☐Memberships are open to all people in the book world where there is a
chapter. Send SASE for a list of local chapters and full membership information. Contact: Sylvia H. Cross, President.

The Writers Community, 120 East 89th Street, Apt. 1 D, New York, NY
10128. (212) 348–0160. Founded 1976. The writer-in-residence program
awards $5,000 in return for a public reading and the teaching of an advanced
writing workshop. Workshops meet for two hours one evening a week for 13
weeks, with individual conference hours to be arranged. Past residencies have
been held by Alan Dugan, Charles Simic, and Ai.
☐Write for application details and deadlines. Contact: Bonnie Midnica.

A SELECTIVE INDEX TO ASSOCIATIONS

What follows is not a comprehensive index, but a convenient cross-reference to entries classifiable into important categories.

Association for Magazine Editors

Coordinating Council of Literary Magazines

Associations for Poets

The Academy of American Poets   The Poetry Society of America
Haiku Society of America

Associations for Poets and Writers in Other Genres

Associated Writing Programs   PEN American Center
The Authors Guild   Poets & Writers, Inc.
The Authors League of America, Inc.

Association for Translators

American Literary Translators Association

Associations for Women Writers

Feminist Writers' Guild   Women's National Book Association
International Women's Writing
  Guild

SUPPLEMENTARY LISTINGS

The following list includes writers' associations that made no response to *The Poet's Marketplace* questionnaire or whose response did not permit a full entry in the directory. Send a query letter with SASE for information.

California

John Dunmore, Director, **American Poetry Association,** Box 2279, Santa Cruz 95063.

Committee of Small Magazine Editors and Publishers, Box 703, San Francisco 94101

Lin Oliver, Executive Director, **Society of Children's Book Writers,** Box 296, Mar Vista Station, Los Angeles 90066

Colorado

The Poets of the Foothills Arts Center, 809 15th Street, Golden 80401

New York

Lydia Kaim, **American Academy and Institute of Arts and Letters,** 633 West 155th Street, New York 10032

Dorothy M. Stearn, Executive Director, **American Society of Journalists & Authors, Inc.,** 1501 Broadway, Room 1907, New York 10036

Association of Hispanic Arts, 200 East 87th Street, New York 10028

Phillip M. Perry, Treasurer, **Council of Writers Organizations,** 1501 Broadway, Suite 1907, New York 10036

National Association of Third World Writers, 373 Fifth Avenue, Suite 1007, New York 10016

Mercy Cobell Wolfe, President, **Pen & Brush, Inc.,** 16 East 10th Street, New York 10003

Poetry Advocates of America, c/o New York Literary Society, 417 West 56th Street, New York 10019

The Poetry Kibbutz, c/o Dworkin, 455 West 34th Street, #2–G, New York 10001

Support Services Alliance, Inc., Crossroads Building, Two Times Square, New York 10036

Teachers and Writers Collaborative, 84 Fifth Avenue, New York 10011

Leonard Wasser, Executive Director, **Writers Guild of America-East, Inc.,** 555 West 57th Street, New York 10019

Texas

Associated Artists Trust, Box 5871, 3809 West 35th Street, Austin 78763

Washington

David Romtvedt, **POW,** Box 484, Port Townsend 98368

Wisconsin

Edna Meudt, **Wisconsin Fellowship of Poets,** Dodgeville 53533

APPENDIX A
WRITERS' DIRECTORIES

Sometimes poets want to get in touch with other poets and writers—to get information or advice, make proposals, question, criticize, or praise. The following biographical sources will help poets make the contacts they want.

One book, readily available from the publisher, is:

A Directory of American Poets and Fiction Writers. Poets and Writers, Inc., 201 West 54th Street, New York, NY 10019 ($14.95).

Reference books available in libraries include:

Elmer Borklund, *Contemporary Literary Critics*. New York and London: St. Martin's and St. James Press, 1977.

Contemporary Authors. 108 vols. Detroit: Gale, 1962–83.

Contemporary Poets, ed. James Vinson. 3rd ed. New York: St. Martin's, 1980.

Contemporary Poets of the English Language, ed. Rosalie Murphy. Chicago and London: St. James Press, 1970.

The Writers Directory 1982–84. Detroit: Gale, 1981.

APPENDIX B
GUIDES TO SELF-PUBLISHING

To poets without a collection of their work, the self-publishing alternative invariably suggests itself. Lacking success with book or chapbook publishers, you will recall the precedent of Edgar Allan Poe, Walt Whitman, and others who published their own poetry. After all, this practice is not very different from one trend among some small publishers: publishing themselves and their coterie. And as more people choose this alternative, more information becomes available on how to do it well. A list of some useful guidebooks follows, along with a list of subsidy publishers who will publish your manuscript for you, as written—at your expense.

Charles Chickadel, *Publish It Yourself*. Trinity Press, Box 1320, San Francisco, CA 94101. $5.95.

Bill Henderson, *The Publish-It-Yourself Handbook: Literary Tradition and How-To*. Pushcart Press, P.O. Box 845, Yonkers, NY 10701. $12.50.

L.W. Mueller, *How to Publish Your Own Book*. Harlo Press, 50 Victor, Detroit, MI 48203. $5.95 paper; $7.95 cloth.

Dan Poynter, *The Self-Publishing Manual*. Parachuting Publications, P.O. Box 4332, Santa Barbara, CA 93103. $9.95 paper; $14.95 cloth.

Subsidy Publishers
Dorrance & Company, 828 Lancaster Avenue, Bryn Mawr, PA 19010.

Exposition Press, 325 Rabro Drive, Smithtown, NY 11787.

Mojave Books, 7040 Darby Avenue, Reseda, CA 91335.

Vantage Press, 516 West 34th Street, New York, NY 10001.

Note: Poets who self-publish will be taken more seriously than those who choose a subsidy publisher. Also, those who self-publish pay only for the actual cost of typesetting, printing, and binding. Subsidy publishers will add a cost override to assure themselves a profit—without letting you make final decisions on design, paper stock, and binding. Self-publication not only is better economy but offers you more control.